P9-DMH-053

If Strangers Meet

Also by Gladys Brooks

Three Wise Virgins
Gramercy Park
Boston and Return

Translations from the French
Mitsou *by Colette*
Salavin *by Georges Duhamel*

Gladys Brooks

If Strangers Meet

A Memory

Harcourt, Brace & World, Inc., New York

To Kenyon

Copyright © 1967 by Gladys Brooks
All rights reserved. No part of this publication may be reproduced
or transmitted in any form or by any means, electronic or mechanical,
including photocopy, recording, or any information storage and
retrieval system, without permission in writing from the publisher.
First edition
Library of Congress Catalog Card Number: 67-10758
Printed in the United States of America

The poem "(once like a spark)" by E. E. Cummings is copyright,
1944, by E. E. Cummings, and is reprinted from his volume *Poems
1923-1954* by permission of Harcourt, Brace & World, Inc. The excerpts from John Hall Wheelock's poems "The Gardener" and "House
in Bonac" are from his book *The Gardener and Other Poems*, copyright © 1961 by John Hall Wheelock, and are used by permission of
the publisher, Charles Scribner's Sons. The quotation from Robinson
Jeffers's poem "The Old Stonemason" is copyright 1951 by Robinson
Jeffers, and is reprinted from *Hungerfield and Other Poems* by permission of Random House, Inc.

"if strangers meet
life begins . . ."

—*E. E. Cummings*

Contents

I   *Strangers Meet*   3

II   *Keystone*   14

III   *Silo*   21

IV   *The Side of Light*   32

V   *Privacy of Storm*   45

VI   *Men and Phantoms*   56

VII   *A Kelson of Creation*   69

VIII   *Sun, Wind and Stars*   82

IX   *Eight Golden Daffodils*   94

X   *Sanctuary*   108

XI   *The Poets of the World Lie Sleeping*   122

XII   *Several Times Farewell*   144

XIII   *Makers and Finders*   156

XIV   *Hope, Fear, Time*   167

XV   *Wit and Wisdom*   179

XVI   *Stones in the Sea*   193

XVII   *Transmutations*   214

XVIII   *Clear and Free*   237

XIX   *Conversazioni*   253

XX   *Seven Maids with Seven Mops*   263

XXI   *Storm Warnings*   279

XXII   *Desolation and Diversion*   300

XXIII   *A Kiss for Caroline*   313

XXIV   *The Meaning of God*   324

    Index   333

Envoi
to
V. W. B.

"Dying leaves beneath the snow being a promise of new leaves opening in springtime. Thus does a life fluctuate between past and future, moving with a rhythm as regular as the denials and promises of earth, as repetitious as the drifting of waves upon the shore, forward and back, forward and back. . . ."

I copy these lines from a book called *Boston and Return,* a book about my first marriage and the rearing of my children. In this earlier time, despite many happy hours, I looked forward, looked ever ahead with a sense of coming fulfillment, a sense that did not err. Now, I can only look back. The waves have ceased their forward motion, denial outweighs promise, old leaves lie dried beneath the melting snows and I cannot see the new ones, I cannot feel the spring.

Memory may serve to stir the sap, to rekindle a little of the joy that has gone, "headlong joy," as Milton called it, joy brought me through the years of our marriage by Van Wyck Brooks. His was a presence. He has died. Perhaps I can do no better than to think of him.

If Strangers Meet

I

Strangers Meet

ROM the window of the New York–New Haven train, in November, 1946, running at evening southward through clusters of factories, movie theaters, dime stores, small frame dwellings, shabby apartment houses, I could see far away the lights of New York. I closed my book, setting one fold of its jacket against page 229 to mark my place. I did not want to stop reading. I did not want to disembark at New York. Neither had I wished, agreeable though the visit to my children had been, to stay longer in Boston. I wanted only to remain suspended somewhere between these two fixed spots while I continued to inhabit the World of Washington Irving, a world introduced to me by Van Wyck Brooks on a day of the previous week. His photograph was on the jacket. It faced me now as I glanced downward, the face of a scholar intently serious in the way that a child is intently serious and as many people grown older seem not to be seriously intent. "He is one of those who give us heart to face and build the future," the caption said.

These words were stirring to me and admirable as they described

3

the man I knew. I did not know him well, having been in his company only three times. Our face-to-face introduction had occurred in 1944 at the New York apartment of the John Hall Wheelocks, a party in honor of Van Wyck and Eleanor Brooks, his wife. The Wheelocks were old friends of the Brookses as well as of mine; John Wheelock and Van Wyck Brooks had been classmates at Harvard. My heart had set up a beat far beyond normal as I entered the room where he stood beside his hostess. I saw a man of medium height, of medium weight, dressed in a well-cut, discreet English suit with short jacket, handkerchief neatly folded in breast pocket, his thick black hair brushed back to stand straight up from his forehead, his color high in a face almost without lines and bearing the distinctive feature of a white moustache, which he wore clipped. He held a teacup in the manner of an ordinary mortal, but his presence, remote rather than familiar, set him apart from the others, held him from the clatter of the party. He seemed a being governed by some unobtrusive yet commanding force. This impression, swiftly gathered, like a glimpse of a mountain peak unveiled by clouds, was to remain with me always.

Our hostess, on my arrival, introduced me to Eleanor Brooks, and I noticed her air of pleasant competence, her steadfast and attractive bearing. This was my first meeting with her, and it proved to be my last. She died before I saw her again, and I have since, more than once, wished that on that day we might have been longer together. Instead, unaware of the course of destiny, I followed Phyllis Wheelock, who led Van Wyck and me down the long room to place us on a sofa beneath a large, realistically assembled painting, a family heirloom depicting a flock of sheep who fought against a blizzard with the aid of a bowed but persevering shepherd while one black sheep among the others and a black raven tenacious of the foreground brought an ominous note to the scene. This, at least, had been my feeling when I had observed it previously. On that day, no awesome specter diminished the moment. I forgot the Meisner above our heads, huge though it was, in the talk we undertook together.

4

I spoke to him of his book *Oliver Allston,* reminding him that I had written him in September, 1941, to ask about a transcript of a speech he had made at Columbia University. Therein he had defined "primary" as opposed to "coterie" writers and had stirred my imagination in describing the latter, with their tendency to deny progress, as "bats that had flown in the twilight between the wars," whereas primary writers who represented "the life drive" spoke, he said, to "the constant mind of man." I was a novice in this sort of thinking but I felt the courage and profundity of those words, something memorable, something to be treasured. Where, I had asked in my letter, could I read the speech in full? An answer had arrived without delay:

I have a copy of the speech which I am glad to send you. Don't bother to return it, as I was just on the point of throwing it away. It consists of two chapters, in a somewhat different form, from a book, *Opinions of Oliver Allston,* which will be published next month.

"It was good of you to have sent me the speech so promptly," I said to Van Wyck Brooks now. "I bought the book and I remember that I came down with the flu soon after it arrived, so that I was able to read it through almost without a break. A wonderful book!"

He bowed his thanks, the bow of a courteous but somewhat detached man, and I understood that he turned me away from the subject. In later days I was to learn, watching other laymen as they attempted to convey their praise, that he avoided compliments with the agility of a squirrel leaping to a safe branch. They seemed to confound rather than to delight. We went on, then, to talk of Edmund Wilson's *Shock of Recognition,* published in the previous year, and I was glad to learn that Van Wyck admired the book, for it was one that I much liked. In retrospect I cannot say why we chose to dwell on it just then. A current of sympathy running between us seemed to have illumined the subject. For me it did, at any rate. And although a reserve held him still, I could sense his pleasure as he spoke of this fellow writer.

Such was my outward recollection of Van Wyck Brooks on that day at the Wheelock apartment. But in memory there clung about him an air of inner focus which was compelling. It had to do with his eyes, grave yet luminous, intent on his thought rather than on the person he faced, eyes speaking of burdens beyond the ordinary yet lit by occasional darts of excitement, eyes one would not forget.

Our next two encounters were more than casual meetings because of the querying demands each of us made on the other, the need to explore, to discover. For we were both vulnerable at that moment in time, our lives hanging between past and future while loneliness wrapped us each like some dull mist. He was alone because of Eleanor's death; I was alone in consequence of a recently and unhappily established divorce. Our being together was somewhat like stepping the minuet, a decorous pattern of forward and back, circumspect, watchful, noninsistent.

We met for the second time under the guidance, once more, of John Wheelock, who brought Van Wyck to my New York flat to dine in November of 1946 on my return from Boise, Idaho, and the divorce court. They came, the two men, without Phyllis, for she had flown on a brief trip to England. I had earlier called Jack to invite him to a small party, and he had proposed that I include Van Wyck: "I think it might be well if you were to write him a few lines of invitation," Jack had suggested over the phone, "to make it more regular." Again I wrote, and again Van Wyck's reply arrived without delay. In my letter I had reminded him of our meeting in 1944 and he said:

Indeed I have not forgotten. I remember the moment very well and could tell you in some detail just what we talked about. So I am thoroughly delighted to be brought along on Tuesday next the 26th at 7.30. You are very kind to suggest it.

The party was a pleasant one. I believe we all felt it a special occasion. Among other friends, Felix Winternitz was there, a violinist and my teacher during the years I had lived in Boston. Philosopher and contemplative, he had stepped again after a long

6

absence into my temporarily suspended life to assume the role of generous counselor. There were also present Allen and Caroline Tate, writers both, whom I had come to know well during the last years. Allen and I played violin duets together, and although technically we were far below professional standards the music that engrossed us was composed by the great. The presence of Allen at the table was at first disturbing to Van Wyck for the reason that the two men had not agreed in the attitudes which governed their writing. "You're a literary enemy," Van Wyck exclaimed. There was humor in his eyes as he glanced at Allen. He had taken the measure of his enemy, I could see, yet had not, I decided, cared to engage in battle, even a minor battle of words. Hence the withdrawal, the temporary absence from the scene which later I was so often to observe. Was not this habit due to a consideration for another's feelings and, possibly, to a sense of futility in the end and aim of argument when it could not become air-borne? It was as though Van Wyck chose to retreat until the dangers of altercation had passed. I had been unaware of any possible rift in advance of the party and I remember introducing the two men as though they were awaiting this moment, long overdue. Perhaps it was just as well, for, as it happened, there now began an easy friendship, bringing pleasure to them both.

When dinner ended we sat about the fire to drink our coffee, and I recollect that Allen Tate asked to have a close look at my Stradivarius, which he much admired. I opened the case lying on the Steinway grand piano and brought the violin over, removing its swaddling wrap of chiffon.

"A beautiful violin," Allen exclaimed, taking it in his hands, and looking at Winternitz for corroboration.

"This is an early example," my Viennese friend replied, instructing us, "known as the 'Avery Strad.' It has the fine big tone of an Amati. But it takes a special strength to get this tone into the open, to make it sing."

"Oh, do please play something for us, Felix," I said. "Allen never hears it properly when he listens to me."

7

Winternitz took the instrument from me, the bow from the case, and stood for a moment reflecting with his back to the silent piano. After the tuning sounds had subsided he improvised briefly, permitting his fingers to wander over the keyboard with bow in attendance, then paused. Presently he began to play the swiftly running sixteenth notes that constitute the allegro movement of the Bach E-major sonata for unaccompanied violin: sounds nasal as the hum of wind in the topmost branches of trees, poignant as the cry of loneliness, bright as courage ever renewed.

There was a sigh as the music ended when, quietly, Winternitz put the fiddle down. Then voices took up their cadences, and we were back in the ordinary world wherein the human heart beats unaware of glory, and the ties binding it to others are dimmed.

I glanced at Van Wyck, and something in his mien held my attention, brought a reminder of that earlier meeting when, entering the room, I had seen that he was apart from the rest, those who laughed easily at the passing joke. He had not laughed at all; his expression, his face immobile, the muscles smooth and firm as a boy's except for those of the forehead, which were deeply indented. But his eyes gave one the essence of the man, in sorrow, intensity, or, now and then, humor. I had not forgotten the glint of mischief they held when at dinner he accosted Allen Tate. As the others began to move about the room, I went toward a sofa near the window, and Van Wyck followed. For a few moments he was quiet, as though confronting something beyond the present. Then he began to speak of his friend Jo Davidson, newly arrived from Paris, of this sculptor's unusual talent for likeness in the portrait busts he was at present occupied in making.

"I've been sitting for him," Van Wyck said, "and now he's taking me in hand and introducing me to New York night-club life. He thinks I need jogging out of my rut. I've twice been with him to the 21 Club, where the waiters are his devoted admirers. Jo has a genius for making people love him."

There was real pleasure in Van Wyck's voice, the pleasure and insistence of an adolescent who loyally praises his friend. Loyalty, I was presently to find, was one of his salient characteristics, and the 21 Club, otherwise a blatant spot as background for so retiring a man as Van Wyck Brooks, he saw chiefly as a challenge to his friend's superior powers.

The good-byes that ended the evening came presently, and I was left by myself. Placing chairs back into position, plumping sofa cushions, setting the screen before the fire, I had a sudden picture of the dinner table when Allen Tate sat on my left and Van Wyck Brooks on my right. I dwelt again on the glowing music of Bach, on the widely open tones of my Stradivarius, and I thought of Van Wyck, of his upright, self-contained bearing, of his gentleness, his unassuming wisdom, his eyes, his high color, the upward brushed hair, the white moustache. An immutable presence but a man who, for all his achievement, his standing, was somehow vulnerable, in need of protection from the accidents of casual encounter.

Van Wyck came to tea at my flat on an afternoon following the dinner, a polite party call. Something of the repression I had noticed earlier fell between us once again as I sat in front of the low sofa table waiting for the tea leaves to steep in the pot. The conversation lagged and nothing served to enliven it. "My mind is in no way the equal of his," I said to myself, selecting this reason as being more probable than another. I felt inadequate and dull as I attempted to entertain him, telling him of my work in "remedial reading" begun in the war years, of my current job with the slow readers at St. Bernard's School for Boys, of my great desire not only to help these particular students but to discover the cause of their failure.

"Boys far outnumber the girls," I told him, "and no one seems exactly to know why. I do wish I could find out!"

"You very well may, one of these days. An essential discovery it should be," Van Wyck answered with an intensity that almost equalled mine. It gave me heart.

As he prepared to leave I told him that I was soon to go on a trip to Boston to visit my children and grandchildren, three separate families, "quantities of them," I announced cheerfully, ringing the elevator bell in the hall outside. He stood beside me in his tweed overcoat, a bulky muffler about his neck, fedora hat in hand.

"You're fortunate. I have so far only one grandchild, a boy," he said, and a shadow crossed his face as the elevator arrived at my floor.

"I doubt if we ever meet again," I thought, and closed the front door with decision.

There were several days between this episode and the moment of my leaving for Boston. On the morning of the second day my elderly German housekeeper, Dora Dilk, friend of many years, brought me the morning mail with my breakfast tray. A package addressed to me lay beneath the letters, a package holding a book. Written in an upper corner of the wrapper was the name of the sender, *Van Wyck Brooks.* Hurriedly, I tore the package and opened *The World of Washington Irving,* to come on the flyleaf inscription:

> *For Mrs. Billings*
> *with admiration.*
>
> *Van Wyck Brooks*
> *November 1946*

"How very kind!" I spoke to Dora. "Perhaps we shall see each other again after all," I said to myself, and went on hurriedly with breakfast in order not to be late for school.

All the way in the train to Boston and all the way back, I read. The initial chapter, on Philadelphia in 1800, drew me at once, passages telling of the city's early history in terms of those who had lived it, the writers, the men of books. At the outset came the engrossing picture of Parson Weems, who traveled in his horse-drawn wagon for Mathew Carey, publisher, the book hawker who was a "familiar figure on the roads of the South" with his portable bookcase and his fiddle, a "quill pen stuck in his hat and a little ink-horn hung from one of his lapels." And I read with a pleasure based on sustained experience about the New Englanders: "famous for their schools as well as the stones in their fields and the stiffness in their necks . . . the most literate of all the Americans . . . industrious and orderly."

The chapters on Audubon and Poe were especially moving: Audubon, "with deep gray eyes as restless as the glance of an eagle," who taught his wife French while he drew birds on the wing and she, in turn, taught him English, the two remaining a devoted and united pair during the many penniless crises of their early marriage, drifting down the Ohio in a flatboat crowded with cattle, horses, pigs, or while he contended with the difficult tangled forests, snaring the birds as models and surmounting the day's disappointments by playing at evening the guitar or the fiddle or the flute. As for Poe, I wondered if ever before he had been so eloquently described: "There were no mornings in the world of Poe, there were only winter afternoons or dull, dark soundless days in the autumn of the year and one sometimes had glimpses of a river or a lake that was saffron or sickly in hue or sullen or livid in the light of a setting sun. . . ." Poe "had heard the strains of the mad waltzes that echoed in his poems and his stories and seen the wind-blown arrases, tattered and dark, fitfully swaying on the walls of some house of the dead."

A work of art, all this, art that ranged with the great in painting, poetry, music. And I pondered the talent, the heart of the man who thus set down in the beauty of flowing words the core of what he chose to describe, feeling the essence of his material as one feels the sun and rain and the vibration of the stars. With his mind of the scholar he perceived also the basic value of his subject's output, the long-time value rather than the hasty, often ill-tempered edicts of lesser men.

I continued to read, and I dwelt on the tragedy of Thomas Paine, hero of America's early history, as his labor and his life were described in the pages of this book. I learned that "the grand phrases of Paine, expressions of courage and principle, rang through the country; and that he had used first the greatest of all perhaps,— the United States of America,—in one of his papers." Paine wrote

The Age of Reason while imprisoned by Robespierre, and Napoleon had slept with Paine's *The Rights of Man* beneath his pillow. Benjamin Franklin had said that "while others could rule and many could fight, 'only Paine can write for us,'" and Lincoln, presently, was enthralled by this patriot's ideas. Yet he lived unhonored and died dishonored, the meaning of his words comprehended by none but the very great. "People," Brooks wrote, "said he drank too much, but so did the most respectable men, and this would never have been held against him if his mind had been commonplace also." He was unshaven and unshorn, "his fingernails like those of Nebuchadnezzar," and he had "the battered, melancholy look of an old eagle moulting." Men crossed the street when they saw Paine coming. Thomas Jefferson, however, invited him to dine at the White House and walked out with him arm in arm.

There came to me then, as I dwelt on these words, certain phrases from *Oliver Allston,* the book I had come to know so well, phrases which disclosed the unworldliness, the sure sense of timelessness belonging to their author: "A great writer," Allston had said, "is a great man writing, and the greatest are those who speak for all mankind." And I remembered that Allston had asked to have cut on his tombstone Pope's summary of Dryden:

> He was not a very genteel man,
> He was intimate with none but genteel men.

Was not Oliver Allston a pseudonym for Van Wyck Brooks?

As much as any writing in the pages of *Washington Irving* I enjoyed what Van Wyck had to say about the correspondence flowing on during their old age between Thomas Jefferson and John Adams, that famous correspondence "so regular and long . . . that all the postmasters along the route became aware of it, and the post riders watched for the letters." Difficult it was for Jefferson to keep up his end, drudging away at his writing table civilly answering his mail from dinner to dark, while Adams chiefly ignored his duties in this respect. But the two men received much satisfaction from one another. They discussed "the uses of grief about which Adams had found a fine passage in Molière and both agreed that the world on the whole was good."

This conception of life, I was happily to discover during the coming years, was also that of Van Wyck. Even though attacked, frequently, for his "unclouded," his "unrealistic" views in a world that despaired, a world of lacerated mind and brutal statement, he remained ever sanguine and on the side of courage, his mind filled with "the largeness of hope." And I, seated in the window corner of a coach on a New Haven train during that otherwise unmarked day, was destined to hold to my indoctrination in the writing of human history by a man of faith, a man whose name was Van Wyck Brooks.

II

Keystone

"*T*HEN they were married and lived happily ever after."
This fairy-tale ending, the child's formula for existence, did truly
apply to Van Wyck and to me, to our union. It applied until death
strode between us, a ruthless act not a part of the fairy tale.

Our marriage took place on June 2, 1947, at City Hall, the witnesses
being two each among the children of our individual families. Afterwards, wearing on my finger the new gold band inscribed "G.D.R.
and V.W.B. 1947," I placed my arm within my husband's to leave
municipal requirements behind and I felt myself "tripping the light
fantastic toe" as we made our way on foot through the streets of
lower Manhattan toward the Third Avenue Elevated. Our children followed us, and we were a compact and cheerful party presently to be seated in an uptown train. I remember having glimpses
through open second-story windows of sad-eyed women leaning
on dusty sills, and my heart went out to them because they were
seemingly without the joy vouchsafed me. Van Wyck, meanwhile,
sat politely talking with our children, his emotions held in abeyance.

We were headed for the Ninety-sixth Street station where, on descending the long stairway with its own special smell of cinders and damp, we entered a taxi to drive to the house, in East Ninety-fourth Street, of Dr. Carl Binger and his wife, Clarinda, who had most agreeably volunteered to give us our wedding reception. The party was held in their garden, one of a series at the rear of a stretch of brownstones in the block. Lovely the garden was with early blossoming shrubs and peonies and borders of forget-me-nots. The weather that day was betwixt and between, alternating shadow with the brief emergence of sun. But there was no rain and the wind over the garden held its breath.

In charge of the champagne was a West Indian Negro by name Emmanuel who was at that moment in Van Wyck's service, an inheritance from his friend George Foote, the composer. Emmanuel served the wedding party with an agile hand, one trained when he had been page to the Governor's Lady in his native Jamaica. There, as a small boy, he followed her among the garden flowers during the cool of sunset, bearing in a basket the blooms she clipped from rose bushes, from the bougainvillaea. Then, back at the palace, under her tutelage, he arranged them into pretty bouquets. His fingers became so deft that in later years, plucking wild flowers in a Bavarian meadow to make them into bunches for the trade, he was summoned to the side of a royal carriage driving by. Their Majesties wished to compliment the young man on his artistic prowess. Something of the grace of that earlier time went now into Emmanuel's serving of our guests. There were present not more than twenty or thirty of family and friends, but among these, we were glad to remember later, was Maxwell Perkins, editor and fond counselor to many a writer during his long editorial years at Charles Scribner's and notably responsible for the difficult task of cutting some of the overweighted bulk of material from the books of Thomas Wolfe. Max was Van Wyck's oldest friend, having grown up with him in Plainfield, New Jersey, and roomed with him at Harvard. Now, in the period immediately following our marriage,

Max was struck down by pneumonia. This was the final meeting of the two men.

On an afternoon of warm sunshine several days after the wedding, Van Wyck suggested that we drive out into the Connecticut countryside in the region of Westport to call on those friends with whom he and Eleanor had been intimate during the twenty years they lived there.

"It's a fine day," Van Wyck said, "and there are several people I'd especially like you to meet."

I rejoiced at the idea. The country beckoned, and a temporary stop to the labor of settling in at Van Wyck's apartment offered an agreeable respite. My husband, on this afternoon, looked very festive in a lightweight jacket of black-and-white checks, and I went at once to change into something similar in spirit. We set out in his new small black Chevrolet, which we had named "Sheba" because of its sleek and dusky perfection, and the visits were easily made, five or six of them. I had done my best to convince each of Van Wyck's adherents that I should make a suitable wife for him and, incidentally, I had enjoyed myself. On the drive back, however, both of us rather tired, I had mentioned a painter, a friend of mine, whose hobby it was to train gamecocks for fighting. Van Wyck, as we talked, was much stirred. "A savage sport," he exclaimed, "along with bullfighting. It ought to be condemned." Although in my deepest heart I agreed with him and came later to respect his wide opposition to all forms of cruelty, I wondered then at his vehemence, which seemed to me unduly stressed, and I was glad when, soon, we spoke of other things.

At home, on our return, I noticed Van Wyck's unusually high color and his look of malaise. Was he still harboring animosity against the sanguinary cock fighter, I wondered? Placing my hand on his cheek, I found it burning hot, and the thermometer marked his temperature at one hundred and two degrees. In great agitation and against his wish, I telephoned the doctor. "You didn't tell me you were ill," I said. "I shall have entirely recovered after a night's rest," he answered. "It's nothing at all. Why not let things be?"

Such was ever to be the pattern in the event of his illness, the brushing aside of symptoms as of small importance. Little in his life was significant, meriting notice, save his work and the people whom he loved. "Was not this the measure of a hero?" I asked myself.

The doctor's first diagnosis was alarming. Van Wyck's blood count, he told me, was very far from normal, and, as we waited for a final report from the city laboratory, I was given a warning: "Your husband, Mrs. Brooks, may be seriously ill and will almost certainly have to be taken to the hospital." Hearing these words, watching the doctor's grave expression, my thoughts flew to those young war brides whom I had endlessly pitied, brides of a week whose enforced separation from their husbands was oftentimes forever. Was I now to become one of them?

The laboratory report arrived next morning, and the doctor was less anxious. Van Wyck's disease was not leukemia, as he had first feared. It was infectious mononucleosis, an illness contracted in the main by young students and caused by overwork and lack of sleep. It was serious enough and most unpleasant in its pattern, and I should have to be a composed and diligent nurse, the doctor warned. "How simple!" I thought as my spirits rose, "by comparison with what I might have been compelled to be."

Then it was that I began to learn, basically, about the remarkable nature, the superior habits of the man I had married. Because of an innate modesty, or should it be termed humility, he had so far kept many of the intrinsic aspects of himself hidden, out of the way. "Why talk of myself?" he would ask when I pressed him. "Isn't the egoist an impossible bore?" And, feeling this explanation to be sufficient, he had turned to other things. Our day-to-day exchanges during the period of courting had been based chiefly on those ideas closest to him, on the state of the world and his hopes for the betterment of mankind, on the books he read, on the qualities he found admirable in his friends, on his daily labor of mind and pen, a need similar to the average man's need for bread. When other aspects of himself demanded more clarity, fuller explanation, his manner of withdrawal, familiar to me in the pre-courtship era, fell over him as night descends upon a meadow obliterating the shape of the growing crop. Thus, there had been never a mention of his current physical existence, the long stretch of his hours, from early morning and on to midnight, the hour when, usually, he had said good night to me. His sleep had been as fitful, his concentration as protracted as those of the most ambitious student. And his illness, therefore, had been of the student category.

On ahead, a goal to be reached by both of us during those suffering days, lay the weeks of our honeymoon, those we had promised ourselves. They were to be spent on Martha's Vineyard, where I had lived for a part of each summer during almost forty years. At Edgartown, at an inn overlooking the harbor, a room with a balcony awaited us, one long engaged, and to this vision of paradise we continued to cling. It helped Van Wyck to bear the fever and the pain, it hurried his convalescence, it cut short, eventually, our stay in the summer city of unmitigated noise and heat. "I've seldom seen a man so severely ill or one who recovered so quickly. What determination! It's remarkable," the doctor said when, finally, we were granted permission to leave town in the latter part of June.

How lovely was the sight of far-reaching waters as we approached the sea on the second day of our drive away, how delicious the smell of salt coming toward us on the wind. With our load of possessions at our back, these in large part Van Wyck's books, slowly, judiciously, because of the invalid within, we approached Woods Hole in my old Ford station wagon, which had for many years served me well in spite of its draughty windows, its elderly engine, and which was as necessary to my existence as some creature of flesh and blood. I clung to this feeling in spite of Van Wyck's amusement at my point of view, his charges of animism. "You must reread the *Golden Bough*," he advised.

He had first seen the car on the evening in the city six months previously when I had driven down from 82nd Street to dine with him and Margaret Cobb at his apartment. That evening had been my introduction to the agreeable small parties he gave with Mrs.

Cobb's aid. She was the widow of Frank I. Cobb, known for his work on the New York *World* at the moment of its greatest influence, and she it was who had left her place in Westport to keep house, after Eleanor's death, for Van Wyck in the city. Her upbringing, as the daughter of the celebrated Harriet Hubbard Ayer, had combined the exotic and the favored with arrant neglect, an unusual amalgam, but her character, as a result, was courageously true and strong and tender.

On the evening of the party at Van Wyck's apartment, I had made my preparations with care and pleasure, choosing to wear a long skirt of black taffeta and a white chiffon blouse with sleeves buttoning at the wrist. This was a favorite costume of mine, and I had hoped it might please Van Wyck. It did, in fact, seem suitably chosen for the evening's company, which consisted of the painters John Sloan, Walter Pach, and their wives. A single man had come to match me but he has been forgotten in the shining memory of the host himself. After dinner, I remember, when I asked Van Wyck a question concerning his book in progress, he left the room for a moment, to return with a cardboard box holding a manuscript, the almost finished *Melville and Whitman*. This he had placed in my lap, and it seemed as though he were presenting me with a portion of his life. Later, when the moment came to leave, he had gone down with me in the elevator as far as the street. "Will you have a taxi?" he asked as the doorman waited. "No, thank you," I answered somewhat airily, proclaiming my independence, "my car is parked on Second Avenue, a block up." And I held out my hand to say good night. "Let me take you to your car," Van Wyck had said in a voice showing finality and, I sensed, something of disapproval. It was apparent that he did not favor solitary expeditions for ladies in the nighttime streets of New York. We walked to the noisy, wind-blown corner on Second Avenue, where he opened the door of my elderly vehicle as though it were the door of a palace and I its reigning monarch. I entered and, with the engine started, I turned to look. On the sidewalk he stood motionless, at attention. He might have been receiving honors at a dress parade. "What a very nice person," I had said to myself, as each time I said when we had been together.

And now here we were, in the glowing present, permanently together, seated side by side in the old Ford and headed for Martha's Vineyard, for Edgartown with its room overlooking the harbor.

"How rarely does attainment match the vision of joy," I whispered to myself when, later, we drew our chairs together on the sunny balcony of a June afternoon.

III

Silo

U P Island, toward Gay Head and the Indian settlement, stands a silo of unusual aspect, in place at Chilmark, near Menemsha Great Pond, a salt-water pond giving through a narrow inlet to Vineyard Sound. "The Silo," as it is named, is painted white, is tall and of equable circumference, and on fair days from the vantage point of Menemsha Bight, its casement windows can be seen opened wide. It resembles the tower of a French castle, but unfortified, and lacking a moat. Indeed, in its graceful, shining stance on a distant knoll, it has a look of innocent participation in the landscape, in the low-lying meadows about it, the flower-bearing bushes of summer. A perpetual monument to beauty becalmed.

On a day at the end of June, leaving the inn at Edgartown, Van Wyck and I took joint possession of the Silo. It belonged to us, ours to inhabit at our pleasure. Van Wyck's recovery was now well established, and with Dora Dilk, arrived from the New York apartment to help us, we began to settle in, to dispose our clothes, our books and pictures, china, glass, silver, umbrellas and walking

21

sticks, the accouterments of existence. I had owned the Silo for several years and had been present when the circular foundation of concrete was poured by fishermen-carpenters who, with companions standing by to see the new marvel, shook their heads at the risk of the undertaking, the uncertainty of the building's future. "Come a gale and this here round house she'll roll over and down into the pond," they predicted, "and there she'll lie." But the Silo rose nonetheless, its parts fitted together according to plan. And there, in spite of several hurricanes that have blown about its rounded surface, it still stands. Inside, to avoid upright shafts as support for the two-storied ceilings, an architect friend had evolved the idea of corner struts made in the shape of a swastika. Thus the circular rooms were left uncluttered, the dining room on ground level, the living room above, and the bedroom at the top, all three served by an inner stairway clinging to the silo wall—a pleasant binding, easy of tread, that brought the sense of upward impulse leading toward the blue sky. In our heaven-high bedroom we felt we belonged with the sky rather than the earth, lying at night an intrinsic part of the stars that enveloped us; at daylight, a part of the awakening universe.

The early-morning pattern soon became established here. Up at six each morning, Van Wyck in his red foulard dressing gown went to the living room below to sit in a deep chair overlooking the sea, there to prepare for the day's writing. At eight o'clock, bathed and dressed, we met for breakfast in the ground-floor dining room with its lean-to kitchen, where casements stood open and the smell of damp grasses came in along with the ever-present smell of the sea. Blueberry, plum, and wild rose grew everywhere about us; the birds darted and sang their songs of first morning while slowly the sun moved above the rounded roof that sheltered us. No other house could be seen, no four-footed creatures, save an occasional rabbit leaping, broke the lovely rhythm of our solitude. We were alone except for our friendly Dora, alone with each other, with the sum of our two lives, with the hope of a far and united future.

"Thirty years of this are what I count on," said Van Wyck with his half smile that outshone the smile of other men. This wish, if fulfilled, would have brought us to the age of the Biblical prophets and their spouses. But it seemed to both of us a plausible idea.

Below the Silo, close to the shore of the pond, there had been placed a one-room portable building as a study for Van Wyck. To this spot he went each morning when breakfast ended. He followed a path cut in the tall damp grass and marked at the halfway point by an apple tree of low-grown habit, its branches bent by eagerly prevailing winds. Van Wyck at that time, as respite from long and intensive labor, was at work compiling a book to which he later gave the title *A Chilmark Miscellany*. This was to be a collection of previously printed essays taken from various among his books to represent what he considered the best of his writing. The pleasure brought him by this sort of pastime was entire, like gathering from an orchard a crop of unblemished peaches. The fourth volume of his history of American literature, *The Times of Melville and Whitman,* had recently gone to press, and was to appear during the autumn. With this behind him and so much on ahead, he walked the morning path with confidence, moving toward the pond with as much alacrity as a boy would have shown on his way to swim in the water.

Boys, small boys in fact, did arrive now and then to stay with us. These were two grandsons, Peter Brooks, who belonged to Van Wyck, and Stephen Saltonstall, who was a part of my family. Peter came later in the summer when his father and mother brought him on from California. Stephen, aged seven, was our first guest, a precocious boy, large-eyed and serious. One morning, over the breakfast cereal, I remember, there had been a brief conversation between Van Wyck and me concerning our social engagements in the weeks ahead. During our first months together, Van Wyck had feared that we should be overexposed to outside pressures, to social engagements. I wished only for his confidence in me while I attempted to balance his wishes against the demands of others, a task which was then, and continued to be, arduous. Striving that morning to conceal my momentary hurt at his doubt of my motives, I must have brushed away his questions in a manner far from suave, a momentary lapse which Stephen, sitting in silence, did not miss. Soon after, when I had gone up to our sky bedroom to practice my violin, a daily rite, and Van Wyck was already at work in his study, I noticed from the window that the boy was walking down the path toward the pond carrying under his arm a stiff paper board. As I watched, I saw him climb the two steps to the study door and turn the handle, a forbidden act. He entered and came out a moment later returning minus his burden. This was, in fact, our Phillips Brooks engagement calendar with which the child had hoped to reassure or to inform Van Wyck, to answer the question of our commitments more fully than I had done at the breakfast table. "We men must stand together" was the adage, while I stood alone and chastened.

On occasional mornings, just before lunch, Van Wyck emerged from his little house, which had grown hot beneath the sun-beaten roof, to join me on our small private beach at the edge of Menemsha Pond below. Here he went cautiously, almost reluctantly, into the water, as if fearing its power to disorganize, to disintegrate his faculties, but once engulfed in the restoring flow, swiftly he became another person, reverting to earlier moments in time when a delight in pure sensation was paramount. It was never easy, then, to persuade him out, to get him off his back, where he seemed to be floating to some far and beckoning shore. At afternoon we went for walks over the meadows and dunes, along the beach. Our pace was slow, the pace necessary to Van Wyck in order to spare his heart, which once had suffered a thrombosis, and the ground we covered was not extensive. Van Wyck carried a cane, a habit of long standing, and on his head was an ancient Panama hat, pliable, of broad brim, which took untoward shapes in the damp air. A bow tie was in place, or a longer one of dotted foulard, but, as a concession to the informal life we led, and possibly because it had become a friend, he kept on his old working jacket of faded blue linen.

"Why not leave off your jacket entirely, or at any rate your tie, in this hot weather?" I now and then asked during that first summer.

"Because I'm more comfortable when I'm fully dressed," he answered briefly. "And if I leave off my jacket, even wearing a sweater instead, where can I carry the odds and ends I must have with me?"

These were lead pencil, ball-point pen, a gilt box holding nitroglycerine tablets, and a small notebook filled with almost indecipherable scribbles of vast importance to him. Also he carried a little silver matchbox, once his brother's. He himself had been forbidden to smoke but, with his perfect sense of civility, he was meticulous in lighting the cigarettes of others. I was to discover that the element of decorum was an added factor in his manner of dressing. It seemed to my husband an inexcusable lack of manners to appear in the company of a lady tieless and in shirt sleeves.

Beyond the Silo in the middle distance, a small cabin became gradually visible as we moved forward. It belonged to a farmer whose days drove him without respite to the necessary chores on his large farm and along the wild stretches of moorland wherein his cattle strayed. His son, and former helper, had been drowned in the pond on a quiet day of summer, caught in clinging grasses that entwined him beneath his boat. And so the farmer spent the long working hours unaided, forever harassed, forever behind in his dawn-to-dusk routine as milkman and caretaker to the summer folk. His cabin, however, stood on its bare dune, a constant beacon to light the inner man. I had seen him pause on his rounds to stare at the windows aflame in the late afternoon, a minor glory, and I thought that the cabin's staunch immobility must have been a comfort in a world so filled with the unpredictable. Now and then, as summer unrolled, he took the time to place a patch of tar paper on its wind-torn roof. But never did we find the place inhabited by any living creature. "A gunner's camp for the autumn migrations," someone explained. Van Wyck was much drawn to the spot, and we went often to peer through the windows, to share in some measure the life that once or twice a year filled the small room, the oilcloth-covered table beside the two-burner kerosene stove, the cot with its rumpled blanket, the empty chair. Gazing through the murky windowpane Van Wyck was drawn like any youth who flings himself into a tale of his own choosing.

"Come along, darling," I would sometimes have to say, so lengthy was his preoccupation.

"I've always envied a man this sort of life," he explained. "No crosscurrents. All the elemental things."

On the beach we gathered shells and water-smoothed stones, I, rather more thoroughly than my husband, whose mind was on intangibles. But he liked to feel me at his side, a part of the pursuits he did not entirely share. Sometimes I paused to clip a branch of bayberry or the rugosa rose, and Van Wyck stooped to take up the ample red-cheeked haws from where my shears had let them fall. I was glad when this happened—when, for the moment, he became an integral part of the scene. On occasion I wondered, striving to understand his nature all the way, how much he felt the physical changes in our universe, the day-to-day changes in climate, in scene, felt them in force as many of us do, whether the pleasures brought by a newly thrust sun into a cloud-encumbered sky, the smell of brine sweeping a heat-enclosed meadow, the gait of the yellowlegs beside the little waves of the beach, whether these things charmed him or remained unnoticed. Then, opening one of his books, I found the answer spread beneath my eyes in its enduring form of black on white. He wrote about the fresh joys of the recurring days. He did not exclaim in the words of everyday speech. His instinct was less for what men call self-expression than to preserve himself for his work.

Below the Silo to the west lay a small body of fresh water surrounded by thickset, twisted, virgin beeches, ancient inhabitants of this spot. Years ago a dam had been built here by the owner of this land which thrust itself out into the low-lying meadows toward Menemsha Pond to form what on the map is known as Pease's Point, a point, according to one branch of tradition, which was the initial meeting place of Indian and white man. The pond was a romantic and languid spot protected in summer from turbulent winds and heat by the leaves of the beech trees. The waters of the pool were lily-laden, shadow-crowded, and the overhanging boughs had become a nesting place for a colony of night heron, a haven designed, seemingly, by the master of the universe for just such a habitation. When sunset swept the circle of the sky, the heron went forth on their nightly foraging trips, a kind of sustained darting full of strength and purpose. From the windows of our circular tower we often watched their flight away, became for a moment a part of it, an accompaniment to evening. We sat beneath the casements over our pre-dinner drink while below us in the soft, salt air the fishing boats came home to port, plodding creatures of the sea, the nets on their decks, their holds filled with mackerel and scup and flounder. And our talk, Van Wyck's and mine, was of quiet things, in the majesty of the moment. Difficult to pick up once again the thought necessary to spoken words, to verbal communication, and we dined in happy, almost silent content, going early to bed.

The elemental pattern of this world of our choosing was broken on occasion by encounters with friends from the various parts of the island. Chilmark, where the Bentons, Tom and Rita, lived nearby on a far-extended knoll with the Great Pond, through the branches of pine, their outlook, and never-ending hospitality in charge of their life within. Beyond Beetle Bung Corners, to the south, was the ocean beach belonging to Evelyn and Roger Baldwin, a fine and beautiful place for swimming, for picnics at high noon, for conversation at morning or afternoon. Vineyard Haven, where in the various markets we bumped into shopping friends; West Tisbury, at the center, where Farmer Green grew his vegetables and flowers; Edgartown, with its white-fenced, rose-covered fishermen's houses taken over now by an ever-increasing colony of year-round inhabitants come from the cities to live. Here, for us, a nucleus formed about Leslie and William Dinsmore, he the composer-pianist who, since the years of my first marriage, had played violin and piano sonatas with me.

At Lambert's Cove, on the waters of Vineyard Sound, lived

Katharine Cornell. We came first to know her through Helen Keller, long-time friend of Van Wyck, our dear Helen. She and her companion, Polly Thomson, arrived each summer from Westport, Connecticut, to visit Miss Cornell and her husband, Guthrie McClintic, in their widespread house of stucco standing on the dunes. Here, delighted with the odor of brine mingled with fog, with the meadows caught in the warmth of sun, Helen was gay as a girl; and here, when a musician friend of the McClintics played on their Steinway grand, Helen stood close to the instrument, one hand upon it to feel the vibrations while with the other she beat time to the rhythm. She might have been an accomplished conductor involved in a score of Schumann or Rachmaninoff. At tea, Helen much enjoyed having Van Wyck at her side. Placing her hand on his lips when he spoke, she was able to feel through her sensitive finger tips the words she could not hear, to feel his love for her; and her smile was a charming thing when she had seized the import of his idea. Watching the two, I heard with pleasure the sound of Helen's voice as slowly, carefully, she pronounced his name. The two syllables "Van—Wyck" became a murmured eulogy.

There were weeks, as summer went on, which crowded the Silo with human beings, children and grandchildren who slept in the ground-level wing added to the westerly side. Those arriving most frequently were my son, John Saltonstall, Jr., with his wife, Peg, and their three children. My daughters and their husbands came rather less often because of lives established elsewhere: Elizabeth Tower, living in Santa Barbara; Priscilla Catlin, who spent the summers in Maine; and Jean Bradlee, my youngest, who was committed, then, to a residence in Manchester, New Hampshire. The sounds of youth passing to and fro, the heavily closing front door below the living room, car engines whirling at the take-off for beach or tennis court, farewells called to departing friends after nightfall—these things brought a boisterous element to the scene. At such moments Van Wyck continued with his inner-directed routine, apart from the commotion and hazards of the day, while I, of necessity and with a good deal of pleasure, adapted myself to outer demands.

I was always happy when Van Wyck's two sons appeared in our midst: Charles and Kenyon Brooks, in whose background lay a love of nature on her own terms. Both were proficient in dealing with the sea, the land, both were filled with content when close to basic things, those determined by the elements of life on our island. Kenyon went forth carrying shovel and pail to return with clams or mussels for our table and, with his rod and lures in late summer, to hook a striped bass from the waters of the long south beach. Charlie, whose initial visit was brief, his wife and son still at home in San Francisco, became a close and steadfast companion during the hours we spent together working to clear an overgrown road through the woods to Menemsha Bight; a short cut to civilization, it would become, enabling us to avoid the lengthy outer highway route by way of Chilmark. Along the old abandoned road, open once to horse and wagon, a massive tree had fallen to block progress, cat brier clung to our clothing, and poison ivy was rampant. But the viburnum was in lusty bloom and the delicate stalk of a red wood lily rose here and there at our feet, while the sweetness of pepper bush edged our passage, filling the air with its perfume under the intensity of the noonday sun. Gradually, Charlie's ax and saw, aided somewhat by my clippers, brought us the clearing we had sought, and an outlet to the Menemsha road, on foot at any rate, became an actuality.

Serene days these were, destined for long memory, serene also for Van Wyck, who from his cabin above the pond, from his worktable there, clad in the old linen jacket, pockets weighted and sagging, sent out his blessing to wife and son as they toiled beneath an open sky denied to him. We strove to reward his solitary hours, his monastic pattern, with the flowering boughs brought him on our return to decorate his study, and the smile he gave us in thanks united us again, obliterated the distance the morning had set between us.

29

There came a moment during the second or third of those summers which changed the free-flowing course of delight, bringing strain and sharp momentary danger, the moment when Van Wyck became ill with that illness dreaded and suffered by so many men as they go on in years. This was a heart attack, his second, that struck on a Sunday evening of full summer when he and I were alone in the Silo except for the company of young Peter Brooks, aged seven or eight. Many of our children had been about during that day and had tired us with their comings and goings, their dartings, crass as those of the blue jay, in addition to the hullabaloo created by varying ideas, divergent temperaments. At any rate, my own heart stopped its beat when, on settling down to read after supper, Van Wyck said quietly, as though announcing the arrival of summer rain, "I have a pain in my heart." His fine color had left his cheeks, and there was a bewildered look in his eyes. What to do? There was no one to help us. Even our old Dora was unavailable, at the movies in distant Vineyard Haven. And the Silo had no telephone.

We got through. We were not permanently crippled. Automatically, at moments such as these, one's motions are impelled by orders from some invisible source and there is no hesitation. I left my husband on the living-room couch with young Peter beside him and I drove the necessary winding two miles through dark woods to a house on the highway, a house with a phone. From there, I managed to reach a doctor in Vineyard Haven who agreed to gather up Dora on his speedy way to us. Van Wyck and Peter were, on my return, as I had left them, and not long after, the doctor arrived with the necessary quieting drug. The attack proved not of the severely hazardous sort, and a few days later, but sooner than the doctor wished, Van Wyck was at work again before a card table in our blue-sky parlor at the top of the house. He had said to me: "This is nonsense, keeping me on my back in the living room. A momentary fatigue. That was what the attack amounted to. I'm far more likely to die of being kept from my work. I'll stay upstairs in the bedroom if you like. That's all that's necessary. I'll write up there." The specialist sent out from Boston by my son, an eminent man who arrived shortly after Van Wyck's attack, agreed that the incident had not been unduly grave, but he shook his head when he discovered my husband's weight. He was ten or fifteen pounds too heavy, a situation that courted danger. Van Wyck was to forgo sweets and butter and many of the other gustatorial delights on which he counted, those which pointed up and recompensed him for the difficult labors of the mind. When he was told of the new regime, he exclaimed: "What a thing to subject a man to! Taking away much of the pleasure of life. Besides, I'm a critic. All good critics are known for their excessive weight. Look at Sainte-Beuve. Look at Edmund Wilson." There began then a fresh attempt to conform, but it did not become easier.

The magic of summer had been dispelled, the mirror at the gateway to our castle shattered. Over the years, our visits to the island tapered, and after a time lost all semblance of regularity. One day, I gave the Silo to my son, and we moved, Van Wyck and I, to live in the shelter of a Connecticut village, a spot more suited to those for whom the hazards of life are best not challenged.

Is there an excellence, an increased luster, brought to the human condition by the device of onerous change? Now and then I pondered this question in my attempt to override a nostalgia for a beckoning past. Are we the better for being denied the pleasure of earlier moments, bright moments beaten into the pliable stuff of our marrow? Do we gather fresh awareness from having to renounce, to forgo? Should this be a solace?

"Anyway," I said to myself when the flowering of sweet pepper mingled in my memory with the winged flight of the night heron, "I hope I shall not forget."

IV

The Side of Light

*I*N the apartment once again at the end of our first summer together, we soon became established in permanence. Van Wyck's study was the core from which our lives emanated, a square, book-walled room, basic, indestructible. It contained his mahogany, drop-leaf writing table, which held the silver-capped inkwell of cut glass, the wide blotter spattered with ink spots, some as large as half dollars, a pen tray crowded with ball-point pens and pencils, and, close by, the carton of nibs on which he relied for serious writing, a fresh one each morning to be held between his lips while he read the page written yesterday, thereby properly conditioning it before it was inserted in the dark-green holder, companion of many years. Scattered over the surface were small boxes of silver or Japanese lacquer or cloisonné, disbursers of stamps, clips, rubber bands, and other clusters of necessity. Dominating the rest at his elbow as he wrote were two dictionaries and the Thesaurus of Roget in worn covers, while a Century dictionary of massive weight lay open on a tip-table against the bookshelves. The classic Harvard chair, black-

lacquered, gilt-adorned, was in position before the table, the chair
in which each morning in his cold-weather tweed writing jacket,
patched at the elbows, Van Wyck placed himself for the new daily
page of his composing. He wrote with jet-black ink on heavy white
Hammermill paper, in a small-sized longhand difficult to decipher
but distinguished and conditioned by his intricately woven mind.
Below the writing table near the window stood a deep overstuffed
chair, his reading chair. A sturdy bench of walnut at its side held
a pillar of books, a pillar endlessly changing, endlessly balanced but
never diminishing. How was it possible, I frequently asked myself,
to continue on as this man did without ever the hope of reaching an
end?

"But to come to the end of my work would mean the end of my
life," he would have answered had I put the question aloud.

About the room on top of the bookcases stood the collection of
fetishes, family heirlooms, in the main, to which my husband remained loyal. These were dominated by a large, black-framed
Piranesi engraving of the Arch of Benevento at Naples. Below this
was a facsimile of Trajan's column, the jar holding a collection of
his father's pipes, a converted whale-oil lamp, a replica of Romulus
and Remus, another of an Iron Maiden with doors that opened to
display the death-dealing iron prongs; also a dancing faun, a pair of
hourglasses enclosed in spiral teakwood columns which had once
belonged to his grandmother, an Egyptian cat of fine dignity, an
artifact from the Holy Land, and, finally, the death mask of Ran-
dolph Bourne contrived by Arthur Dove. At the back of these objects, leaning against the wall two or three deep, were the framed
photographs of Van Wyck's forebears at Plattsburg, New York, and
in Plainfield, New Jersey, city of his birth, as well as pictures of the
rooms they had inhabited. Of these there were so many that in
order to give each its chance at the light of day I began the practice
month by month of placing some at the rear, bringing others to the
front. The larger pictures I let stand: the trial of Louis XVI by the
French National Assembly, an engraving of Lincoln holding his
silk hat, a framed letter with accompanying photograph of Sainte-

Beuve. The stamp of the study was deeply personal. On entering one felt not only the presence of the single being to whom it belonged but also the aura of the many who had gone to compose this being's substance. And Van Wyck's fidelity allied to his proud sense of the long past kept the whole a living unit. People coming here for the first time, fresh from hurly-burly and routine trivialities, paused a moment on the threshold as they encountered that superior force that men name character.

Indeed, his character, for me, was a whole new charted course in a foreign land, with its peaks and its plains, its shaded groves, its burning sun. I had not only to explore it, to gain a foothold within its boundaries but also, as William James wrote of entering his country on leaving Europe, I was obliged to "pitch my whole sensibility within a different key." For I had encountered a man whose personality, fixed as it was, had been established in stark necessity, and served him now, served his readers also, as a vehicle for his thought. I had come to learn that his was a "daylight mind," rather than "nocturnal," alert each day in the fullness of its power as soon as the dawn broke, but fading toward evening, that he possessed both knowledge and wisdom—seeking wisdom, holding to it as to a life line, while knowledge came to him naturally, a product of his reading and the quality of his mind. I found that he held to a native goodness, a gentleness and an acceptance of obligation based on a decent awareness of right and wrong tied to a perception of the dilemma of the other man. I found that he clung to verity rather than to the flashing light of fame. Had he not warned: "Everything . . . tends to repress the creative and to stimulate the competitive impulse"? And, somehow allied to his dignity, his modesty, there were the contrasting moments of melancholy or of high rage, when his sensibilities had been attacked, the fortress breached, when, hands in his trousers pockets, rattling his coins, striving for composure, he paced the study floor. Back and forth, back and forth he continued until the thunder subsided, violence giving over to the reins of melancholy and thus to patience and courage in renewing the more familiar encounters of the daily round. His humor, I had found, was largely quizzical, aware as he was of the foibles of men but abstaining, through forbearance, from overt reaction to their absurdities, while his gift for discrimination and sympathy held him back from the easy pronouncements of censure or irony usual in ordinary intercourse. He saw each being through the fringes of his own inwardness, rather than taking a person on hearsay. His innocence, his purity were elemental. They reminded me of my carefully limited indoctrination when I was a girl into the standards of the Parisians: "The French are immoral." He was unsophisticated, also, in meeting the routine matters of daily life, as, for instance, his walking the twelve blocks to the New York post office to mail off some urgent note rather than using the telephone, his driving his car through the difficult traffic of lower Manhattan instead of taking the subway. For punctuality he had a passion. I was not to forget his aspect one afternoon early in our friendship as I came on him watch in hand walking the pavement before his apartment-house door, timing the minutes of my nonappearance at a moment of tryst. Yet he could linger on that same day, as if a child from the country, in front of a window holding a group of small dolls from Japan. He was taciturn by habit but voluble when the person or the talk interested him. The shyness of which he spoke took the form of an immobility which held the quality of mystery. "What fine or painful thing went on beneath?" I asked myself. His resolution was a part of the earth revolving on axis, and his power to focus was that of the sun at noon. But there were certain shortcomings in his nature which distressed my husband. Earlier in his life, on graduating from Harvard, he had made an acquaintanceship later to become a fast friendship of great influence, that with John Butler Yeats, the father of the poet. At the age of seventy Mr. Yeats had come to New York and had so happily established himself there that he did not return to Ireland. He lived at Petitpas', a house in West Twenty-ninth Street run by three sisters from Brittany. Here it was that many younger men, writers and painters, gathered about him in the small restaurant at lunchtime, and the conversation flourished.

He painted three portraits of Van Wyck, hanging now in our apartment, and Van Wyck delighted in the old gentleman's wisdom, his genial yet courageous philosophy. Along one of the pages of his book *Oliver Allston,* I was to find that my husband had written:

I have always been a most injudicious letter-writer. I have always been too impulsive,—J. B. Yeats called me the most impulsive of men and he did not say it in praise. My way has always been to say Yes, and then think it over and, thinking, I often found that I was wrong. I had said not what my nature necessitated, but what first came into my mind, because I was touched or pleased or flattered. . . .

But his predominant beliefs, I was wonderfully to find, were more often on the side of light than of darkness and his imagination, with the talent he had to re-create on paper the picture of a forgotten character, a disappearing scene, was a part of his essence. Was not a phrase from his essay on Edwin Arlington Robinson applicable as well to himself? "He revealed a fact which Americans had almost forgotten, that poetry is always opportune."

I admired this man, product of so potent an amalgam, wherein were force and discipline and disappointment and ingenuous faith, and I loved him, seeing in his eyes, about which men spoke, eyes of magical clarity, that he loved me.

On a fine October day, six weeks after our arrival in town, I celebrated a birthday. As reward, Van Wyck had Sheba sent around from the garage and took me for a drive. These afternoon drives about the city delighted him notwithstanding traffic problems, of which he seemed largely unaware. He was like the driver of an eighteenth-century coach, established by right of domain on the box seat, snapping his whip in pleasure at the scene about him, at the smart pace of the vehicle. Now and then I shuddered at what appeared to be escape at close range from accident, but invariably we got through. Our destination on this particular day of Indian summer was the Whitney Museum of Art on Eighth Street, still, at that moment, directed by the artists' friend and benefactor Mrs. Juliana

Force. The exhibition we had come to see was one of Albert Ryder, a representative collection. For many minutes in the quiet of late afternoon we stood before the somberly worked canvases with their flashes of inner light. Van Wyck was reminded of Poe and he was loath to turn his back on them, on a personality thus intent, throughout the years, in so gravely formulating the deeper vision.

At home, after a return drive beneath the sunset-lighted towers of the city, we prepared for the small birthday party of friends who were to dine with us. We had gone out earlier, Van Wyck and I, to buy flowers, wine, and the birthday cake, stopping at the local five-and-ten-cent store for the candles to light it. This shopping together had already doubled the festive quality of the scene to come, and pleasure continued throughout the evening as we gathered our guests in the long living room beneath the mantel vases that held Jo Davidson's towering American Beauty roses. Even after the party ended and guests were gone there remained a permeating sense of their presence in the aspect of chairs drawn together at angles of friendship.

During the soft days of autumn that continued, Van Wyck drove us out sometimes to visit his intimate companions at Westport. I remember one such afternoon when we called on Eugénie and Charles Prendergast. Charles was the beloved brother of the painter Maurice, who had died some years earlier. They had studied together as young men in Boston and together they had gone to live and work in Paris, where Charles had met his wife. It was Charles who stood by to help the more successful Maurice in carving the frames for the canvases that accumulated, and, with his talented, well-trained fingers, Charles contrived also the adornment in color and gold leaf of those wooden chests which traditionally have served as storage space for the careful housewife. Beautiful they were, skillfully done, yet possessing the innocence a novice might bring to the work of art. Indeed, there was something essentially innocent about Charles Prendergast, a quality that drew him to Van Wyck. He and Eugénie greeted us in the garden of their house, where we sat talking and eating her cakes. Then we were taken to the studio to see some paintings of Maurice recently come to light. Charles rubbed his hands together and skipped about the room in pride and pleasure as, one by one, he placed the pictures on an easel. He appeared to enjoy them as though they had only just that moment been completed. "If they'd been discovered earlier they would have been sold and I wouldn't have them here to look at now," he said with his gentle smile. As we drove away presently under the newly risen moon in the sudden chill of an autumn evening, the little old man, over eighty now, looked shrunken and infinitely lonely, waving us good-bye, his gaiety gone. I had a sense that he realized he might not see Van Wyck, whom he trusted and loved, again. The approach of winter must often bring this fear to the elderly.

We went next, early that evening, to call on Karl Anderson, the painter brother of Sherwood Anderson. En route, Van Wyck told me the story of an experience he had once had with Karl, of a book of Karl's composing. Van Wyck, when invited to criticize it, had found the writing florid, even gaudy, and in kindness had set to work to simplify it. But when he had brought the job to an end, rereading the manuscript in its new form, stripped of excess verbiage, he was amazed to find himself confronted with the prose of Karl's brother, Sherwood. As we saw Karl that day he appeared to be rather sadly aging, although he had kept an alertness in his dark-brown eyes and a fine candor in his manner.

We dined in Weston, presently, with Hamilton and Toto Basso. These two friends of Van Wyck had been particularly good to him during the weeks and months following the death of Eleanor Brooks. Toto, with her grace of manner and her beauty, had endeared herself to Van Wyck as she took charge of the sorting of books and household equipment when the Brooks house was sold, helping him with the onerous task of settling into the city, tending him with care, that there might be a minimum of the lonely hours. Ham Basso and Van Wyck shared a common concern for their craft. Ham, a small, eager, articulate man, had the expressive black eyes of his Italian forebears as well as their talent for vivacious argument. His name for Van Wyck was "Pop," a term of endearment usually accompanied by a hug. In our talk that evening Van Wyck defended a certain writer for the quality of his work while others present condemned him for being a knave. The question then arose as to whether Van Wyck was sometimes taken in, fooled by people. Listening to the argument, trying to decide the question for myself, it came to me then, easily perceived, that my husband's magnanimity, his generosity were wide, being related to the breadth of his other powers, and that inevitably he strove to give the devil his due. But fooled he never was. Later, at the dinner table, always a fertile spot for conversation, Ham read us a letter he had recently received from Sigrid Undset, and in connection with this we came to the subject of collecting letters from one's writer friends, and how best to keep them intact, a unit. I was reminded then of the letters belonging to Van Wyck and of the library at the University of Pennsylvania, which already had requested that they be placed, eventually, in its Rare Book Room. Professor Robert Spiller, of the English department there, a friend of Van Wyck's and an admirer of his work, had been the instigator of the plan. When, at the time, I asked Van Wyck why he had overlooked Harvard, his alma mater, in this connection, he had replied, in the voice of a parent who settles a minor dispute between his children: "It doesn't matter where my papers go," and had turned back to his work.

My own existence in the course of the winter was very full, a quantity of everything poured into my lap, a magical world. During five days of each week, I went on with my work in reading instruction at St. Bernard's School for Boys. I continued also with the practice of my violin, making music with whichever among several pianists came to play sonatas with me. Then there were the books that Van Wyck brought me. "See what you think of this," he would say, handing me one of the numerous volumes sent him by authors and publishers in the course of the week. In addition we had a continuing involvement with our friends, the mounting total of two recently united lives, and, blessed and best, our special and most private life together. As a by-product, there was also the means of a new acquisition for me under my husband's guidance. He had, on my birthday, handed over a splendid, vellum-bound book of blank pages sent him earlier by Ruth Stephan, a young poet admirer who hoped he might use it as a daily diary. "I haven't time for this," Van Wyck said to me. "Why don't you keep a journal for us both, an account of our life together?" And he inscribed the book to me. I took it over, along with the obligations that such a task involves, and soon the story of our daily existence became mine to recount as a permanent duty and pleasure. Much of my writing was done in bed. It began before sunrise when, glancing now and then out into the darkness, I saw the gradual lights that came to scattered, solitary windows as the sky went from black through gray into blue. On Sunday mornings, especially, there were long, lazy hours to be enjoyed as the sun pressed into our bedroom and Van Wyck, close at hand, worked uninterrupted in his study, the sort of respite the city offers to a crowded week. The pause in vibrations brought by gigantic trucks on weekdays, roaring beneath us as they did, was like a deep natural breath following asthmatic convulsions, and a sense of similar experience for the other myriad New Yorkers added to the miracle of peace.

There came the day which was the anniversary of our first meeting, Van Wyck's and mine, or, rather, the renewed meeting at my flat in November, 1946, bringing us permanently together. To celebrate this important date I gave my husband the first volume in translation of André Gide's Journal. Far more romantic, especially because he knew of my feeling for this Yankee poet, Van Wyck presented me with a slim volume of poems: *I x I* by E. E. Cummings. I found them fresh, virile, humorous, tender, and of lilting exuberance. On that afternoon I read several aloud to Van Wyck, perching myself on the book bench close beside him. A certain poem had seemed written to commemorate our meeting:

> (once like a spark)
>
> if strangers meet
> life begins—

40

not poor not rich
(only aware)
kind neither
nor cruel
(only complete)
i not not you
not possible;
only truthful
—truthfully,once
if strangers(who
deep our most are
selves)touch:
forever

(and so to dark)

The color of our days at 350 East Fifty-seventh Street during winter and spring was to an extent dependent on the reviews of Van Wyck's *The Times of Melville and Whitman,* published that fall. First the interviewers, often young women, arriving at odd hours to wring from him all that they could of his personal life, his habits, his method. Next the reviews themselves. In advance, Van Wyck had told me that the newspapers should, following the pattern of the earlier books of the series, be favorable. The magazine reviews, however, controlled in the main by the "advanced guard" heads of the English departments in colleges, he expected to attack him. These men, he believed, would not forgive him for certain, by now, notorious passages in *Oliver Allston* wherein he had stated that the influence of Joyce, Proust, Valéry, Gertrude Stein, et cetera, had left a dubious stamp on those of our writers who were concerned with the American literary tradition.

Van Wyck's forecast was correct. The newspapers were, in the main, eulogistic. William Shirer, for example, writing in the New York *Herald Tribune,* said that the combined weight of the four volumes of Van Wyck's history was "one of the few monumental works of American letters." Other reports in the nation's press were largely in accord, soothing words to me, the writer's wife, but lacking in significance for Van Wyck, who awaited the holocaust. It arrived presently, a searing flame, pitiless in the extent of its wish to annihilate. The least injurious of these utterances was one which referred to the "magic moonlight radiance of his style," but which admonished the writer for the reason that "instead of constructing or operating systems for the precise analysis of our literary culture, Mr. Brooks has preferred to create what amounts to an original art form of his own devising." This, it seemed to me, might be considered an enviable achievement. Not so to the author of the piece. Other articles were wounding in the extreme.

"Look at this," Van Wyck said one morning at the breakfast table, thrusting a magazine toward me as he jumped up to pace the floor, frowning, outraged. "The kind of thing that makes one wonder why one writes."

It was a dark, rainy day, heavy with oppression, but he walked to his study, shutting the door with decision to continue his work, pushing into momentary oblivion the day's gloom and the day's disappointments. Now and then I praised my husband for his courage in pressing on as he did. In answer he said merely: "But I'm a professional." Later, I was to read in the pages of *Chilmark Miscellany* words which pointed up his courage even more:

In forty years of writing, I have not gained one ounce of confidence. . . . Every day I begin my work with the same old feeling, that I am on trial for my life and will probably not be acquitted.

A momentary lift into fairer spaces, respite from purgatory, came to Van Wyck from an article written for the *Saturday Review of Literature* by Lewis Mumford, a piece balanced by a happy combination of head and heart:

In reading his history, one has a sense that Mr. Brooks has repeopled the American continent. On his benign Judgment Day, the dead arise from their graves, throw off their shrouds and become flesh and blood again, ready to take their place in eternity. The writer who in his youth called for a usable American past has, in the full tide of his maturity, created that past for us; and has shown us that it was far richer, far sweeter, far more significant than we could, in our rebellious, dissident, adolescent days, have dreamed of.

Even these words, however, were somewhat splashed with the gray hue of a neutral stand. For, in concluding his article, Mumford questioned the choice Van Wyck had been obliged to make between history and criticism. But here, the choice, I believed, had been made necessary by the complexities of subject matter tied to the qualities, the constitution of the writer himself.

As the reviews continued to arrive it was apparent that the so-called avant-garde had largely reversed their feeling for the earlier books of the series and were out as a body to attack the fourth volume. I decided then to try to spare my husband, as much as might be, the further darts of sharp-edged torture by withholding the more objectionable pieces, removing pages from incoming magazines before he had seen them. One day, scissors in hand, I heard his footsteps and hastily I tried to hide an issue of a university quarterly behind a sofa cushion. I was caught. "You mustn't do this," Van Wyck scolded, eyes flashing with anger. "I mean to keep every one of these reviews and some day, when the moment comes, I shall answer my critics together at one time." I ceased to intervene, and the reviews, piling up, he gathered into a labeled carton. Later, in 1953, he replied to his critics in a book entitled *The Writer in America.*

The dispassion necessary for the writing of this book, the self-containment, the candor, the stamina, were complete. Seated at his desk, day after continuing day, engrossed in this lacerating but unalterable task, he faced those who had attacked, exhorting his hosts in the manner of the military forces of tradition. I thought of Henry the Fifth before the field of Agincourt. In the final chapter Van Wyck arrived at the statement of his credo, a summary of belief, a finality, also a plea. It was based, because of the color of his disposition, of his nature, on a shining hope for the future of the world. This, in spite of "the catastrophic defeat of man,—once thought to be noble in reason,—in two world wars." The climate in which we were at present living was described by Van Wyck as a "devil's brew that destroyed the secular hopes of mankind together with its faith and trust in human beings," while the novelists then at work, he said, wound about the unconscious of our time a "mystique of masochism." He called on them to break the evil spell, to tear away the "negative aspects of life." To those writers whom he here addressed, those intellectuals who, in Padraic Colum's phrase, "conceive it to be their privilege and duty to write in favor of that which the great interests of the world are against," he sent a plea, urgent, pressing. He begged them to "be astride again of the instincts that are natural to them and that are paralysed at present." He challenged them to seek, to find, to establish within the collective literary mind an ever-growing faith and grace.

"For that way," he assured them, "lies the line of human growth."

V

Privacy of Storm

*A*T Van Wyck's side in our elongated living room, while the months of winter unrolled, I was now and then swept into the whirlwind of large party giving. The smaller gatherings of our friends were those we chiefly enjoyed, dinner followed by protracted conversation among us all, but on an afternoon of April many people crowded the apartment. This party, I remember, was a double one. The first was the result of Van Wyck's invitation to the house of Dutton, publishers of his books. We hoped that many members of the company would come to us at the end of the working day, everyone from Elliott Macrae, president, downward. They did come in quantity, an event that pleased Van Wyck very specially, and they filled the study as well as the living room while he moved with alacrity from this person to that, almost effervescent in his greeting to those human beings who had assisted him in one way or another to place before the world the burden of his labors.

Added presently to this initial group there arrived from the

Wheelock apartment across the hall several relatives of Phyllis on a visit to the United States, the ancient Italian family of Rucellai. The variants forming this picture were not easily assimilable, but despite confusion and clamor an aura of good will permeated the scene. Late in the afternoon Van Wyck and I had a conversation with the dowager Countess Rucellai, who told us a tale concerning her palace in Florence on the Via della Vigna Nuova. High on the top floor, the story was, stood an attic filled with discarded furniture. Here, workmen arriving to repair the roof came on a series of painted wall decorations. These seemed to be something out of the ordinary, and the experts were called in. It appeared and might soon, the Countess hoped, be verified that the decorations had been executed by Paolo Uccello, famed artist of the fifteenth century, lovely and invaluable works of art, bestowed by happy chance, after centuries of being hidden, on the existing family.

Van Wyck was delighted with the story, as I was. But there it stopped. For it was impossible, then, to foresee the moment fifteen years later, after his death, when I was to find among my husband's youthful copybooks several sheets clipped together and labeled in a child's hand, "My First Composition." The subject was "Paolo Uccello and the Art of Perspective," a learned dissertation by a boy of thirteen. In the course of our talk with the Countess Rucellai on that afternoon Van Wyck had not mentioned the composition, nor did he tell me of it when, during the years of our marriage, we lingered before the work of this painter in the Dublin Museum and in London's National Gallery. As always in his scheme of things, in his personal life, the past seemed less urgent than the possibilities lying ahead. A note among his papers, later, confirmed this, a phrase from a letter of John Jay Chapman written him in 1933:

There ought to be some proverb in Greek or Sanscrit to the effect that one should take no interest in one's past, and self-study should be styled auto-toxic biography.

Among those who came to see us that first winter were Molly and Padraic Colum, intimates of Van Wyck, a friendship sprung from the days of the *Freeman,* that magazine of four years' distinguished standing, edited in its literary department by Van Wyck. Molly had ably helped him at that time. Now, with her redheaded Irish extravagance of tongue, she nonetheless summoned admiration for her extreme but concise judgments of men and books. She possessed the valiancy exhibited on the battlefield when men used spear and crossbow. Padraic, "the pure saint," as Van Wyck called him, was equally knowledgeable but less obtrusive. It was fascinating to hear him recite the ballads of his land, to listen to the tales of Ireland in the long past, Ireland and its writers in the present.

Another connection with Ireland was brought us by James Stern, whose mother had sprung from the Ascendency North. Jimmy and Tania lived then in New York, having temporarily renounced their European citizenship; a closely united couple, whom Van Wyck had inherited through me as I had come to the Colums through him. Tania was part Polish, part German, generous and beautiful. Jimmy, deeply sensitive, a prey to confusion and noise, with his lean body and diversified mind, was a writer by profession, a conversationalist by avocation, a convinced and persistent friend. Like Molly Colum, there was much in him also of biting intellectual keenness and the passion for analyzing the minds and motives of men. Van Wyck immensely enjoyed his company and could never have enough of his talk. When, later, he visited us in Connecticut, the two men were together during many hours of the day, following each other about when work was over like a pair of horses turned out to graze.

One afternoon in early winter, as a friend and I were playing the final movement of a Mozart violin and piano sonata, Van Wyck came in bringing Professor Alexander Meiklejohn, a brave and lovable man, always defending the cause of freedom in academic conduct. Alec had flown on from California, where he lived, in order to address the students of Yale and Dartmouth. We left presently, Alec, Van Wyck, and I, for West Eleventh Street and dinner with Evelyn and Roger Baldwin. In the Baldwin dining room, shut away in quiet below street level, one heard a species of enlightened argument difficult to find elsewhere. Roger, head of the

American Civil Liberties Union, had just returned from Japan, where he had spoken with the Emperor and presented the royal children with boxes of candy from Schrafft's. We listened to his tales of the new Japan as it had been set in motion by MacArthur and we were glad to learn of Roger's general approval. During the evening the talk was chiefly carried on by Roger and Alec, while Van Wyck, I noticed, remained almost silent. But on the way home, seated with my hand in his beneath our taxi roof, he gave me so penetrating a summary of the two men that I was able to value them as never before: Meiklejohn the dreamer with the mind of a scholar who had inadvertently been drawn into the battles of men, Baldwin a fighter by vocation who carried his saber happily, lustily bared.

A meeting of the Literary Awards Committee of the National Institute of Arts and Letters took place one afternoon in our living room. Van Wyck was its chairman, and I was permitted to remain, though not a member, after pouring the afternoon cups of tea. The awards to be decided on were sums of money to be presented at the big spring meeting to candidates allied with literature. Glenway Wescott was there. His aristocratic detachment and benign humor gave him an insight into the motives of writers. He was the author of several books which I particularly enjoyed. There were also William Rose Benét and Marianne Moore, whose conversation, in spite of her tailored, foursquare exterior, had by implication so many mysterious undertones that she became a kind of soothsayer or sibyl. Her smile was kind. Louis Untermeyer was a formidable and most knowing guide to budding talent, it seemed to me as I listened to his downright, humorous pronouncements, and Lillian Hellman was her customary intelligent and tactful self when she wished to make a point in someone's favor. Mark Van Doren came in late from teaching a class at Columbia. His manner of quiet restraint obviously covered strength. It was decided, on Van Wyck's initiative, after the forty-three contestants had been divided into three groups, that one prize be given to a refugee, two to established writers who needed greater recognition or money, and the remaining four prizes to young people not yet known. The first two groups were disposed of without much discussion: Bertolt Brecht was the European refugee chosen, Genevieve Taggard and William Carlos Williams were the two older writers, and a reward was to be given to Djuna Barnes, who, after many years of silence, had begun to write again. Van Wyck had kept the meeting in order so quietly and with such consistent purpose that his leadership had been nearly imperceptible; an example to me in my dealings with disparate elements, an example, possibly, to each person present.

An evening spent with the Theodore Maynards and the Ridgely Torrences, two poet friends of Van Wyck, was interesting to me for bringing an unforeseen encounter with my past. I discovered that Torrence was familiar with the house in which I grew up at 81 Irving Place, near Gramercy Park, because of his friendship with Edwin Arlington Robinson, who had lived at number 71 in the block below us. Often as a child I had skated past that house, and walked by more demurely at a later age, with no notion that a poet lived within. Even had I known, I should not have been impressed, for I was all for adventure then, preferring to be with people of strong vitality rather than with those whose hidden lives held them apart, alone, lives motivated by reflection and sorrow. The merits of these opposing worlds I had later to weigh before I was able, finally, to reach and hold the rewards which are to be gathered from the company of poets.

The days of holiday were suddenly upon us, days of preparation for Christmas that sent us into the shops. Returning home one day we had a happy surprise when Van Wyck opened a package brought to the door and found several copies of a book of his, *The Malady of the Ideal,* a book originally published in England in 1908, when he was twenty-two. It had long been out of print. The new edition, small in size and beautifully designed, had come from the University of Pennsylvania Press, and Professor Robert Spiller had written as preface a sympathetic commentary on Van Wyck's work and on the book itself, which for so long had lain in oblivion.

Christmas breakfast in our living room brought a quiet aura to our personal world. Our tree looked a docile pretty thing, and beneath it, among the presents, a virgin white azalea spread its Christmas petals, an offering from Kenyon. Over coffee, Van Wyck talked about current values, those subscribed to by many of the modernists of our day, values he decried because of their so limited and ungenerous extent. It was the fashion, for instance, he said, among the "bright young men" who wrote criticism for the literary magazines to say that "no one can read Balzac today." Whereas, my husband insisted, Balzac gave you the panorama of life, each cross section replete with nourishment as is honey in the comb.

"Just what is this thing called 'literary criticism'?" I asked my husband now. "How would you describe it?"

"Criticism exists," he answered, "to determine values, to cherish them, define them, and maintain them. That's the reason why criticism is central to civilization. Our criticism is too high-pitched."

Van Wyck's feeling as he talked, his wisdom combined with the innocence of his heart, made for an amalgam of profound sincerity. How not be moved by it?

At the end of the morning we went across the hall to eat our Christmas dinner with the Wheelocks. Caroline and Allen Tate were there, and we were thus able to thank Allen for his Christmas card, "Fragment of a Meditation."

> The signs and portents screaming in the air
> The Nativity in my thirtieth year
> Will glow in the heavens. . . .

A friendly gathering wherein, as always, the Wheelocks acted in the guise of family: Jack, tall, lanky, benign, a perfect host, with his sweetness and his equanimity; Phyllis, with her pretty face, full of a suppressed but vital excitement at the presence of her guests, whom she shepherded with maternal concern. The end of the day became, in our apartment, the setting for an eggnog party, and presently, with lamps extinguished, tree and mantel candles softly glowing, the music of César Franck coming from our recorder, it seemed as though we were a part of the spheres.

An old-fashioned drama was brought to New York in the days after this Christmas of 1947 when a twenty-four-inch snowfall, exceeding the great blizzard of 1888, disrupted services in the city for several days. Cars marooned along the streets resembled in their white shrouds the sheet-draped pranksters of Halloween and pedestrians moved at their leisure along the center of highways, usurping the place of the usual traffic. Over all hung a prospect of new freedom, the sense of playing a carefree game, one based on the collapse of a great city. A giant dislocation. Van Wyck delighted in the game. We walked about in the sparkling cold that followed the storm, and we might have been ambling along a village lane. At evening, in overshoes and heavy coats, we set out for the Third Avenue Elevated in order to keep a dinner engagement in the East Forties, proceeding on foot for a large part of the way.

"I shall be sorry when we're returned to civilization," said Van Wyck as we walked the final block, his cheeks glowing from exertion in the chill air.

"So shall I. Let's go live in the country," I said.

Finally we were back in a workaday world, the various holidays at an end. We had lived happily through them. People living alone at such moments cannot greatly enjoy them, I had found. Van Wyck gave as a reason for this that holidays create a hole through which we drop to the foundation of our being, whereas on the ordinary days, he said, there was formed a covering or insulation which helped to obscure the hole. Anyway, we hoped never, either one, to be obliged to live any future part of our lives alone, we told each other once again.

As the winter continued I learned to narrow the visits of our friends. Van Wyck himself was naturally a guide in choosing those important to him. One day, for example, he invited James Farrell to lunch with us. Farrell had attacked Van Wyck and his work at an earlier date but now asked for a meeting. *Studs Lonigan* had been published ten years previously, but successive books had not attained a comparable popularity. With a manner as unkempt as the shock of hair above his eyes, he was a stimulating talker, intensely loyal to his origins in the slums of Chicago and, in the present, swept with enthusiasm for the theories and insight of Freud, whom he continued to study. His summaries, on that day, of writers, including Max Eastman and John Dos Passos, seemed to Van Wyck acute and amusing.

The Eastmans asked us to dine with them in the small Thirteenth Street walk-up which they used as a *pied-à-terre* when not in their house near Gay Head, on our island. Max seemed a rather constrained presence on that evening, lacking the gusto which was his at Martha's Vineyard, where his white hair flew in the island wind as he drove here and there in the small roadster with which I chiefly associated him. Eliena, too, his Russian wife, seemed more at home in those wider spaces, which were better fitted to her gestures. The Raymond Fosdicks were at dinner. He, as head of the Rockefeller Foundation, had had much to do with the publication of Kinsey's report on the sex life of the American male, an issue which latterly had brought acrimonious debate. Fosdick's reasons for supporting the book hung on the uses of frank statement versus secrecy.

"If we admit certain fundamentals of behavior to be the norm," he argued, "we abolish the sense of guilt, a crippling emotion."

"But often necessary, nonetheless," said Van Wyck.

"Rather than making the attempt to legislate man's life," Fosdick went on, "it should be judged on the basis of good versus bad taste."

"Do you believe we can rely on taste when it comes to morals?" Van Wyck asked. This question seemed not easy to answer.

After dinner the E. E. Cummingses came in. He was full of an elfish kind of humor and was particularly in vein as he described a recent encounter with T. S. Eliot. "A one-man institution rather than a racket, which presupposes a motive for putting himself over. Eliot just *is*," he said. I was glad that the image of Cummings I had held in my mind, sprung from his verse, need not be disturbed. He seemed that evening very happy to remember that Van Wyck owned one of his paintings, a wind-torn sunset reminiscent of a Ryder gone vivid. Marion Cummings was wise and simple and lovely to see.

At cocktails one afternoon in the Tates' Perry Street flat there were gathered many people to crowd the two small rooms which seemed to have become magnets to draw them from the waning winter sky. Three of Allen's fellow poets were present: Léonie Adams and Robert Fitzgerald as well as his particular friend, Jack Wheelock.

"You may some day find that Frank R. Stockton was a more important novelist than Henry James," I overheard Jack say to Léonie. This was spoken doubtless in jest, but, I reflected, Van Wyck would not have been shocked. The weighted pressures of the James cult, at the moment, annoyed him.

A young man entering the party with Marguerite Young, later to be known for her extraordinary novel *Miss MacIntosh, My Darling,* was Truman Capote. He had not yet justified himself as a clever writer, and I watched him in astonishment touched with pity. He was very short, his blond hair above a child's face cut in a bang, and he clung to his stalwart friend as they confronted the others. He might have been a shy boy brought to school on the opening day except that he was not made to relinquish a hold on his protector. We stayed on for dinner, and afterwards Allen read to us from his own poems, from those of Louise Bogan and John Peale Bishop. He brought a solemnity to the words and a caress to the last lines, as if persuading them to linger along the floor of eternity.

Every now and then, at the apartment, we offered overnight shelter to friends who sought us on their trips to the city. One of these was Hamilton Basso. He arrived, once, bringing Peter De Vries, a writer whose variety of humor seemed made of cynicism and kindness and ingenuousness and despair, a wit well suited to his moment in time. Ham stayed on talking to Van Wyck until bedtime, and I enjoyed watching his excitable gestures and the affection he spilled out on Van Wyck as, by degrees, my husband's staying powers diminished and his eyelids drooped. "I guess you're about ready for bed, Pop," said Ham presently. "Oh, not at all," Van Wyck answered hurriedly, pulling himself up to a rigid position.

Another overnight guest was Margaret Cobb, who came in occasionally from Westport, where in her large house and from her large heart she gave shelter to a numerous family. She wished to see how we progressed, Van Wyck and I, as man and wife. "Don't forget that I gave you two the initial push that brought you together for good and all," she often said. I answered with a smile while Van Wyck remained silent. He believed that the impetus had been his own. But he loved Margaret. And we were both glad of her approval.

A guest whom Van Wyck greeted with especial pleasure was Newton Arvin. They had become friends during earlier days at Westport but now met rarely because of Newton's teaching job at Smith College. Dining with us once when Arvin was there, were the young poet Ruth Stephan and her husband. She had for several years subsidized a magazine of poetry—*The Tiger's Eye*—an immense boon to the many unpublished poets, and it pleased Van Wyck to learn that the circulation had already reached the four thousand mark. Newton, at that moment, was at work on his book about Melville. I found him a subdued and sad man and I wondered if to teach the subject of English to a fluid population of young women year after year might be a life-sapping experience.

A trip away by myself took me to Boston to visit my several families there. A severe snowstorm blanketed the train windows during my return to New York, and I sat driven in on my thoughts. Train trips had ever been a solace to me. They brought a kind of rest which I found in no other way, my actions circumscribed and the bugaboo of choice exorcised. The ideas, the images, arising at such moments were often valuable. I remembered train trips which had had an undeniable effect on my life. But the best on that day of storm was to come. Van Wyck awaited me at Grand Central, markedly visible, muffler wrapped high about his chin, snow clinging to his Burberry. He had walked the long way through the blizzard to meet me. He stood in the front line behind the rope that holds the crowd in place, and once again he appeared somehow separated from those about him, as though the forces within had sloughed off the ordinary, the usual, to give him some particular essence of his own. I ran to him persuaded that I had been away forever rather than for thirty-six hours.

Our arrival home became a literal shelter from the tempest without, and the apartment was a welcoming place, flowers fresh in their vases, a fire on the hearth. Over the evening cocktail we spoke of Van Wyck's book *Three Essays on America,* an early work which on the train I had been reading, the style graceful and confident, product of youth and precocity. He talked to me now of a man's writing style, saying it was the emanation of his nature at the moment, a mysterious elixir compounded of experience and emotion and the exigencies of the subject matter. I listened with care. For what could be more immediate, more binding for me, than words direct from my husband's mind and heart?

VI

Men and Phantoms

*J*OURNEYS undertaken together, away from home, from routine and the effort of the daily discipline, were occurrences that now and then drew us. But the manner of Van Wyck's return, streaking for his study like a bird dog intent on its prey, showed where his deepest heart led him. We seldom accepted invitations to spend a night in the house of a friend and had not as yet exchanged our own bedroom, except during the days of our honeymoon, for that at a distant inn. It was thus, for me, a matter of the maximum excitement, "heart-pounding," as the children called it, to drive from our door with bags and books behind us and anticipation before us.

The first of our trips away from New York was made in early fall in order to visit the Poughkeepsie warehouse where many of my possessions were stored. Van Wyck had agreed to accompany me, and in order to add to our pleasure we had accepted a long-standing invitation to stay with friends living at Kingston in an old Dutch house built when this town had been the capital of New

York. We left, driving Sheba, soon after breakfast on a Sunday morning when Fifty-seventh Street was quiet and open as a village highway and the air as fresh as innocence. We crossed the George Washington Bridge and found youthful zealots, knapsacks on their backs, walking the footpath. It was a day of fair blue skies, and the orchards and sloping vineyards above the Hudson were lovely to see in their autumn guise as we drove northward along the west bank of the river. So, also, were the glimpses we had of imposing houses and parks on the opposite shore built in the eighteenth and nineteenth centuries by the gentry of our land. Van Wyck, pointing them out, was widely aware of their history, of the names connected with them, so that I was given a running instruction tied to anecdotes amusing to hear. Reaching Kingston rather ahead of the appointed time, we drove on to Woodstock, where I had once spent five years within the colony of artists who lived there, hard-working painters, many of them with wide reputations, some of them living on the minimum of income, men whose wives were staunch and gallant in meeting the daily needs. The center of this community, known as the Maverick, was an open-air building where concerts took place on Sunday afternoons, concerts in which various New York professionals played music magical to hear while oftentimes thunder and lightning clattered through heavy-weighted clouds and raindrops freighted with hail competed with the running sixteenth notes of violin and flute. I had been invited one summer to join a group of established musicians in playing second fiddle to a string quartet. How flattered I was to be thus included, how long I practiced, how frightened I was at the opening concert and again on a later occasion when an A string snapped during the performance and the music had to be halted while with trembling fingers in the tenacious heat I wove a new string from tailpiece to peg and up to the required pitch.

In the course of my exhibiting this portion of my life to Van Wyck, we reached the hour when we were due in Kingston. We drove, then, down to that city of stone houses and demure aspect, a city wherein turbulence seemed to be unknown, where the small neat baskets attached to white door fronts, awaiting the postman, brought the sort of security one would choose as background for convalescence after severe illness. Also belonging to the old New York tradition was the ancient Senate House, which we visited in order to see the Vanderlyn portraits hanging there. In advance, Van Wyck had given me the story of this local farmer's son, John Vanderlyn, whose talent had so impressed Aaron Burr that he sent the boy to Paris for ten years of application in French studios and had supported him there. Born at the moment of our Revolution, Vanderlyn had been the first of our portraitists to study in Paris rather than London. He received a gold medal from the French for his large picture "Marius Amid the Ruins at Carthage," and he had painted a wall decoration for the Capitol rotunda at Washington. He died in Kingston, of absolute want. A sad tale, but fascinating as my husband recounted it.

One of our brief visits, which did not include the night, we made on a lowering autumn day to Arcan Ridge, at Westport, home of Helen Keller and Polly Thomson. Van Wyck had wished to have me see Helen within her own setting and he himself was curious to view the new house which had risen above the ashes of her former one, burned some months before, when Helen and Polly had been on a visit to Japan. He was delighted on our arrival to find the new house identical with the one he had always known. A benevolent and all-seeing donor had been responsible for restoring the familiar from beginning to end, even to the pots and pans in the kitchen. Inside, one was conscious of the smell of paint and paper hanger's paste, and yet, already in position, a kind of miracle, was a collection of ornaments sent on the long journey eastward by Helen's Japanese admirers to decorate the house, mementoes on a grand scale. Her library, however, of patient Braille books and her collection of letters from the far, wide world had vanished.

We were shown into the living room, with its background of flowers, where for a moment we stood waiting within the aura of Helen's ineffable presence, which hovered like the scent of flowers above a garden bed. With Polly's arrival there was an end to hidden awareness. She was openly hospitable, brisk, and, in her person, conveyor of that "carry-on" attitude basic to the British. Her Scottish upbringing clung fast to bring the dour courage which was a part of her character and most useful in her dealings with the dual world which she endlessly inhabited.

"Shall we go upstairs to see Helen in her study?" she asked us now.

My heart took on an extra beat as I moved slowly upward. Van Wyck followed, and presently, on the landing above, Polly threw open a door, reaching inside to turn an electric switch. A ceiling light leapt to change the study from night to day, to fall on a large writing table where, motionless in her chair before it, hands clasped above her Braille copy of the Bible, Helen Keller sat alone in her private world. She was unaware of the light, as also she had been unaware of the dark. She did not know that we watched her; she knew only her inner thought, enkindled as it was by the great words she had been reading, her fingers moving across the page with deliberation so that the purport of the writer became a veritable part of her. She smiled as we stood at the side of her world and she spoke aloud in answer, no doubt, to one of the Hebrew prophets, while her gesture, in the lovely way that she had, seemed to include us in the joy which was hers. The luster that emanated from her was like the original act of creation, the source from which life springs.

Presently Polly moved forward to touch her, to tap on Helen's hand the fact of our presence, and Helen arose, brushing the dream aside.

"Time for tea with Van Wyck and Gladys," said Polly in her cheery tone, which communicated itself to her charge in ways invisible to the eye and inaudible to the ear. Helen embraced us in turn, murmuring each name, then placed a hand on Polly's shoulder for guidance as far as the stair landing. She was on her own as she descended, negotiating the stairs by means of the special rail along the wall.

Below, before a blazing fire, Herbert brought in highballs as well as tea, for both Helen and Polly enjoyed their Scotch at the end of day. Herbert's last name I soon forgot. It seemed not an essential part of this unusual man who acted as general factotum and host to Helen's household. He had begun his service at Arcan Ridge in the role of gardener and chauffeur but had soon achieved, because of his superior bearing, the right to play diverse parts, and had become, gradually, the mainstay on which all depended. He had mastered the difficult art of Braille and was a fluid technician, now, in the manual of the deaf and dumb, so that he was fully capable of taking charge of Helen when Polly left her side. Herbert it was, also, who with clever fingers carved the numerous birdhouses spread about the place, houses for wrens, for bluebirds, for orioles. His quiet attitude in dealing with human beings had as beneficent an effect on them as it had on the birds. To Van Wyck and me he was especially kind, building us a feeder for our birds when we took possession of our place in Connecticut. It saddened us to learn on a day that followed another of our visits to Arcan Ridge that Herbert had died, falling one morning to the floor of the living room, never to rise again. Helen and Polly were bereft. They were not to fill his place.

The Washington's Birthday holiday in 1948 we spent with John Carroll, painter, and his wife, Georgia, at Chatham, New York. Their house was set among the open hills of the lower Berkshires, a farmhouse of the 1860 period and little modernized. Inside, clinging layers of faded paper had been stripped away from the walls, the plaster beneath left bare and uneven. This constituted a disordered but romantic background for John's fanciful paintings and for the scattered pieces of English walnut and Sheffield plate decorating the rooms, while at evening, the picture currently occupying the place of honor was lit by a seven-branched silver candelabrum placed beneath it. The wide floor boards were stained almost black, uncovered save for a white bear rug before the fireplace, and at the high narrow windows hung embroidered muslin curtains in fairylike delicacy, permitting us to see, beyond, the stark limbs of an ancient ash. On a pedestal, tall as a man, in place before the front wall, a wrought-iron urn held a cluster of spring primulas, and their uncontaminated white was lit by the sun when it entered the room from the far-ranging snow-covered meadows without.

John Carroll, a turbulent, sensitive, unhappy man, ever in search of his Irish mystic's soul, which would not let him rest, I had known for all the years since the First World War when he returned from serving in the navy as seaman and specialist in camouflage. His first wife, a talented pianist, had come to Washington during John's absence, from the Cleveland Conservatory of Music, on the invitation of Nicholas Longworth, to act as accompanist to his violin playing and mine. We had established a friendship then, and my affection for her and for John, although they were presently to separate, continued. He had now married a young former student, a tiny creature, frail and rather silent, with immense hazel eyes, a child's upturned nose, and a wide mouth. It was an unusual face, appealing, haunting, which John painted over and over again. It appeared, as if by unconscious compulsion, in his portraits of other women, bringing to these an attenuated reminder of their painter's preoccupation. John and Georgia seemed the ideal counterpart of male and female: John strong, capable, quick of decision; she gently pensive, amenable, but coming to life in her culinary achievements, which had the quality of high art. John was master of the local hounds, a breeder of gamecocks, a farmer, and he moved with a kind of fury from early till late. He it was who started the fires in the morning stove, filled the kettle, supervised our breakfast while Georgia lingered in her room, emerging finally in unobtrusive fashion to sit on a low bench before the living-room fire, where she read her book in the way that small girls read the romance that fascinates them.

On the Sunday morning, soon after breakfast, I looked about for Van Wyck but did not find him. Later it appeared that he had gone with John to the studio to pose for a portrait. Georgia presently came in, her housecoat trailing the floor, her hair down her back, looking like one of Gabriel's attendant angels. We talked, but I could not persuade her to speak of her own paintings, which were, I had been told, in the nature of small and charming fantasies. These she sent off to the city of her youth, and they were promptly sold, the proceeds going toward the ornamental enhancement of the house. Thus did she fill the days when John was away from home, gone to teach in New York at the Art Students League or to make one of his commissioned portraits, which emerged from the final brush stroke with the stamp of Georgia upon them. Was this, I wondered, a consolation to her, homage unspoken in return for her many lonely hours?

Van Wyck was twice able to sit for John during our visit, and the portrait that grew in the studio was strangely like and yet unlike him, a blend of reality and the painter's vision: a lofty form of caprice which immensely drew us. It gave out the inner quality possessed by my husband, which no other painter had yet discovered. And then on a chilly morning we said our farewells to the angelic Georgia and to John, who loaded Sheba for us and leaped into the driver's seat with a gesture to Van Wyck to sit behind. Brusquely he seized the wheel and drove us along icy lanes as far as the highway, his handy man following in a truck. There John descended and presently left us, we to return to our quietly ordered routine, he to headlong activity and passionate accomplishment.

In late March we undertook a three-week trip to the South, our first extended journey as man and wife, a real holiday. Van Wyck had chosen Lexington, Virginia, as our objective, site of Washington and Lee University and a spot, he said, centered on Southern history. Before leaving, I bade my farewell to St. Bernard's, after several years of intensive teaching in that agreeable and friendly school. We were both tired because of obligations and constraints fallen upon us during the last months in New York, Van Wyck in particular, his nerves taut and his spirit burdened. Wonderful to drive away, going deeper and deeper into new spaces where no soul had the desire, the power to stop us. At Baltimore, our first stop, being novices still in the matter of motels, we drove to a hotel recommended by the guidebook, and for me it was a most gratifying pleasure to follow behind the porter carrying our bags into the lobby, to stand beside my husband as he signed the register "Mr. and Mrs. Van Wyck Brooks." We might have been getting married all over again.

Next morning we wandered about the residential portions of the city, and Van Wyck talked to me of Mencken and of the German colony from which he had sprung, his father a German manufacturer of cigars and his mother a German-American. The family barber was a German, as was the farm hand in the country. Mencken had attended a German-language school, where he learned to sing *Volkslieder* and where those unfortunate students born of pure American stock were regarded as dunces. These beginnings, Van Wyck believed, were unalterably to influence Mencken and his point of view, and perhaps accounted for his enduring bellicosity toward many of his fellow Americans. He had spent his life in one house in Baltimore and he valued the tradition of his past as he pitied the New Yorker for his inability to establish long-lived relationships. His major work, Van Wyck said, *The American Language,* was born of a facile ear for music added to the experience gained as a young newspaper reporter in the jargon of the city room.

From Washington we set out rather late on the journey to Lexington, driving as often as possible along the roads of Van Wyck's choice, the less-traveled ones. Once we lost our way, and in order to retrieve our error took a short cut of twenty miles along empty ridges caught between mountaintops and valleys. I drove while Van Wyck followed the map intermittently, the countryside being to him of more importance than our direction. The sun came and went and came again before its final setting between clouds freighted with water, and the glory of its recurrence each time brought a fresh promise of unnamable joy. There is something magical, midway between the solemn and the festive, about the last hour before sunset as one motors through a countryside. I had known it in the Rhone Valley between Cluny and Mâcon, in the hills of Dutchess County bordering the Hudson, and in the Dolomites of Italy.

Lexington, on our arrival, was a disappointment. The hotel room engaged in advance was small and the general atmosphere without any sort of appeal. After dinner, however, our spirits rose as we walked through the university grounds by moonlight and saw the ancient brick buildings spaced in dignity, their intensely white columns standing tall and forever upright. Van Wyck told me the story of General Lee when he was invited to become president of this poor little college at the Civil War's end. He accepted, and bidding good-bye to his family, with whom he had only recently been reunited, he mounted his horse, Traveller, companion through all the battles, and rode slowly and alone over the Blue Ridge and into the Lexington Valley. As we went back to the hotel we came on small groups of students moving between dark trees and branches of flowering plum. Each in turn bade us good evening in a gentle Southern voice.

Next morning we searched for rooms, calling at several houses of broad and ingratiating aspect that stood near the university, where we should have liked to be. But while people were courteous in responding to Van Wyck's queries and several attempted to help us, we were told that university students and their families were already in tenure. Finally, we drew up before the Hotel Natural Bridge, south of Lexington, a huge place of white painted wood three stories high and hung with massive porches displaying empty rocking chairs. The ravine below, heavy with the sound of rushing waters, was the base of the chasm spanned by the Natural Bridge, that towering spontaneous creation of stone. Inside the hotel during this pre-season period, all was quiet and gleaming, and the dining room promised us generous fare. We were shown a bedroom with twelve-foot studs, and furnished with two double beds. Through white muslin curtains we looked out on a gentle grass terrace embellished with jonquils and hyacinths and a Judas tree in the act of opening its buds. An elderly gardener was at work below the window. It seemed an altogether pleasant spot, and it was at this moment free of tourists. We engaged the room, and soon our books were ranged on top of a tall highboy, one of the beds was turned into a sofa, and a vase of jonquils, which I had gathered from the lawn below, was on the dressing table.

On Easter day, cold and overcast, we did not linger long at the dawn ceremonies beneath the Natural Bridge, a tradition that drew massive crowds, but escaped to our quiet room as soon as might be. In the afternoon, when Van Wyck's work had ended, he took me for a drive. I had been eager to find a spot where one summer during the first war I had gone with my children to live in a house along the Blue Ridge summit in order to escape the heat of Washington, a place named Buena Vista. There, that summer, the Russian ambassador to the United States and his massive wife, with their numerous servants, had occupied the local hotel, pre-empting it for themselves alone. On the narrow piazza, I remembered, formerly in possession of traveling salesmen, feet on balustrade, the Bakhemetieffs had established their aviary, birds in gilt cages that glistened in the sunshine, and here the young servant, whose duties were exclusively to them, fed the parrots, the parakeets, the macaws, while her master and mistress sipped tea drawn from a silver samovar close by. We did not manage to reach Buena Vista that day, but passing through a small settlement on the way back I heard Van Wyck exclaim at a sign he saw on a house front.

"Did you notice that name?" he asked. "How curious to find it here, 'Rose Aylmer.' "

"Who was she?" I asked.

"Walter Savage Landor wrote a poem to her. You don't know it?" I did not know it, and he recited it for me:

> Ah, what avails the sceptred race,
> Ah, what the form divine!
> What every virtue, every grace!
> Rose Aylmer, all were thine.
> Rose Aylmer, whom these wakeful eyes
> May weep, but never see,

A night of memories and sighs
I consecrate to thee.

We went on to speak of the death of this beautiful woman, of death in general, and Van Wyck said it had always seemed impossible to believe that anyone could die on a day of bright sunshine. But the mystery of Landor's lovely Rose Aylmer in this remote spot was never solved.

Difficult to realize that our holiday could have an end, that one day we should no longer see the sunrise touching pine trees whose tall trunks had remained our weather gauge during the happily unrolling days: a soft pink for a fair day, a dull mauve for an overcast, like the colors on the petticoat and knickers belonging to the tiny dolls who inhabit the toy houses of Switzerland announcing the weather as the lady or her partner dances to the forefront. Gone also our trips afield and the return at evening, our hands filled with white violets, primrose, and the delicate pink of sweet viburnum. When the day of leaving was upon us, we drove slowly past Washington and Lee University, that place of dignity and self-containment. I had come to associate it with the adornments of duty and the purpose, tied to authority, that governs these splendid attributes. I was loath to bid it farewell.

We reached Washington late that afternoon, and Van Wyck took me to dine at the Hotel Hay-Adams. I had last been on this spot when Henry Adams's house stood there next to that of John Hay, the house of red stone designed for him by the noted H. H. Richardson. Uncle Henry had made me one of his "nieces," a latter-day honor, at the moment of my meeting him as a girl in Paris. Many times during World War One, which followed my first marriage, I had lunched or dined at this Washington house, and I had been summoned one early morning by his attractive young companion, Aileen Tone, to see Uncle Henry on his deathbed, a magnificent figure of stern and lofty presence surmounting in death the frustrations of his life. Since my alliance with Van Wyck Brooks and reading his *New England: Indian Summer,* I had added to my knowledge of Henry Adams by means of the perceptive account written there of his proud failure and his flight from the world. These were the memories that came to me as I sat in a dining room belonging to any who would enter, to those presumably unconcerned with the past.

We lunched next day, at Van Wyck's suggestion, in Newcastle, Delaware, that small seventeenth-century city which sat, quietly unaware of progress, between pressures ferocious enough to have squeezed the life from anything less archaically determined. We ate at a restaurant within the old Court House, under the high dome, our table close to the raised dais once used by the judge. Afterwards, we walked through the town, slowly, at Van Wyck's pace, stepping on ancient cobblestones marked with the hollows used for open drainage in years past. Few people were about, but in a house of brick soft with age overlooking the square, a young girl sat writing at her desk in a sunny window, a tumbler of squills beside the inkwell. A portrait by Vermeer.

Leaving this remote paradise, we set out for the ferry to New Jersey. On the far side of the river we headed for Plainfield. We had decided that I was to be shown the house in that town at 237 East Ninth Street where my husband was born. It was an inconspicuous place, inhabited now by strangers, and small enough to have made a family move necessary when he was still a little boy. We drew up our car before the house front and remained for a moment in silence. I tried to picture a young woman seated on the far side of lace-curtained windows, a baby in her arms, a baby with solemn, staring eyes, Van Wyck and his mother, of whom he did not often speak, seemed unable to speak. I knew she had been charming beyond the usual, but it was not he who had told me of this. He spoke instead about his grandmother, whom he had much loved. We continued, now, to sit in silence until finally my husband said: "Let's move on, shall we?" I glanced at him and saw that he sat rigidly upright, that the frown was in place on his forehead.

"Of course," I answered, and started Sheba's engine. "Would you like to see the second, the later house?"

"No. We'll put that off to another time. Best to get home."

"Yes, you're tired. We shouldn't have stopped here at the end of a long journey."

We drove on, making for the highway, and I wondered how to break the spell that wrapped him. In a moment he broke it himself:

"As a matter of fact, it's just as well we came. You've helped to exorcise the ghosts surrounding the past. They have a way of clinging. Thank you, Gladys."

"Oh, my darling," I said, and took my eyes from the road for a moment, turning my cheek for my husband's kiss.

VII

A Kelson of Creation

*T*HE concerts that Van Wyck and I attended in New York inevitably held us as one. For him they became a solace, quieting his mind. One of the events which had increased our friendship was an evening of music by Robert Shaw's choral group heard, not long after we first met, at the Metropolitan Museum. I had invited Van Wyck to go with me on that occasion. Playing music and hearing it played had been a major part of my life. Van Wyck, by contrast, had not closely followed it. His mind was more intimately concerned with the other arts. We sat that evening, I remember, side by side in the gallery above the main hall, and from afar we heard the beautiful sound of mingled voices as they rang out, floating upward. The program itself I can no longer name, but I shall not forget its impact on Van Wyck as well as on me.

"You've opened a door into new pleasures," he said. "I realize now what I've missed."

Occasionally as the winter wore on we selected programs of modern music. One in which we were particularly interested was a portion of a festival series in honor of Ernest Bloch's compositions given by the Juilliard School. Van Wyck and Bloch had been writing to each other for more than a year. Bloch felt that they were kindred spirits, and the letters arriving from the Pacific coast, where Bloch lived, were monuments of length and thought and feeling. On that evening we heard his psalms, which were laments for the singing voice, and a viola sonata which held a quality of whispering wisdom in the bow's soft pressure. The outcome was a lofty accord rather than discord. Thus do the great speak to eternity.

Another evening was given to hearing the Bennington College choir sing fifteenth-, fourteenth-, and thirteenth-century music. The singers stood grouped in the Metropolitan Museum Armor Hall, casting a bright sort of renewal over the embattled yet somnolent figures in their glass-fronted cases, music matching their own period; nothing at variance. On our way out at the end of the concert, we encountered Buckminster Fuller and his wife; he was a cousin of mine whom I rarely saw because of his many absences from New York. Curiously, I had come only the evening before on Fuller's *Nine Chains to the Moon,* and I had asked Van Wyck to glance at it, a difficult book for the layman owing to the complexity of the writer's ideas. At Bucky's command lay variations of thought fostered by several different disciplines: architecture, mathematics, geography, history, engineering, and poetry. Emerson's friend Margaret Fuller had been a forerunner of his, and he shared the courage of her imagination. He seemed worthy of carrying on the great tradition, if in a different form. At any rate, I was glad to see him again and to observe how happy he was to find me at Van Wyck's side.

During January we undertook an experience new to us both. This was at the instance of Van Wyck's friend Lee Simonson, who had just then completed a series of sets for Wagner's Nibelungen Ring at the Metropolitan Opera House. He was eager to have us see them, suggesting that we attend dress rehearsals for one or two of the performances. Van Wyck liked the idea and decided to forfeit several mornings of work, playing hookey from school in order to see and hear. With Lee's passes in hand we found ourselves groping our way one morning along the dark aisle of the Metropolitan parterre toward seats not far from the stage. The rehearsal of *Rheingold* was in progress, with its astonishing flow of preparation for the final performance: the tornado of emotion pouring from the stage in the voices of singers, the fumes from underworld fires, the shouts of despair uttered by the conductor when one of the singers missed his cue. This was Wagner and the German myth in crudest essence. Gradually, we were able to focus our attention on Lee's scenery, compelling as it was, and suitable to the background of the story. It had a fine austere quality, jagged rocks and rude cliffs, while the color and lighting possessed an affinity with the sensuous line of the music. Thus barbarism and sentiment were perfectly allied, in keeping with the tradition. I liked especially the staunch composure of the little fir trees, kept low in growth, as at that altitude they are, trees bordering the spaces of Valhalla, where the gods confer. There was a charm in the fixed curve of their branches suggesting the tales of Grimm, as also they reminded me of the tiny acid green trees on their stands that belonged to the toy sets given us at Christmas when we were children, toys from Schwarz, made in Germany.

Among the exhibitions of painting, during the winter months, we saw many. Here it was I who became the pupil and Van Wyck the docent. For my husband had begun his indoctrination at the age of eleven when, on a trip to Europe with his family, his father had taken him, on first arrival, to the Zwinger gallery in Dresden. This event Van Wyck liked to dwell on. It had been a decisive moment for him and for his future. "We were in Europe for a year," he told me, "and I was seldom out of a gallery. A kind of adolescent passion."

At the end of that year, when he was twelve, he had chosen his career. He would become an art critic. Someone, when the family had settled in at a pension in Dresden for the winter of 1897, had given the boy a copy of Mrs. Jamieson's *Lives of the Painters,* which he read with application and lingered over for weeks. From

71

this he advanced to Ruskin, thence to Vasari. His seven small diaries, written and illustrated in ink at that period, give the story of this boyhood preoccupation. "Mamma and Ames have gone shopping in the rue de Rivoli," was one of the entries in June of that year, "but I decided to visit the Louvre." And had not his first composition been principally concerned with the art of perspective?

Thus, I was to benefit from his extended application, Van Wyck's *violon d'Ingres,* which during all his life was to remain his second love. Many were the occasions, modesty notwithstanding, when he was able to exhibit his learning. Once, I recollect, during a visit made by several of us to a private gallery at a short distance from Saratoga, New York, and near the painter-writer colony of Yaddo, where we were staying, the director of the gallery and Van Wyck found they had a common bond. Their conversation was overheard by several of the visiting Yaddo artists, who later commented on it.

"What a lot about painting that man Brooks knows!" I heard one of them say on the drive home. "A whole lot more than any of us."

Early in the 1948 winter our first encounters were with the work of two friends: Jo Davidson and John Sloan. The Davidson portrait busts were on exhibition at the Academy of Arts and Letters, one hundred and ninety of them. It was an impressive assemblage. The group in which Van Wyck's bust stood held the full-length sculptured portrait of Gertrude Stein, with Joyce and Pirandello on one side of her, Sandburg and Van Wyck on the other. Many of these pieces had come from Bêcheron, the Davidson place in the Loire district of France, and were the result of years of labor. The fashion in sculpture was then in process of change, turning its back on realism, but anything as authentic as these likenesses of Davidson's should, we believed, have a meaning for posterity.

The opening of John Sloan's exhibition of paintings was crowded with his many supporters. It was a retrospective showing which included some canvases from as early as 1902: tender pictures of women within the setting of their unadorned lives which gave out the tranquillity of this long-lost time. Sloan's later work had become higher in key, gathering intensity as he grew older. He was to die not many years after this exhibit without having established the later manner, and he will undoubtedly be remembered as one of the romantic proponents of what is known as the "Ash Can School."

The month of May brought a Grolier Club showing, with the work of Rudolph Ruzicka on display, designs for the enhancement of book printing: varieties of type, engravings for head and tail pieces, illustrations to serve the text. Ruzicka it was who had originated the Fairfield type used for Van Wyck's *Chilmark Miscellany*. It seemed the best possible vehicle for conveying this author's prose. We examined it all, therefore, with great pleasure, marveling at the minuteness of detail, at so much elegance and control, at the clarity of black on white and the delicacy of color.

As we made our way home through the wood-bordered paths of Central Park, we talked of Ruzicka. And we agreed that his work held the essence of a day in early spring when rain had washed the earth and the tender twigs of trees with a limpid freshness.

Pleasures such as these could not entirely erase the vexing thoughts that lurked in Van Wyck's conscience, to dwell there in an obscure foreboding, somewhat as the fear of coming rain haunts the mind of the person who counts on a fair day. The political scene hovered on the outskirts of his life. He called himself an "old-fashioned socialist," but this could be construed by other people in any way save that of the far right. In fact, the left made many demands on him, oftentimes little removed from the Communist angle of vision, with which he was not in sympathy. Difficult to brush off requests in the face of tenacity. The hundred-word telegrams asking for a speech or other endorsement were the easiest to deal with, for the two words "Sorry. No." seemed enough by way of reply. These were written with sundry amplifications on one of the post cards which were my husband's habit and expedited with a linear regiment of one-cent stamps, thus avoiding the use of the three- and later four-cent designs which he disliked.

At the moment of our marriage and for a long time thereafter, the Committee on Un-American Activities was in the ascendency, and many were the meetings which Van Wyck was invited to attend in protest of its methods. The Spanish Loyalists needed support, and, more immediately, there loomed the cause of Henry Wallace, who hoped to become our next President. Van Wyck's friendship with Jo Davidson entered here—Jo, who regarded Wallace as the basic prop of mankind and believed that Van Wyck's support might enhance the prospects for his election. This, as Van Wyck readily saw, was implausible, but so insistent was the demand for action, the weight of obligation, that Van Wyck's early-morning hours, those he chiefly prized, were attended by anxiety, and his work suffered.

"How am I to get out of this without hurting Jo, hurting our friendship?" he asked me more than once.

"Why not go to Radio City, be on hand the evening Jo is to sculpt a head of Wallace before the crowd, as propaganda?" I finally suggested. "That ought to please him."

We did so, edging our way toward the deeply encircled Jo, as with deft fingers, and in serene unconcern for the milling audience, he built the portrait of his candidate. Our appearance, though minor in extent, served as a gesture of loyalty and somewhat allayed Van Wyck's feeling of guilt, as also it helped to extricate him from any arduous part in the campaign. He was now able to return to the hours of reading necessary as preparation for the last of his histories, a life line as imperative as any thrown to a drowning sailor on the high seas.

Requests sent Van Wyck by the younger writers were given precedence over others. Interviews were granted, when for long minutes the study door was closed and the caller established himself in the small chair that faced Van Wyck's large one and profited, I hoped, from the encouragement and unassuming magnanimity that hovered about him in that room. Usually, I noticed, when I knocked to interrupt with a tray of sherry and crackers, the young aspirant appeared relaxed, reassured. Yet now and then some nervous tic or other sign of uneasiness spoke of a nature too complex or wavering to gain from a brief exchange: one among the more tortured devotees of a difficult craft. Manuscripts submitted by mail, and often without the return stamps, were carefully read by Van Wyck and commented on in writing, while the continuous flow of request letters he managed once in each ten days to answer, taking them up from an untidy pile on the floor near his desk, where they had been tossed. These included letters from high-school students hoping for autographs, or the story of Van Wyck's life and "influences," or advice on a career; others were written by proud descendents of those who had been a part of the literary scene in one of his histories. He dealt with all but the obvious crackpots, whom he ignored, turning their sometimes amusing, sometimes bantering or even insolent words over to me to be filed with the letters from other correspondents in the tall metal cabinet at the head of the back stairs in the country house we were presently to inhabit, where they were placed in a folder marked "Fans and Cranks." The filing of Van Wyck's incoming letters was a job which became imperative every two or three months, during our years together, one which I attempted to deal with. I remember the dark, rainy afternoons, the winter evenings, when I sat on the living-room floor, furniture pushed out of the way, lights blazing, while, encircled by the symbols of the alphabet inscribed on pink pad sheets, I sorted letters for hours at a time from the high, slippery stacks Van Wyck had brought out of the study cupboard and from cartons in the attic. I tried to concentrate on the signatures alone, in order to place them in the proper category, but I made, often, slow progress because of the interest I had in the letters that referred to passages from Van Wyck's books, to points of view in agreement or disagreement.

One of many evenings with Allen Tate that winter brought a quasi-political discussion of T. S. Eliot, with whom Van Wyck was at variance. An antipathy of temperament as basic as the canine and feline existed between the two men, the infrared as opposed to the ultraviolet, a contrast used elsewhere by Arthur Koestler, which seemed to Van Wyck applicable here.

"How can you admire a man," Van Wyck asked Allen, "who

stands for the Cavaliers against the Roundheads, who denies the American Revolution and deplores our Civil War? How can you continue to respect a writer who, along with a renunciation of his citizenship, has reversed his opinions on several of the English poets, notably Milton and Tennyson, moving headlong from denigration to affirmation, presumably to serve the literary loyalties of his recently adopted land? I grant his skill as poet and essayist," Van Wyck continued, "his ability to express the temper of the era, but I don't find it possible to admire him. We're in opposition everywhere. He represents all that I dislike and opposes all I stand for."

In answer, Allen said he understood the respective viewpoints of the two men and could see that the barrier for Van Wyck might be insurmountable.

"I've explained myself in *Oliver Allston*," Van Wyck said, "but perhaps not clearly enough."

"That may have something to do with it," said Allen. "If only that one chapter on the 'coterie writers' had been left out, how much happier we should all have been." And the unresolved dispute was laid aside in favor of fiddle playing.

A meeting of the American Philosophical Society took place at Philadelphia in the spring. It was my first encounter with this venerable organization, founded by Benjamin Franklin "for the advancement of useful knowledge." The experience was by no means new to Van Wyck, who had been a member for many years and had once delivered the "Penrose Memorial Lecture," at the apex of the meeting. It was all a delight to me, the gathering of members and their wives in the Benjamin Franklin Hotel, where for several days we were the guests of that affluent society, attending lectures in the fine old building which forms a right angle with Independence Hall and gives out on a small park where tiny leaves in springtime are gay with the new life that animates them. Inside, from high paneled walls, the faces of American statesmen and philosophers painted by Stuart, Sully, Copley, and Peale watched proceedings, their faces touched with nobility. At the buffet lunches members talked earnestly in small groups, present, all, because of some distinguishing mark, some noteworthy accomplishment. Following conversations with several among our friends on the opening day, Van Wyck and I went off to visit a comprehensive exhibition of the work of Matisse at the Museum of Art, a view of vast extent. We were interested to note the simplification of manner reached by Matisse in his later work, at the end of a fully creative life, a reward, I believed, for having so long and laboriously come to grips with indigestible material, incongruous ideas, almost insoluble intricacies, for having regained at last the contentment and wisdom of the child who is engrossed and charmed with nothing more complex than the evanescent patterns made by a butterfly's wings in poise over a summer flower.

On a visit to Princeton some weeks later, we called on Christian Gauss, a former dean much beloved by faculty and students. He presented Van Wyck with a small book by Ortega y Gasset just translated from the Spanish and published by the Princeton University Press. It was *The Dehumanization of Art,* and in its thesis was to have an unhappy effect on my husband, who had long been an admirer of Ortega. As his theory unfolded, Ortega seemed to proclaim the end of the human pulse in art, a factor which, Van Wyck felt, would nullify all that he himself had accomplished, believed in, and clung to in a lifetime. But the book had been written in 1920, when the effects of the First World War had been harrowing to a generation of artists. Finding no further reassurance in the romantic tradition, they had turned, rather, to the harsh, the dissonant, the mathematical, the unadorned, and even to the irresponsible, leaping from one half-finished thought to another. Like the hand grenade of the recently ended battles, the process became a short circuit between death and the human heart. And so the current preoccupation with enigmas, with cursory manners in criticism, with superstructures that lacked a base, with new directions along paths bearing no signposts. Van Wyck knew that the chief law of being is impermanence and change, that the spiral

77

draws man's course, and he hoped that once again, more than once in their history, men might turn outward toward a beneficent and believing world.

On a bright day, the American Academy and the Institute of Arts and Letters gave their annual ceremony. The aggregation of events at the Academy building in West One Hundred Fifty-fifth Street brought, on this particular occasion, a series of duties to Van Wyck, the secretary, obliged, now, to substitute for the president, Walter Damrosch, who was ill. Certain academicians, with their wives, gathered at eleven o'clock in the morning to hear the tributes spoken in memory of those members who had died during the year. Such gatherings were very moving, assembled as the audience was in a small sloping amphitheater, the great windows, framed by somber curtains of velour, overlooking the uptown cemetery of Trinity Church. Facing us was the speaker, who turned his pages slowly on a high desk, and told us of the life and labors of him who had gone on his far way. I looked forward on that morning in 1948 to hearing my husband's tribute to Willa Cather, which he had read to me in the study several weeks earlier, written with discernment and imagination, and I thought it a pity she herself could not have heard it. A tone poem it might have been called had it been made of music.

During the cocktail hour preceding luncheon the conversation rose like a sea buffeted by storm. At lunch in the library, where the background of books mounting high conveyed a sober tone to the frivolous process of eating, I sat between Thornton Wilder and Bruce Rogers, the book designer, then over seventy and about to receive the Gold Medal of the Academy as reward for his life-long and shining work. We talked of the Bible in process of design by Rogers, a large one for use on lecterns. It was to be illuminated in color and might well become a historic masterpiece in printing. During the ceremonial in the large auditorium I watched proceedings from a box, wishing I were closer to the stage at ground level and nearer Van Wyck, whose duty it presently became to bestow the Institute's Gold Medal for History on Charles Beard.

A difficult moment. Because of Beard's isolationist views during the war and his denunciation of Roosevelt for embroiling us in world affairs, there had been several murmuring comments of disapproval within the Academy concerning the award, and Lewis Mumford had resigned. Van Wyck had taken time from his work to review Beard's qualifications, the salient facts of his life, and had come to the conclusion that he was a supremely honest man and courageous, that his views sprang from his Midwest background, something instituted in childhood, like the taste for sauerkraut. "A country man from Indiana," my husband called him, "of the most quintessentially American type." In the presentation speech Van Wyck spoke of Beard's loyalty in defending at the outset of his teaching career two pacifist professors in danger of dismissal for their political beliefs, thus jeopardizing his own position. And had not Beard taught us that history can never be entirely objective? To be sure, Van Wyck admitted, "Beard was a generally troublesome man, bellicose himself and causing bellicosity in others," but admirable no less. Beard, I noticed, helped by his hearing aid, seated there close to the lectern, lean, long-legged, with his high cheekboned Yankee face and the detachment brought by years of deafness, smiled at these words of my husband. The ceremony ended with the induction into the Institute of our friends Padraic Colum, John Wheelock, and Virgil Thomson, while Judith Anderson received the medal for fine speech on the stage. It was with pleasure that I rejoined Van Wyck on the terrace later for tea, with the sound still in my ears of the applause which had greeted his speech.

Helen Keller and Polly Thomson spent an evening with us, a farewell party previous to their leaving for Australia and the Far East. These long-range tours of theirs were made for the purpose of raising money for the blind in the various countries they visited. From photographs shown us by Polly, we saw that Helen's arrival at foreign airports resembled that of royalty: huge welcoming crowds of natives, bouquets, children strewing flower petals. The effort required from both women on these trips would have overwhelmed the average person: the fatigue of travel, public appearances, the speeches which Helen must deliver. Confronting crowded auditoriums, she stood patiently beside Polly addressing audiences in her deaf-mute's voice, her enunciation labored and difficult, while Polly repeated the words after her, that all might understand. But in spite of the rigors of their life, of being ever on exhibition, in spite of their never-ending concern for the sufferings of the blind, they retained their gaiety and were quick to communicate it to one another: "like two birds on a branch in springtime," as Van Wyck put it. To give them pleasure at our house that evening we had also invited John Sloan and his wife. The combination proved fortunate. Helen Sloan spoke with careful deliberation, so that Polly's translated tap-tapping of words on Helen's hand should not be too far in arrears, while Sloan himself, an old socialist, was the right man to talk politics with these two women of warm and liberal viewpoint. Just before leaving, Helen placed her fingers on Sloan's head to feel the contours, her one sure method of appraisal. "A noble head and strong," she said it was.

A day toward the end of May became the moment for a meandering walk uptown when Van Wyck and I left Wanamaker's on Eighth Street to go slowly northward toward our flat. For me it was chiefly an exercise in architectural education. We stopped first at Grace Church, which Van Wyck admired as an especially fine example of the Gothic. We walked through Union Square, familiar to me as a child, still inhabited by homeless, wandering men who sat straggled along its benches and still the base from which like some errant flame a crowd springs to life about the soapbox orator. We went up Broadway to Madison Square. The streets had emptied because of the approaching holiday, and we were able to examine the buildings that peaceably lined the streets. One of these, Van Wyck said, had been designed by Louis Sullivan, a building ornamented with care and pride in the 1870's, to house one of the great retail stores of that period. In the center of Madison Square, Van Wyck brought us to a standstill before the Saint-Gaudens statue of Farragut, a dignified work which admirably depicted the admiral's uncompromising attitude and was charming in detail: a corner of the tunic blown back by the wind, the hair ruffled, the marks of insignia on the sleeve.

These walks with my husband were ever a pleasure. Such walks were undertaken, I imagined, by few inhabitants of Manhattan, that eager, frantic race inevitably on the move toward something beyond grasp. I had once been a part of their jerkily propelled number, moving like a wound toy along the sidewalk, until Van Wyck helped steady my gait and turned my eyes toward the enduring things, product of man's creative labor and imagination.

Now the winter had ended, our first winter together. Soon, we were to make our way to Connecticut, to occupy a house belonging to friends, as we searched for something more permanent, something that might become home. Many people, many ideas, many conversations had ornamented the days of our stay in East Fifty-seventh Street. There was much to look back on with pleasure and with gratitude. The words of Whitman came to me:

> And I know that the spirit of God is the brother of my own,
> And that all men ever born are also my brothers, and the women
>   my sisters and lovers,
> And that a kelson of the creation is love.

VIII

Sun, Wind and Stars

*I*T was among the cluster of Connecticut villages and small towns in the general neighborhood of Danbury that we had made up our minds to search for a permanent home, a place where we should find the lovely and simple façade of a high-steepled white church and, along the green, one or two dignified elderly houses among the lesser ones. During our various trips we had motored through many of these minor harbors of humanity, often in full sunshine when the dormant quality possessing them was as apparent as under the aura of a full moon, and inevitably we became a fleeting part of their existence.

Westport, Van Wyck's former home, had become rather too large and crowded to suit our needs, and although Van Wyck and I had not gone into our future in any great detail—indeed there had scarcely been time for this—we discovered that each had in mind the picture of a placid, pastoral setting for any house we might acquire. When, therefore, the Matthew Josephsons suggested that in June we go to occupy their house in Gaylordsville, Connecticut, lending them the Silo at Martha's Vineyard in exchange, we at once accepted. The finger of fate appeared to be directing our course.

The subsequent move from one place to another held the usual elements of stress and fatigue, and, finally, we drew up before the Josephson house late on a rainy June afternoon with a sense of foreboding added to the rest, so different, so fundamental, did this change in our surroundings appear. The last half-mile had taken us along a narrow dirt road of primitive aspect, bounded on our right by hills of towering darkness, and it was as though we were being irrevocably shut away from the civilization we had heretofore known.

At the house door a light shone steadily, and as we drew up, Eric Josephson, son of Matthew, came out to greet us and help us with our luggage, to lead us into the book-filled sitting room. Immediately, a lovely peace enveloped us. Civilization, though of a different sort, seemed yet to be with us. Tautly spun tops that we were, we began at once to unwind, to accustom our eyes to something beyond a city sophistication. After dinner, in the tremendous stillness, we read for an hour that seemed like a moment on the borders of heaven until we found, presently, that we were capable of nothing other than sleep.

On the following morning we awoke to find the sun and rain clouds playing tag with each other until at last it was the sun that won. The dining room in the Josephson house faces east and south, a spot responsive to fine weather, and we were able to open the door leading to the terrace, where grew an enormous elm, haven for a catbird that continually gathered unto itself the songs of the other birds to send them forth again in a wild sort of passion. After breakfast Van Wyck left the house for Matty's study beyond the garden; it was a large room holding a wide table, reference books, a couch, a potbellied stove to ward off the damp. He spent the morning, as always when we took up new quarters, assembling the notes to be used when he began writing again. At lunchtime, on my going to fetch him, he was happy, his mind free of needling pressures. Together we walked back through the grass, and I took off my shoes and stockings to come closer to the earth, while the sun beat down on our heads and I knew of a sudden that we were a part of summer. Our old Dora knew it, too, celebrating the knowledge by going forth from her kitchen tasks to pick a bunch of buttercups, which we found on the dining table arranged in a stiff little bouquet like those a child hands its mother at happy moments. In late afternoon, with our unpacking accomplished and the house already a part of us, I went for a walk along a road in the valley where a vivid small stream breaks its way beneath beeches and alders. Purple flag covered the water-strewn borders, and I stooped to gather some, lingering so long at this delicious task that I was late for dinner and ran all the way home, feeling that I was a girl of ten. And then, as I reached the piazza, all out of breath, I found Van Wyck seated in a deep chair contemplating the last of the sun. He smiled at me, and I was even happier than before. Of such moments is the essence of life.

We drove, in the deepening dark, down the road to dine with Muriel and Malcolm Cowley. The Peter Blumes were there, and we were all very pleased to be together. I was especially glad to be surrounded by the Cowleys' bare white plastered living-room walls, smooth and fresh as a newly drawn bed sheet. Wonderful, I thought once again, to be able to keep a room uncluttered, as this one was, unornamented save for a tall flowing mobile designed by Alexander Calder, its languid metal arms on a base of blue and red moving delicate white metal flowers as an unseen hovering spirit gave them the whispered command. We talked at random, we six, about nothing very much, content because we were basically of the same kind, the men, all three, adepts at persuading forth the written word or the graphic scene, the women sharing with their mates the joy and the despair that such a vocation brings.

On the next day, as he had promised himself in advance, Van Wyck's new history began to be a book in the making, one eventually to be entitled *The Confident Years;* it would be a protracted, over-all engagement because of the immensity of the task. At the same time it fell to me to pursue the matter of the still-elusive house in Connecticut, the house we hoped might become a long-term residence. Hour after hour, I drove out with the persevering agent who took me from one village to another along the roads of early summer. Now and then Van Wyck joined us, his study jacket hurriedly changed for one less worn, cane in hand to further progress, but he was reluctant to confront the various house-holders, wary of approach as a sparrow at a feeder. His power of decision was polite but instantaneous; he left it to me to give it an articulate form. "These people had a gift for the commonplace," he would say to me wearily, as the agent closed one more door. He tired quickly, this sort of labor being alien to him, and he soon closed his mind to further impressions. So it behooved me to en-visage our future in one spot or another, a return to the child's game "Let's pretend."

Two houses at the outset became conspicuous among the rest. One stood in Newtown and was suggested by the Francis Hack-etts, who were then living there. Signe Toksvig, Francis's wife, had recently finished her book on Swedenborg and, more and more, shut away on a hillside enclosed by trees, she chose to dwell in the mysterious world of the occult, the abstruse. Van Wyck could not follow her there, eschewing as he did the mystic arts, but the two got on well. Francis, at the moment, was working on his auto-biography. This was of much interest to Van Wyck, who had known Hackett since the opening days of the *New Republic*. The four of us went to look at a house on the main street of Newtown, close to the post office and the general store. A situation of this sort drew us for reasons of safety and convenience.

"I have a certain amount of daily dealing with the post office," Van Wyck had said, "and I like being within walking distance. In winter we shall have to depend on the local store." This Newtown house, however, proved to be beyond our means.

The second house that interested us belonged to Bruce Rogers. It was possibly the prettiest house in Connecticut, the most graceful, composed by a very special mind in the early nineteenth century. It overlooked Candlewood Lake, and its façade of ancient faded brick was decorated with narrow pilasters of wood painted white, slim and delicate as those on some minor Greek temple dedicated to a very young goddess. About the house grew bleeding heart and pink poppies, and at the rear a grape-grown pergola led off to the barn with a clock tower mounting toward the sky, faced with blue and gold, the whole, with its orchard of apple and nut, bound by a careful stone wall and circumspect as the country place of an eighteenth-century philosopher.

Rogers called this spot "October House," an additional lure for me whose birthday falls in that fairest of months, and he hoped we might relieve him of it so that he could go to live nearer the city. "The years and the months of winter get you down," he told us as we sat together in late afternoon on a bench that faced a stone-lined pool. "The goldfish in that pool hibernate under a board we throw in before the water freezes. But men can't live that way. I plan to leave." We were sorry to say good-bye to Bruce Rogers and his October House, the more so as we knew by some undefined means that we should see neither one again.

In my journal, an entry for June 17, 1948, I find the paragraph:

The agent and I stopped for a few moments at Bridgewater to walk about the grounds and look again at the house on the village street which has been in my mind rather continually since we were first shown it last week. I still like it better than anything we've seen, monstrously ugly though its outer layer is, owing to the gloom cast by close-pressed trees, a wide piazza and the panelling of fumed oak with which the rooms are lined. But with trees cut, part of the piazza removed, the closed blinds opened forever, the dark oak buried under white paint, I believe we might have a sweet old-fashioned house, solid and substantial and, with the really beautiful grounds of shrubs and flowers, a pleasant place in which to work and receive our friends.

This picture somehow wound itself about my mind, and on a subsequent page of the journal I found I had made one more entry:

After lunch on our first consistently clear day when the birds set up a gigantic hullaballoo, Van Wyck and I went off by ourselves to explore

86

the house we have found in Bridgewater. We had no key to unlock the door but we peeked through the windows and wandered about the grounds. The garden is tangled in a most romantic way, honeysuckle linked with climbing rose, mock orange blending with rhododendron and an untidy stretch of old-fashioned moss roses profuse with flowers that smell very sweet. I can imagine a Sargent watercolor: ladies in wicker chairs intent on their embroidery, a handsome bearded gentleman reading Tennyson to his love on a long, summer afternoon. Van Wyck was drawn to the garden but the house pleased him less: "Too much like the houses of my youth in Plainfield with their broad piazzas and their rocking chairs. I managed to get away from those. Let's put off any decision until autumn," he said.

That ended our month of house-hunting and also our stay at Gaylordsville. On July 2 the Josephsons were to arrive in order to take possession of their premises once again, and we were to motor to Martha's Vineyard. In fact the two cars would pass each other on the road. I said my private good-bye to the serene world about us early on the morning of our departure, when I walked to a small deserted house to cut the last blooms from the pink rosebush planted there long ago by a vanished hand, and a silent communication took place between me and the spirit that emanated from hills and hollows and meadow grass and scattered roadside flowers and the rampaging little brook and the birds flying in and out of its overhanging alder branches.

We left presently, with small Sheba loaded like any beast of burden, and the Connecticut countryside as we moved under a sparkling northwest light in the stillness of early morning looked, as Dora said, "just like a picture."

At the Silo and the outset of our second summer there, following the initial days of our settling in, serene days entirely our own, the first going forth occurred on the evening of July 4, when we attended a beach party spread on the wide sands below sharp, upgoing cliffs known as "Evie's Beach," the Baldwin beach. We sat in the darkness, ten or twelve of us, around a magnificent bonfire made of driftwood, while children climbed the cliffs, their bodies wet from diving the waves, until presently we settled down, old and young, to watch the fireworks brought by Van Wyck and me from the mainland. They were set off on the dunes high above our heads, and the children looked, Van Wyck said, like the Nibelungen in the grotesque shapes they formed against the sky, the rockets and sprays becoming the aerial symbols of the gods' golden hoard.

On the days after this celebration we became engaged in following the progress of a nest of barn swallows high in a corner of our breezeway. At first they were no more than a series of avid mouths, but after some time we noticed that the tail feathers of one bird were being sharply agitated, in rehearsal, doubtless, for the flight from the nest. Later that day, I was called by Van Wyck to be shown the little bird hunched and solitary on a neighboring beam, and, as we watched, this motionless lump of feathers was joined by two more, then another three, to make a total of six. For long moments they clung seemingly powerless and dazed by the immensity about them, while the mother bird attacked us with rapid darting strokes of vigor and prowess. Then they were gone, all of them, leaving an empty nest and the cluster of droppings that told of the prolonged labor of mother and father. Van Wyck was sad at losing these island friends, closer to him than those he found at cocktail parties, and he turned a dejected back on the breezeway. Late that afternoon, returning from down island, we found the parent birds back at their old game of attack at the breezeway entrance and, seated on the home beam, the six fledglings. From over the sea a spread of inky clouds moved toward us, and the wind had begun to disturb the still waters. Mother and Father had winged the brood back to safety only minutes ahead of the storm that presently struck in fury, breaking tree branches and driving an army of whitecaps across Menemsha Pond. The thermometer dropped rapidly, and soon there was no distinguishing one bird from another, as, sheltered beneath the roof, they had become one breathing mass of feathers. During almost twenty-four hours they sat thus, until the storm passed and the sun appeared. With it, they were once more off. That night, seeing our dinner guest out of

88

doors, Van Wyck and I stood side by side beneath world upon world of stars sharply bright and so low-swung as almost to be caught and held vivid and throbbing in our hands.

The summer brought many callers including those writers who asked to talk over their work with Van Wyck. People seemed to discover the Silo for themselves and my husband along with it: a kind of annunciation repeated many times, some of those who came finding their way on foot when they lacked a car. Often, in the afternoon, Van Wyck returned to the study by the pond that he might more surely get on with his reading. He had read about five hundred of the books necessary for the completion of the fifth volume of his history, but there were some fifteen hundred more to be gone through. Indeed, the titles of the books placed in his copybook reading lists, a habit he had kept from boyhood on page after page of neat script, were a kind of marvel. Something, it seemed to me, to be regarded as one did the wonders of the Taj Mahal.

We had a prolonged visit during that summer of 1948 from Van Wyck's older son, Charles, who arrived from San Francisco, this time, with his wife, Inez, and their small boy, Peter, aged eight. They moved toward us on the ferry one afternoon in August, and with beating hearts we waved across the gradually diminishing distance. Van Wyck was much moved by this reunion, one of the moments when the core of life's expectancy and hope flies between those who arrive and those who wait. Later, these things are somewhat dimmed in the familiarity of repeated hours, but they seem, nonetheless, to be closest to truth. During the month that they were on the island, living in the nearby camp which Van Wyck had engaged for them, we saw them continually, and when a moment in September brought their departure the clock in the Silo dining room appeared to have slowed its beat and the marsh grass below us lost some of its sheen. On the final morning Van Wyck left his work with the haste that sudden dislocations force upon us and, as I sat beside him, he drove over to the camp. The frown of unhappy involvement, I noticed, was in place on his brow.

We found the Brookses preparing for the long transcontinental drive in characteristically casual and appealing fashion. Their 1938 station wagon, minus the middle seat, had become a repository for objects such as clamshells gathered as presents for the Pueblo Indians whom they were to visit on their way, a flock of horseshoe crabs for the decoration of Peter's room at home, bed quilts, worn sneakers, paints, and canvases. Beside the window on the rear seat, above a pile of army blankets, a nook had been arranged for Peter, its boundaries marked by boxes and bags. At the moment he was barefoot, a staunch small boy of upright bearing, sun-bleached hair, and sun-browned body, restless and elusive as a small fish.

Van Wyck was silent as we drove from the ferry back to our end of the island, a silence weighted with the intangibles born of complex pressures, of crowding emotions.

"What a good time they had!" I said, trying to reassure.

"They're innocents, each of them. I hope the world will let them be," he answered me.

I pressed the car forward into higher speed so that we might the sooner be at home, where, in the study by the pond, my husband could forget anxiety.

The second of Van Wyck's sons to visit the island that summer was Kenyon. He also came with his wife, but missed us, because of our return to the city, by a few days, and so went to inhabit a small bungalow in West Tisbury instead of being with us at Menemsha. The bungalow was in the nature of a wedding present from Van Wyck to the bride and groom. Kenyon's recent marriage to Kappo Phelan seemed an essential one and, we hoped, long-lasting. The two had been much together during the last years; indeed, their friendship outdated Van Wyck's and mine, and was one based on mutual intelligence. Kappo at that moment wrote the theatrical reviews for the magazine *Commonweal* and, in private, wrote poetry. Kenyon was on the point of leaving the office of E. P. Dutton, Van Wyck's publishers, for work on *Life* Magazine. We looked forward with a good deal of pleasure to their future, and now Van Wyck was able to dispense with much of his former unhappy preoccupation, the fears for this younger son which had long possessed his mind. "So unnatural to be alone," he kept on reiterating at the moments when at evening's end Kenyon had made his solitary way back to the small walk-up flat which since our own marriage had become his home. "The chief motive for living is to be with the person you love."

One evening in early autumn Van Wyck drove me along our winding wooded lane of heavy sand to dine with Rita and Tom Benton. The light was still bright enough to illumine Tom's studio, and he came to invite us in as we stopped the car. He showed us his work in progress, a still life of fruit and flowers meticulously painted on a gesso panel, glowing like those done by the Dutch masters of long ago yet as essentially American as his earlier canvases of the horse-and-buggy period. I found the picture very fine, and, I believe, Van Wyck did also. Difficult to be certain of my husband's deeper feeling because of his mistrust of a casually expressed verdict of the sort common to most men. He was an unobtrusive but perhaps the more authoritative onlooker. At the house, Rita greeted us with the wide breadth of her Italian nature, and we made our way gradually through her kitchen to the living room beyond. Leopold Mannes and his wife had arrived ahead of us with old David, Leopold's father, who had started me on the fiddle when I was eight. After dinner, over coffee, there took place a discussion between Tom and Van Wyck on the artist's place in the current world, his place in general. Tom discoursed with voluble vehemence; Van Wyck, though disagreeing, was quietly restrained. As the more or less one-sided conversation went on, I remembered a phrase of my husband's which seemed to fit the occasion: "Every man of good sense knows when not to argue and has his mind made up on a thousand matters that are not discussible for him." A case in point. When the argument died for want of fuel, we musicians were invited by Rita to make music. David Mannes and I had brought along our fiddles and, accompanied at the piano by Leopold, we played the Bach double violin concerto. I was glad to be thus reunited with my first master, the last time I was to see him.

As I drove the slow way home, Van Wyck, deep in his corner, told me he had enjoyed the music but had not cared for the after-dinner controversy. This had angered him. More than that, it had brought with it a burden of sadness. For Tom had opposed the notion of progress in man's world, quoting chapter and verse with energy and certainty to prove his point, while the idea of a continued upward swing, the power of man's will toward good, was a belief that lay at the core of my husband's being. One day he was to write of this in the final pages of *The Confident Years,* to analyze the varying viewpoints of those who held negative attitudes, the cynic, the disenchanted, as opposed to him who believed in the natural goodness of men. Quoting Pascal within a similar argument Van Wyck was to say that "nothing could be lost and much was to be gained if, considering which held the greater value, one placed one's bet on the faith rather than the doubt." Small wonder that the evening had saddened him.

Our farewells, before returning to the city that September, included one to the Roger Baldwins, to Evie in particular, continued benefactress, whom again we attempted to thank for the use of her beach, our island sanctuary. "But you are our friends," she said by way of reply. We went also to call on Max Eastman and Eliena, his generous, wide-hearted Russian wife, who filled our hands on our leaving with sprays of the late spirea, honey and rugosa hips to be brewed into a healing infusion. Their house high on a hill overlooking the Gay Head end of Menemsha Great Pond, with its borders of wild plum and bayberry, wind-blown, isolated, fitted the distant yet compelling image of Wuthering Heights, its given name, and I wondered if the occasional guest might wake heart-struck in the night at the sound of a lamenting voice. Max and Van Wyck had known one another chiefly as fellow writers. Their temperaments and the pattern of their lives were not similar. As for Eliena, both of us admired her bright courage and her simple approach to the daily scene, while Van Wyck was especially touched by her devotion to the Indian children of Gay Head. In later years, he and I, as many others, were moved by her gallant death, when, insubstantial as a wraith, toward the end, she was carried each day into the sunshine in the arms of a stalwart Wampanoag. And it was to these Indian friends that she wrote her last letter, one wherein she gave her "dear Max" forever into their care.

The actual leave-taking from the Silo was an arduous performance, our packing not accomplished until after dark on the evening before our early departure. But Van Wyck was in a happy mood and he kept us all laughing over the dinner we ate at nine o'clock in a friend's kitchen. New York, on our arrival, was hot, dirty, noisy, a spot on the borders of Hades. No one can permanently inhabit Paradise, I reflected, and went to receive from my husband a consolatory embrace.

IX

Eight Golden Daffodils

$\mathcal{J}$T became gradually apparent that Van Wyck should not be taken from his study to view houses unless for a final decision. He was unable to swim in the deep waters suited to his constitution if he was asked often to bob up to the surface levels where most of us have our being. Our New York apartment had, however, been put on the market, and before long we should be obliged to pinion the evanescent place in the country.

On a morning of work in the city, as I practiced my violin, the telephone rang and, impatiently, I went to answer it. The person at the far end proved to be Charles Prendergast's widow, Eugénie, who called from Westport.

"Do you and Van Wyck still want to spend the winter in the country? Get away from New York?" she asked.

"Yes, we do, Eugénie, very much indeed. But we've not been able to find a place anywhere."

"A friend of mine who lives in Cornwall, Connecticut, tells me there's a nice house in the heart of the village there and you can probably get it for the winter. Why not drive out to see it? My friend thinks you won't be disappointed."

The matter was arranged, and two days later Van Wyck and I drove to Cornwall. We found "the heart of the village" to be a small, pleasing place and tranquil in its noon setting where, opposite the stone library on the green, stood an eighteenth-century house of generous size, foursquare and white and authentic in its aspect of quiet authority. It was shaded by high elms, maples, spruces, attendant ornaments to Connecticut life, and it was rather apart from the other houses of the center, offering itself, apparently, as benign shelter to the initiated.

With the turning of the key in the front-door lock we entered a pleasant parlor which gave, on one side, to a study. This, Van Wyck immediately went to examine, and, during all the weeks of our search, there had not been the gleam of satisfaction in his eye such as there was when he confronted the book-lined walls, the writing table facing a fireplace, the deep window chair: a spot suited to hour upon hour of tranquil labor, a spot long in use by civilized people. The other rooms seemed suited to us also, and we were in a happy frame of mind when we started on our way home along the borders of the Housatonic, where meadows run even and clean to its banks and the background of hills is covered in virgin hemlock.

At breakfast next morning in Fifty-seventh Street, we decided to engage Mrs. Woolsey's house for the winter provided we could come to terms with her and be permitted to stay until June. We telephoned the agent and later that morning had word that our offer was accepted. We could move in, Mrs. Woolsey promised, as soon as the furnace had been put in order. Wonderful it was to have uncertainty at an end, even though only temporarily so, and with the prospect of an agreeable house in a Connecticut village where we should doubtless find enough congenial people to ward off loneliness yet not enough to constitute a society. The library and the post office faced us across the green, a good doctor was close by, and a neighboring boys' school would presumably contain several pupils in need of assistance with their reading. We had been thoroughly provided for.

That afternoon at teatime we went across the hall to inform the Wheelocks of our good fortune. They were glad for us, they said, but sad also. For we should not be returning to East Fifty-seventh Street as neighbors. This was obvious. And Jack, a bit mournfully, I thought, began to speak of his long friendship with Van Wyck, one reaching back to the days at Harvard when, as freshmen, they had met at a party given by the *Harvard Monthly*.

Van Wyck, off in a corner alone, had appeared to Jack shy and lost. In spite of what he described as "a certain austerity" in Van Wyck's otherwise appealing aspect, Jack had gone up to speak to him, and the bond between them was forged. In fact, during their first year at Harvard, they had jointly brought forth a small book named *Verses by Two Undergraduates*. They published it without their names, one poet placing his verses on the left-hand page, the other on the right. The austerity in Van Wyck noted by Jack at the outset, and often seen by me at the start of our acquaintance, he later discovered to have been born, he said, of "an extraordinary vehemence of thought and feeling held severely in check."

In this connection I had often wondered about the origins of several of my husband's characteristics, some of them small preoccupations, others more disturbing to him and to me. For example, there was his continuing displeasure in his appearance when the fit of his clothes was not as he conceived it, when there seemed to him a conspiracy on the part of tailor, shirtmaker, of the clothes themselves, to go wrong. Standing in agitation before the long mirror on his closet door, trying on a new suit just arrived from the city, he would say: "Can't you see that the right sleeve is longer than the left? I warned the tailor about this. There's almost a half-inch more of shirt showing on this side." The tailor's lapse had somehow become an injury to my husband's person, a purposeful unkindness. On another level, equally unrealistic, were the onslaughts of temper, insurmountable anger based on that sense of injustice which unwittingly persisted in him. It flared at a touch, a tone of voice, a fancied affront, someone's lapse in loyalty toward a friend, and it spread like prairie fire, jagged, leaping high until, with nothing fresh to feed it, the flame sputtered out. Van Wyck himself laughed at these unpredictable attacks, once they had vanished, describing them as due to "placing soap in the geyser." But I sought for other reasons, lodged in the far past: moments when a child's thwarted eagerness, his small desires, his explanations had been choked at their source, his gestures of love cut short, alien patterns superimposed, and ridicule used as a substitute for understanding—in a word, suffering. Such, I supposed, might have befallen a sensitive boy whose spirit and courage, the vehemence Jack Wheelock spoke of, had been enough to carry him through without lament while he learned to bind his wounds and to guard the secrets of his imagination from attack. Thus he had long carried an ill-balanced weight damaging to his native strength, while early sorrow cut a wound whose mark sought the surface now and again. Then it was that the disciplined man became the outraged youth tied to his beginnings, striking out in retaliation until the normal course might be restored. Often, when first we were married, I had pressed him for details of his childhood, but he seemed reluctant to talk of it, brushing me off with some statement of outer fact.

"Tell me a little about your father and mother," I begged. "What were they like? And your brother, Ames."

"My father died of a heart attack while I was in college," he answered. "He'd not been a success in business, living as he did at Plainfield, which in those days was no more than a suburb of Wall Street where fortunes were made and lost overnight. His fiber wasn't tough enough to get him through. My mother married again, a fine man, a mining engineer, Henry Hibbard. They traveled together over much of the world while he was still actively connected with engineering, a companionable marriage. He understood my mother, knew how to handle her. She was somewhat demanding."

"What of your brother?"

97

"Ames was three years older than I. He and my mother were very close. I remember they used to accuse me, when I was in my teens, of being unco-operative, selfish. He went to Princeton and made many friends there. He was often best man, later, at their weddings. People were fond of him but he never managed to find a wife, although he was engaged several times and was very personable. He lived at home, and his attempts at marriage were apparently not encouraged by my mother. He was also miscast in his career. He might have been a scholar, for his mind was excellent, or a professor of history. Instead, he went into Wall Street and was perennially disappointed. His chief pleasure he had from visits to his friends who owned ranches in the West where he could help round up cattle. A romantic."

"How sad!"

"He killed himself, finally, after a stock-market plunge which wiped out most of his investments. He walked in front of the early commuters' train one morning at the Plainfield station."

"Goodness!" I said. "How did you ever manage to become a writer with that sort of background?"

"I was fortunate enough to know what I wanted and I left home for good when I went to Harvard."

"But it was your mother who took you and Ames for that winter in Europe when you were eleven. It made all the difference in your life, didn't it?"

"Yes, it did," he answered abruptly, and the conversation stopped there. It was obvious that he did not want to continue.

Shortly before our leaving town, the Wheelocks asked us to dine to meet the Charles Lindberghs. Jack, at Scribner's, had recently edited Lindbergh's book, *The Spirit of St. Louis*. I had once met them, twelve or fifteen years earlier, at the Simon Flexners when Lindbergh was doing a piece of work at the Rockefeller Institute in collaboration with the French scientist Alexis Carrel. Lindbergh was then at the height of his popularity, and his wife, Anne, was very young and very charming, with the thickest of fringed lashes ringing her intelligent and beautiful eyes. I found her little changed, basically, in spite of those moments when the suffering brought by life's sharp weapons became visible. Lindbergh's qualities of energy, persistence, caution, seemed undiminished by the years, but he had become what men term "a character." At dinner he led the talk, over a large pitcher of ice water, talk which had to do with America's many mistakes, at that postwar era, in her oversevere handling of the Germans, her too great leniency in dealing with the Russians. Anne, during these moments of debate, had little to say. Her wifely reserve and composure were the feminine qualities to be prized by any husband.

Many friends during these our last days in the Fifty-seventh Street apartment came for tea or a cocktail, thus saying good-bye to our pleasant long room as well as to us in the role of city dwellers. And to keep up with the press of errands necessary to our departure we drove here and there about the city with Van Wyck at the wheel of Sheba. These outings had for some time become one of our happy traditions, wherein Van Wyck remained in the parked car to read his current book while I shopped. A pleasant thing to be certain that he was there awaiting me each time I reappeared.

Finally came the day in October when we made the move to Connecticut, driving away to the north knowing that there would be return journeys for the packing of books and china, but a conclusive move nonetheless. The lights were on in the Woolsey house for our arrival late that afternoon, and it was warm. With many bags and cartons to unload, however, and Dora's kitchen to organize, tired as we were, the minor discrepancies in the household loomed large. But we were at last come to live in the country, where for so long we had wished to be, the air smelled of October and the distant bonfires of fallen leaves, and presently the lovely quiet began to seep its unobtrusive way into our being.

"Tomorrow we can begin to enjoy everything," each of us said to the other.

The morning proved us right. The colors were vivid as a dream remembered, and outside our bedroom window a giant maple of gold, under the touch of the early sun, dropped its leaves gently and persistently as fate, a fate which reached in to mark us also.

The days floated by. In reminiscence they did indeed float, if this means being free of urgencies, of duties other than those imposed by the inner man. We lived them among undemanding people who seemed both self-sufficient and openhearted, a minor colony of human beings who had long ago determined among themselves, we were told, to speak no ill of another. This procedure, and the manner of its being lived, made an especially agreeable impression on Van Wyck. He several times spoke of it. "How sensible they are! The pleasures of gossip forsworn." There were whole clusters of serene moments: calm, security, labor unrolling almost of itself. I practiced the Bach sonatas for violin alone, I wrote at my desk beside a sunny hall window above Van Wyck's study, I went for walks along the hills and through wild meadows growing blue gentians, I breathed the air that came from the mountains. And, during the three months of midwinter, I taught the slow readers at the local public school. This was a pleasure, the work with country children who were eager for help, a few of them waiting about the school door for my arrival in early morning, while their parents seemed more understanding than those I had encountered in the course of city teaching. Several of the boys, as spring approached, came bicycling on Saturday mornings to our house on the green bringing little tight bunches of wild violets or a bag of cookies from the family larder.

At home, after lunch, Van Wyck and I walked to the shabby post office across the street to get the mail from the elderly postmaster, who seldom failed to let us know what a favor he bestowed, and whose untidy dog with wheezing bark and ruffled coat lay between him and us. Van Wyck pronounced them two of a kind. When afternoon was upon us, if there were no errands to be run and the day was cold, windy, or snowbound, we lit our sitting-room fire and sat before it reading or telling each other stories out of our separate pasts, drinking tea, or playing Chinese checkers, a game that served to soothe Van Wyck's thought and that he came to play as swiftly and decisively as he turned the pages of his book. When we had a round after lunch and after dinner, our interest seemed never to flag. There were days of rain that fell with abandon, as if from a broken heart, days of sunshine when at noon, as in Switzerland, the thermometer rose high and a frost filmed the ground at morning and evening, days of being snow-enclosed, when the great drifts pressed about our lives to encompass us entirely: a kind of white peace.

Guests came to sleep in the Woolsey bedrooms, our children, our friends. Among these, the Peyton Rouses arrived for a weekend. In discovering the so-named "Rous Sarcoma," Peyton had made an early and important contribution to the dilemma caused by cancer. His wife, Marion, a sister of Phyllis Wheelock, was a childhood friend. Peyton's life was based on two disciplines, the one concerned with his career proper, the other with botany. In college he had written his thesis on the American fern, and when he embarked for the country his approach was that of an expert naturalist. He stepped off the train wearing knee-length knickerbockers, heavy boots, and a Norfolk jacket, and he had a vasculum slung over his shoulder, a repository for the plant specimens collected on his walks. It was a pleasure to follow behind when he set out on his expeditions, and also somewhat tiring, for he walked with eagerness and a forward-trotting gait that made me think of the White Rabbit in *Alice in Wonderland.* His eye was ever on the alert for the tiny plants that press the earth, plants unnoticed by the average man. In autumn, before snowfall, he made a practice of digging specimens of these, wrapping them in newspaper, and stowing them in his vasculum for transportation back to the city, where he awaited the latent surprise of winter bloom inside his glass herbarium kept on the dining-room window sill. At Cornwall during the weekend, we set out together on a November afternoon of clear air when the mountains were under a splendor touched with that dormant sadness which brings a profound stirring of the inner man. At evening over the dinner table, with the Rouses opposite him, Van Wyck sparkled and glowed, to match the fire in the wide chimney, coming to life with fervor as he did when congenial minds met his own.

Friends of Van Wyck who had arrived recently from England were Sir Alfred and Lady Zimmern. My husband's acquaintance with Zimmern had stemmed from his friendship with J. B. Yeats, who had introduced them at the Petitpas restaurant, in New York, that now historic spot where old Yeats, then in his eighties, gathered writers and painters about him for long hours of conversation. Zimmern was a fellow of New College, Oxford, and the author of *The Greek Commonwealth*. He had been in California when Van Wyck was teaching at Stanford and he persuaded the young instructor, then twenty-six, who contemplated a trip to England with Eleanor and their infant son, to give a course the following year in London at the Workers' Educational Association, for which Zimmern was a government inspector. In *Scenes and Portraits* Van Wyck describes the pleasure he had in this venture, supervising, as he did, the studies of working men and women, many of whom were so scholarly as to make him feel an uneducated man. "If any students could soften my stubborn egotism," he wrote, "it would have been these." There was the carpenter who quoted Horace and the young mechanic who studied Aristotle because "You can't read Aristotle without being a good man." And an elderly shoemaker who knew Greek and Latin was later to remind him of the "learned blacksmith" who is described in the *Flowering of New England*.

At the moment of Van Wyck's indoctrination for the course he had gone to stay with Alfred Zimmern at New College, in Oxford, and he described to me the pomp and circumstance, the ancient traditions still extant there: the gatherings about the bottle of port at evening after dessert, the silver and linen, the decorous walks of the dons across well-kept lawns, "the tangle of chimes" in the air. Now, forty years later, the Zimmerns were come to live in a lusterless hotel apartment in Hartford, drawn hither by their faith in America, which, they believed, possessed something more immediate, more genuine in its processes of government than did those at home. Lucie Zimmern was the daughter of a French Calvinist pastor, a brave man who had led an uneasy life among the determined Catholics of a small village, and, at Hartford, she conducted a class for taxi drivers, her theme: "driving through life." She was part feminine mystic, part masculine logician, and her heart was full of a practical sort of kindness. One recognized in Sir Alfred a lifetime experience in the clarification of ideas, and there was a look of Confucian wisdom in his eyes. Seated with these two remarkable people in the dull dining room of their hotel, I wondered if the birdbath dishes of canned corn, the slovenly waitress with frizzed bang were as disheartening to them as they were to me. I decided that the Zimmerns were oblivious of the unpleasant, and I was glad.

Meanwhile, during the winter, continually in our minds had been the location of a permanent residence in the country. Cornwall profoundly drew us, but Mrs. Woolsey wished to hold the house there for her daughters, and no other seemed to us quite as desirable as the one we had found in Bridgewater. To this we had many times returned, exhibiting its exterior to our children and friends. They, as we did, liked the quiet village street on which it stood, the sunny garden sheltered by beech and magnolia, the sound of the church bells. As for the house itself, we knew that its core was sound and its aspect potentially pleasant, that by depriving it of a certain amount of cumbrous ornament, we should be able to give it the grace it needed, thus making it the base for our continuing life together. We decided, therefore, to make a bid for it, and on March 1, our assiduous agent called to say the offer had been accepted. Hearing the news at evening, Van Wyck and I dressed ourselves in our best and drank a champagne toast to our future home. In advance we were able to visualize our comfortably wide round table in the sun-filled dining room, my mother's high French armoire in our bedroom, and, of chief importance, Van Wyck's books along innumerable shelves and his letters and papers safe within the walls of the immense attic, one that covered the entire house.

Spring was coming in, and we had much to draw us toward it.

103

At six in the morning, when Van Wyck went downstairs to brew our early tea, he no longer closed the bedroom window, leaving it wide so that, propped against the bed pillows, I could smell the new freshness and have a glimpse of the living grass, the red of maple buds, and, possibly, a robin. On a morning of this kind, I encountered in a book by the Englishman H. J. Massingham, a passage about the poetry of Christopher Smart:

Smart is one of the illustrious company of our native organic poets . . . free as Blake himself . . . of the current, sophisticated urban approach of his Georgian period. . . . Smart is of the Great Society, ranging through all grades from Shakespeare to the carter hitching a martingale between his horse's forelegs and the hedger heathering his stakes. They are the makers, as poet means, the up-builders, the regenerators, the pure in heart. . . . The man who has his joy in organic labor is a stone in the arch which spans the heavens like a rainbow. . . .

Reading, I instantly thought of Van Wyck, and when I reached the end of the passage I ran barefoot down to the early-morning parlor, where in his warm Turkish bathrobe he prepared himself for the day's work. To his surprise, I flung my arms about his neck. For, as I asked him, had he not also opposed the "sophisticated urban approach" of many writers in our time, was he not the laborer-poet who undertook to liven the memory of our own "native organic" writers, an "up-builder," pure in heart?

At the end of March we took possession of the Bridgewater house, being "seised of the premises," in ancient legal parlance. The ceremony did not occur on the property itself, the past owner pressing a handful of earth into the palm of the new owner, as the custom once was. Instead, we sat about a lawyer's table in New Milford exchanging the deed for a check, and receiving handshakes and wishes for our happiness from the four gentlemen present. Then, key in pocket, Van Wyck drove us to our new home. We walked about the garden and found eight golden daffodils in bloom beneath the south piazza. These we cut and thus were truly seised of the premises. In *Chilmark Miscellany* Van

Wyck speaks of the emotions that accompany the taking over of a new property. They are not simple, or of one piece, for the act resembles that of matrimony, bringing its own patterns, impressing a new way of life, raising the ghosts of the hovering past and the wandering wraiths of the future. We are forced, then, into intimacy with a stranger, and there is no turning away. So, on that afternoon, a sense of curtailed freedom, like the sudden jerk of the chain that tethers the dog, leaped to our hearts to blend with the pride of possession and the peace of finality. Small wonder that we drove away in silence, each striving to reconcile contrasting emotions of grave import.

In New York, we broke the arduous monotony of packing our last possessions by going to call on the Jo Davidsons at their recently acquired studio around the corner. They led us down to the reconstructed garage beneath the house where Jo's busts and figures stood on the high black pedestals lining the walls: Helen Keller, her arms outstretched toward Gandhi withdrawn into his personal solitude; James Barrie confronting Anatole France, a tortured gnome face to face with giant equanimity; Charlie Chaplin's mischievous smile directed at the squat impassiveness of Gertrude Stein; the imposing brow of James Joyce intent on linguistic sequences. A gallery of interplay between the dominating personalities of our era, those who had made their way through talent and patience and tenacity to the upper reaches. Back at Fifty-seventh Street, our job of emptying the apartment was accomplished in part by expert packers, but the books were handled by Van Wyck himself. With the courage and purpose which were his, he set to work in his shirt sleeves on a warm day to sort and pack some two thousand of these. In late afternoon of the second day this formidable labor came to an end with his tying of the final bundle, and we could return to Cornwall. On the way back, as the sun was setting, in the stream beneath the shadow of Coldfoot Mountain, we saw two trout fishermen. They seemed, in the falling light, to be messengers from Mars, wrapped in their bulging paraphernalia, rods held motionless, and I wondered whether they were able to breathe the sweet air of a dying day as we mortals were privileged to do.

A final gathering at Cornwall came into being almost by accident. It began with a telephone call from Carl Sandburg, who in his travels away from base in North Carolina was with friends at Hartford. He asked if we would put him up for the night. Van Wyck was fond of Carl and eager to have him come, even though it meant driving the long distance to fetch him. The Henry Murrays, she a cousin of my children, he a Harvard psychiatrist, were with us for the weekend, and we all waited impatiently for the return of the two men, which was a good deal delayed. Finally, we heard the sound of the car in the driveway, and soon after, Van Wyck entered with Carl, an upstanding man, deliberate, stubborn-headed, intent on himself, dominating the scene. As I welcomed him he said he badly needed an hour's nap but, seeing my consternation at losing him from the dinner table, he said he would forgo the nap if he could be provided with a guitar. This we obtained at once, borrowing one that belonged to the local doctor, who lived close by and who came over after dinner with his wife to listen to the great man play. Several others came also, uninvited, but having heard the news by means of the grapevine, a lusty climber in a small village. For an hour or so, Carl entertained us all. His voice had a fine resonance, and the songs were moving and true, bred as they were of man's immense loneliness on the desolate plains of our West. A little before midnight it was suggested that we go to a party at an adjoining house, a birthday party attended by both James Thurber and Mark Van Doren. I began by declining because of the lateness of the hour, but we were overborne, Van Wyck and I, by Sandburg.

"I must see Thurber," he said. "Seventeen years back we spent a fine evening together and I haven't seen him since."

We went out into the moonlit village and entered a house too small to encompass the people already there, the volume of tobacco smoke, the tumblers of whiskey. Carl was immediately at home and went to sit on an old-fashioned mohair sofa between Thurber and

Van Doren: three mockingbirds on a branch; while Van Wyck, a solitary thrush, watched from a remote branch opposite. Carl continued with his singing and his wisecracking, which was now and then interrupted by Thurber's special brand of humor. Van Doren helped to keep things alert, and it was all very gay. Soon, however, the thought of Van Wyck's early rising pursued me, and I managed to extricate him and the Murrays, while Carl stayed out until four-thirty. "One of the best parties of all time," he said.

On July 1 we made the move to our Bridgewater house, a temporary inferno bred of heat and confusion, the sounds of sawing and hammering and soldering, the smell of paint still wet. Van Wyck searched in vain for a spot wherein he could settle himself and his equipment, wandering about, brief case in hand. Two days later, however, on a Sunday morning, we were of a sudden at peace. On our waking we could see the spire of a church through the open window and its parish house close beside. After breakfast, in the lovely quiet, the identity of our house emerged to confront us, a house awaiting its future. The living room, still empty, had a fine elegance of proportion with its height of ceiling and length of line, while Van Wyck's study, nearer to completion, gave out a sense of coming purpose. There was everywhere an intangible but compelling force toward hidden, elusive things, as unseen patterns, long ago imposed, played hide-and-seek with us, begging for our compliance. It was the spell of another day that wound us about, when the pace of life was slower and time played on the side of those whose gestures were deliberate and circumspect. This house was not one to be treated with casual regard, I could see. But neither Van Wyck nor I wished to treat it so. We knew that we were now "at home."

X

Sanctuary

*T*HE advent of our first New Year at Bridgewater took the form of a gathering in our living room. Our single house guest on that occasion, come from New York to spend several days, was Julius Teller, my friend of many years, a conscientious and hard-pressed lawyer. I had first known Julius when, recently arrived from Vienna and the law courts there, he had gone to study at the Yale Law School and found himself a classmate of my son, John Saltonstall. Notwithstanding the difference between them in age they were much together, and he was brought to my house, where, little by little, he assumed the role of standby to the members of my family. A small man, shoulders bent from work, he arrived at Bridgewater, usually, wrapped in a protracted fatigue from long and burdened hours at the law office, where his judgment was as much sought as it was with us. He was also a talented purveyor of presents, choosing his gifts with a kind of prescience that always hit the mark: "Thank you, dear Julius," was the phrase that came to be routine, one around which he, in turn, composed much of his existence.

To our New Year's Eve party came the Blumes, the Cowleys, the Alexander Calders, the Louis Untermeyers, the Josephsons, the Julien Levys, the William McFees, and Henry Schnackenberg, the bachelor painter who lived in nearby Newtown. His was a rejuvenated farmhouse painted yellow within the confines of a tidy picket fence and bordered by a discreet bit of woodland wherein he had encouraged the growth of the various ferns collected, trowel in hand, over the years on trips to Massachusetts, Vermont, New Hampshire. Here, just beyond his dooryard, he was able to watch the result of his labors in the dignified and circumspect bearing of royal, walking, polypody, ostrich, maidenhair, Christmas, and so on: graceful creatures all.

Also, as background to life in our village, we were paid a visit that evening by the rector of the small Episcopal church across the way, Father Day, who dropped in for an hour of cheer as he made the festive parish rounds. He was an Englishman and had remarkably held to the qualities inherent in the tradition of the English country parson, pink-cheeked as he was, rotund as John Gilpin and a lover of good fare. A warmhearted man whose hidden, far-off, private tragedy wove a figured bass accompaniment to the cheerfully running upper registers of his personality. His sermons were not of the sort to be treasured on paper. Rather, he delivered them extempore, striding back and forth across the rostrum while he rebuked his congregation in the manner of the classical schoolmaster. He was a consolation to the poor and the solitary and a staunch friend to such groups as the girls in the local telephone office, on whom he kept a benign eye, supplying them with ice-cream sodas from his meager purse in periods of protracted heat. A man of faith.

When Father Day departed, our party was pre-empted by Sandy Calder, whose vigor spilled over us as the wine in his glass spilled over the tablecloth. After supper, we lit the candles on our towering tree in the front windows of our long living room and played a recording of seventeenth-century choir music, to which Sandy danced a minuet with Louisa, followed by *pas seuls* of clumsy, light-footed grace, making us laugh at his clowning, naïf obscenities. With his energy and huge capacity for work, Calder, we believed, was in the great tradition among artists: Rubens, Michelangelo, Frans Hals. Van Wyck adored him and his fresh-blown pranks. Sandy had given him at Christmas a miniature mobile of recent design, and this evening Van Wyck walked about holding it aloft that none should overlook its delicate metal arm miraculously sprung from a stone such as one finds by the roadside.

Frequently, as the winter wore on, it was imperative for Van Wyck to drive to the Yale Library in New Haven. Usually I went with him, taking along my journal to bring it up to date, and I sat in the periodicals room situated below the stacks where, above my head, Van Wyck searched for the material needed. "I wish now and then I could read for pleasure," he said occasionally on the way home, the bright red denim drawstring bag spilling out books on the rear seat and "heavy as all get-out," a phrase of my father's. We lunched at Liggett's counter, surrounded by alarm clocks, jackknives, hair curlers, chocolate bars, and the displays of paper-bound books so fascinating to my husband.

Once or twice during the season, we lingered within the Yale boundaries to hear a lecture of especial significance. One of these in the course of the winter was given by Thornton Wilder in a room in Strathcoma Hall, and it turned out to be entertainment of the highest order. Wilder was compelling to watch, with the attributes of the actor as he made his points, telling us of the distinctions and design of our American tongue as it was used by certain writers of the past to whom we offer an allegiance not sufficiently particularized: Thoreau, Melville, Whitman, Emily Dickinson. These few, in the protracted solitude of their lives, had evolved a noble manner of communication wherein the native essence, the fervor, the vehemence of our language had been driven with almost hysterical pressure far beyond its original purpose. Wilder's theme was exciting to follow, and Van Wyck listened eagerly, in approval and agreement. "Altogether fresh," was his whispered comment to me. When the lecture ended, we went to shake hands with Wilder, who told us that he had almost run from the hall on noticing Van Wyck seated below in the audience. But he seemed happy to have Van Wyck's quite obvious approval.

A duty which fell to me in connection with my husband's literary life was that of helping him to compile the indexes for his books as they were finished. The first of these to be worked on at Bridgewater was *New England: Indian Summer,* soon to be published in the Everyman edition. At a card table set beside his desk I took down the list of names appearing in the book as he read them aloud, setting them in alphabetical order and numbering them according to their appearance on the various pages. Pleasant to be in company with so many distinguished human beings, most of them turned ghosts, while the juxtaposition brought them by alphabetic order was odd and amusing: Abélard, the great lover, and Adams, Brooks, a crotchety old Puritan; Lehr, Harry, leader of cotillons, and Leonardo da Vinci; or Bishop Berkeley, the eminent Divine and philosopher, tied to Bernhardt, Sarah. Van Wyck read on as the hours went by, oblivious of all but the existing task, while my mind wandered as I sought the basic value of a human life and reflected on the inevitable interruption caused by death.

On St. Patrick's Day of that year, we played an unforeseen part in an episode such as comedies are made of. It involved an Irish harp that I had owned since early Boston days and that had been bought at Hill's, the renowned dealer in musical instruments, on Bond Street in London. We had taken it with us to New York that day, unmindful of the holiday, one of small consequence in our village, in order to have it appraised at the Metropolitan Museum of Art, which possessed a similar one, the Egan harp, among its rare musical instruments. Arriving uptown during the afternoon to reclaim our parked car we found ourselves blocked by a parade on Fifth Avenue and only then realized that for the Irish it was their great day. The harp, however, remained as yet unseen by the authority at the Metropolitan and we resolved to make the attempt to reach the museum. As we neared the east side of Fifth Avenue the parade was in full swing, the crowds were out in volume, the police lines were firm. What to do? It was the harp that saved the day. For, bearing it staunchly over his shoulder, my husband became the focus of many admiring eyes. Children followed us. A small boy asked where it came from. "Dublin," answered Van Wyck. "Dublin City, is it?" another cried out. "My father was born in Dublin City." A cop caught sight of Van Wyck, with his white moustache, his dignity, his unflinching mien, an Irish harp slung over his shoulder.

"Where do you wish to go, sir?" he asked. "To the Metropolitan if it's at all possible." Instantly a passage was opened through the crowd, the march halted for an instant, and we were waved across Fifth Avenue to the museum steps. On that March 17 Van Wyck and I were no aliens. We were members in high standing of the noble race of Hibernians.

With our settling at Bridgewater, Lewis and Sophia Mumford, in Amenia, New York, had become our neighbors. We were long-time friends and we frequently exchanged visits, driving the twenty-five miles between us for lunch or tea. At first, Van Wyck and I were apprehensive as to the effect that our newly completed house might have on Lewis. It fitted no single period or category, and, with the bulging width of its exterior, had already been christened by William McFee the "Fall River Boat," while in size, because of the height of ceilings and the third-story attic, it seemed far to outdo the requirements of two people. Inside, a stairway confronting the entrance door, its quartered oak banister and paneling painted white, mounted toward a group of Léger water colors hanging above, vivid in essence, while on the wall facing the rail were the Raphael engravings inherited by Van Wyck from his family: two varying styles, symbol of our lives in the past and our conjunction in the present. At the left of the hall, the living room of many windows spread its length from east to west, from sunrise to sunset. Walls of books and a fireplace marked the easterly end, where we sat with our friends and where Van Wyck's deep chair and my sofa corner were centered on a circular coffee table. Three paintings hung in the available wall space. One was a portrait by

J. B. Yeats of Van Wyck in 1907, at the moment he graduated from Harvard, the profile of a slim, sensitive young man in high wing collar, flower in buttonhole and a bust of Sophocles confronting him. Another was John Carroll's fanciful portrait of me, which, in the way that he had, resembled his wife, Georgia, a charming sample of the illusory Carroll style. On the third wall was a maritime still life by the French painter Jacques Emile Blanche, a contemporary of Sargent. This was replaced later by the portrait Carroll painted of my husband when, before our marriage, we spent the weekend with him in the Chatham Valley. Across the front hall, Van Wyck's study held curving bow windows facing the street, and a plush-covered seat below them became the repository for the books and pamphlets in active use. Here, the Venetian blinds, partially drawn, served to conceal him from callers mounting the front steps, so that seated in his Harvard chair at the ink-stained, drop-leaf table of long service, he could continue his daily labor. A window at his elbow brought morning sun and the sight of the magnolia tree beyond. For the rest, the room was the one lived in by my husband on Fifty-seventh Street, the same books, pictures, fetishes pressing him around in the manner which was his alone. The dining room drew the sunshine through its broad south windows, as though a giant magnet were at work, wrapping us about as we sat at a small table to eat our breakfast and our lunch. The walls surrounding the large center table were hung with portraits of Van Wyck's ancestors: the cotton merchant, Grandfather Brooks, with beautiful delicate hands, whose house in New York's Wall Street contained the family below and the cotton above; Great-grandfather Bailey, the Plattsburgh pomologist whose cheeks were as intensely red as Van Wyck's own; Great-great-grandfather Bailey of old Poughkeepsie, friend of Chancellor Kent and patriot of the American Revolution. Bringing the tone and the pattern up to date, there hung on the northwesterly wall a bas-relief in colored plaster, facsimile of my husband made in recent years by the sculptor Paul Manship. Through a southerly door of the dining room, open all summer, we stepped to a terrace of broad paving stones. This hung over the garden, that ancient garden of roses and honeysuckle which had had such power to compel when first we walked its sheltered paths. Here, we sat on warm evenings drinking our cocktail before dinner while the sun set at our backs and water splashed gently from the little fountain in our pool and the birds came to drink before night fell and the flowers sent their sweetness into the unmoving air. House, a shaded front piazza, terrace, garden, we used it all and it became a shelter for those whom we loved. The Mumfords saw it on a day in April, and, to our delight, Lewis appeared pleased with its awkward grace, its substantial quality and the aura of hospitality which it enclosed. He was in a cheerful mood just then, having reached the end of a protracted and difficult winter of bad weather and illness. Also, his book in progress had recently taken a leap into the light. Earlier, he told us, it had been cumbrous in structure, refusing to expand as it should. Then had come the discovery that in essence it was three books rather than one, that anatomically it required tearing asunder. Interesting to watch the log jams that accrue from the volume of a writer's material and the manner in which a skilled artisan persuades it back to the main stream.

A return visit to Amenia at the end of June showed us Lewis lean and vigorous in mind and body after two months' work in the garden. In a few days' time he was to receive a delegation of German youths, trained in architecture and city planning, come to study our methods. He intended suggesting to them, among other things, he told us, that their Germany would be a better place, less susceptible to dictatorship, to regimentation, were it to become decentralized, broken into a series of small states, as it had been in the days before Bismarck's heavily uniting hand had made it a single political and military state. This seemed to us a stimulating idea, the more so as Lewis believed it might be applied on a global scale, the world becoming thus a group of comparatively autonomous units. We drove away, my mind racing, Van Wyck's moving rather more deliberately, so much was there to be assimilated. But we questioned the effect that would be made on the arriving

German students by the Mumfords' house, which, with its wooded background, reminded me of the one inhabited by Red Riding Hood's grandmother: so simple, so small and unremarkable except for the books that it held. Only the kitchen had authority, the spot in which Sophia, handsome and wise and good as some fairy-tale wood chopper's wife, baked her loaves of bread. The planner of modern cities, himself, seemed to eschew the up-to-date where his daily life was concerned save in the spaces of his own mind.

A friend of ours at Woodbury, William Ivins, was curator of prints and engravings at the Metropolitan Museum. His wife, Florence Wyman, a talented and subtle draftsman, had spent several years with us when I was a girl, and many were the records in the form of perceptive portraits from that period still in my possession. Also, she had drawn the illustrations for Louis Untermeyer's early anthology of poetry for children: *This Singing World*. Now, just as Van Wyck and I were settling in Connecticut and looking forward to a much delayed reunion with the Ivinses, who lived only twelve or fifteen miles away, Florence died of a sudden illness and Bill became an inconsolable widower. He had always been a peppery, argumentative man, and his manner of disparagement and disagreement had so increased with his wife's absence that it was more than ever difficult to avoid locking horns with him. Van Wyck was an admirer of Bill, of his mind and his knowledge, and he was well able to understand not only the sorrows of solitude but also the inescapable nature of those explosive attacks of desperation which, uninvited, beset the human constitution. He used, therefore, a gentle tact particularly his own, avoiding verbal encounters of any drastic sort, establishing a *modus vivendi,* so that over the years Bill came frequently to our house, dropping in without warning in late afternoon for a cup of tea. At those moments, as his tea grew cold, he sat well forward on the edge of his chair wagging a vigorous forefinger while prefacing his attacks on some current writer or painter with the phrase "Now, I'll tell you. . . ." Invariably, he did tell us. On our visit to the remodeled white farmhouse in Woodbury after Florence's death, the living-dining room overflowed with her presence, her water colors facing us from the walls, her equipment as housewife everywhere present: cutlery in a wicker basket, teacups of Rose Medallion in place on a tray of red lacquer, oil and vinegar cruets half full in their stand. Beyond this intimate but now superceded core for living, in the passages and hallways were Bill's rarebook collection, row upon row of leather-bound editions of ancient, mediaeval, and modern works on history and art, and the splendid prints which hung in haphazard fashion here and there or stood against the walls along the floor. We were within the confined existence of a scholar. So might the Brownings or the Carlyles have lived. Outdoors, near the house, Bill had planted a colony of tree peonies from China, lovely flowers of long delicate petals and quiet habit in virgin white or rose, and, in the sun-splashed corner of a lower terrace facing his battered wicker chair, a salamander of persisting loyalty made his darting angular movements along a wall grown with unobtrusive rock plants. We hoped Bill's sorrow would abate, that he might live here in peace.

Our garden of annuals we planted on a day when the blue of the sky was fresh and still and the sun so steadfast as to swell the buds on the magnolias and draw the smell of spring from the turf beneath. At the side of old Calvin Bates, the gardener whom we had acquired with the place, I worked in a small outer plot sowing the seed of lettuce and parsley and radish, setting out stands of onion, and placing markers in the rich willing earth overturned a week earlier, the rows to be edged presently with dwarf nasturtiums and pinks. As we labored, a pair of neighbors drove past the house. With their car top down they perceived Van Wyck in a chair on the lawn applied to his book, ancient Panama hat mounting high, and they stopped to fill his arms with daffodils from their meadows. It seemed natural that people should give him what they had, should enjoy doing so, for he was entirely undemanding and accepted what was offered in the rather bewildered way that an unsuspecting pupil might accept a prize handed him for merit by his teacher. I took the flowers to place them in water, jonquils of different varieties: the yellow trumpet, the starlike white, the red-eyed poetaz. And I thought of the lines from Herrick:

Y'ave heard them sweetly sing,
And seen them in a Round:
Each Virgin, like a Spring,
With Honey-succles crown'd.

Later, on that fair day, we made a new acquaintance, who came
to pay her respects and to offer us her friendship. Dr. Mabel
Pearson had come at the instance of Padraic and Molly Colum,
and at once we were drawn to her, a neighbor and retired doctor
of medicine, originally from England. Her concise voice and manner were attributes sprung not only from her background but also
from a severely trained mind, while her way of life, we were to
find, in its dependence on solitude, exhibited the sort of pluck for
which her compatriots had always shown talent. Her house, somewhat apart from those within the village, was situated above a broad
meadow with glimpses of trees and water reminding one of a painting by Constable. We were often to be with Mabel Pearson in the
years that followed, partaking of her clearly presented ideas, her pots
of tea, and the Irish soda bread which was her specialty.

A June Sunday came along when three dear friends of Van
Wyck arrived to spend the day, thereby warming his heart and enabling his tongue to carry him where it willed without constraint
—Helen and John Sloan and Margaret Cobb. Seated on our piazza
under a hot sun, we looked out over the lawn toward the massive
lilac-colored bloom of our immense rhododendrons. Margaret Cobb
was in resilient spirits, which rose, with the genius that was hers,
up and beyond the day-to-day existence making her a willing
slave and dispenser to children and grandchildren. She was like a
tall-stemmed, vividly colored aster outgrowing her sister flowers in
an autumn garden. Sloan, drinking his glass of buttermilk while
his devoted young wife watched with adoring eyes, sat with hat at a
comic angle to shield his face, and for all his seventy-eight years was
droll and spry. He and Van Wyck talked of the state of writing and
painting in our current world of small faith. Van Wyck's conten-
tion was that there are periods of low vitality, which nations must
traverse, when the human reservoir is at slack ebb, and that we
were at present in such a period. Sloan agreed. It almost seemed to

me, then, watching my husband's intensity, his capacity for caring, that with no more than his two bare hands, following the guideline of his mind, he could instill the needed vitality into the places where it belonged, turn minor into major.

A party in our garden during this initial summer at Bridgewater brought twelve or more friends to drink a belated brew of May wine and to listen, during the hour of sunset, to Durant Rice, my brother, playing and singing those French folk songs which seemed a part of his blood, singing in his poignant voice that could not fail to move those who heard, to bring a catch to their throats. As a special member of the audience on that day, someone to play to in particular, Durant quite naturally gathered in Freddy March, who had not heard him before and who listened with apparent delight to Durant's native spirit, to a talent free of training but possessing that grace which springs from acute feeling. Others in the audience were a part of the magic, too, and at the moment of its ending there was a sigh, made of joy and sorrow both, that charged the atmosphere to die in a slow downward floating.

This was the last time I was to hear my brother sing. The summer, as it unrolled, brought a stop to his music, to his line of life, forever. He died, the youngest among us three Rices, after lying helpless in his hospital bed, drifting into that far secret place which is closed to us whose hearts beat on. "Was there ever anyone so beloved and so unaware of it?" One of his friends wrote me thus, one among those who in their affection and sympathy had attempted to protect him. I had loved him since he was a small, silent boy, wide-eyed, absorbed, gripping with his knees a violoncello larger than he. Music should have been his destiny, but the world wrenched him away and set him down in the flat places of commerce, wherein he attempted, more or less empty-handed, to stand beside those who rolled the marbles with ease. Only the years he spent in France during the two major wars were a respite from the monotony of fate. He languished in the day-to-day struggle at home, brave though he was. And on a glowing September day the dream and reality were finally reconciled. His essence lingered on, brushing the sun on summer leaves, mingling with the winds of autumn, often a part of the evening stillness and, of music, always.

The Marches, Florence and Freddy, neighbors and friends, came to dine with us, and the evening established a fresh bond because of our common sympathies. Until almost midnight we sat about our coffee table talking of the tidal wave of red-baiting which swept the land. This was the moment when Hollywood was being excoriated as an example in perfidy, but the Marches, who had given their generous support to many liberal causes, had been able, in the face of glaring publicity, to establish their magnanimity and their love of country. Van Wyck was impressed with the calm and detachment of their viewpoint as well as with the courage of their stand.

Our life in the country was not made entirely of sunshine and serenity. On a day of November we were swept into an eighteenth-century world in which floods and gales cut off the power which bestows light and heat in village houses and we sat numb and cheerless in cold, dim rooms, unable to continue with our tasks, while at our backs wild winds tore the roots of great trees from the sheltering earth and before us, through westerly window-panes, we looked out on a menacing downpour which emptied the streets of all life. We gathered about our kitchen stove, lit by gas, in order to be warmed, but the impression of a sojourn in a pitiless world was not to be dispelled. My sister, Marjory Means, was with us at this moment of sudden attack, the first among several hurricanes in the 1950's, a habit of destruction which established itself during those years, and we were sorry to bid her good-bye on her return to Boston just at the moment of the storm's cessation and the new arrival of sunshine. She had uncomplainingly met the prolonged gloom and monstrous destruction and deserved brighter things to follow.

Once again Carl Sandburg came to see us, this time at the Bridgewater house, which he ornamented for twenty-four hours in his own singularly decorative way, part Western cowboy or bronco-buster, part shy youth at once eager and affectionate, and, lastly, a poet of integrity and power. He and Van Wyck were partners in their reliance on the American literary scene, their labor in its cause. I found it a moving experience to enter the study, to come on the two engaged in depth, Van Wyck, ever courteous, in the visitor's chair, Carl sunk low in Van Wyck's reading chair, a shawl about his shoulders, while only the stresses imposed by an outside world could have dislocated the communion of these two passionate warriors. During the evening, Carl forfeited his usual session of music in favor of reading aloud, with the Peter Blumes as additional listeners, the preface he had recently written to accompany the complete edition of his poems—a stirring comment, it was, on the role of the poet.

A massive bout with winter engaged the village during a certain week in February when the thermometer hovered close to zero and an icy screen separated us from the world beyond. The birds clung to our feeder, and the lump of suet on the rose arbor beyond the study grew rapidly smaller as the woodpeckers attacked it. This was a lovely time for Van Wyck and me. Within the house, day after day, we faced each other across his graceful Queen Anne table, which he carried into a south window or placed before the open fire, laden with two copies of the manuscript for *The Confi-dent Years*. I read the book aloud to him, word by word, while he followed from his copy, listening, meditating, correcting. We read of the aims and achievements of the generation of writers in the years between 1885 and 1915, forgotten men, often enough, whose influence was, nonetheless, a cog in the far-flung chain, and whose books were, in the future, to bring pleasure to readers who, lacking the impetus given them by Van Wyck, would have let them lie.

The completion of this book, and with it the end of the series *Makers and Finders,* had coincided with Van Wyck's sixty-fifth birthday on February 16, 1951. It became a happy and significant occasion, which we celebrated with the Kenyon Brookses and a few friends. Hamilton Basso made a speech telling us that an error had been discovered in Van Wyck's birth certificate, that in reality he had been born ten years later, making him, thus, only fifty-five years old. As I watched Van Wyck that evening, although outwardly quiet, he shone with a luster that seemed to reach beyond the present, beyond the limits of yearly computing, of the immediate day, to be halted, perhaps, by no specific date at all.

Toward the middle of March we drove home to Bridgewater after a day in New York with several momentous achievements behind us. We had dropped off the manuscript of *The Confident Years* at E. P. Dutton, we had bought a new car, and Van Wyck carried in his wallet the slip of paper which insured our passage to Ireland in April on the *Britannic*. There had also been a meeting of the Committee on Grants at the Academy, where, waiting in the office for Van Wyck, I was amused to see committee members come straggling in like any group of schoolboys when the meeting was over, gathering up coats, brief cases, hats, as they joked or gossiped. Malcolm Cowley was among the rest, and presently we drove him back to Connecticut. He and Van Wyck talked of Sinclair Lewis, whose posthumous novel, *World So Wide*, had recently been published following his lonely death in a hospital at Rome. Malcolm stressed Lewis's downhill stumbling from the peak of his *Main Street* and *Arrowsmith* days. Van Wyck defended Lewis's continued importance as a writer who understood men's motives and who fought for a better world, who celebrated, also, in each of his books, despite much inferior writing, some aspect of human behavior which he was able to clarify like no one else. Driving the two men onward through the deepening twilight, I thought of the tragedies which had crowded Sinclair Lewis's life to leave him in the end—possibly all the way through—as solitary as the wan moon above us in the far sky. And I wished that I might have taken his hand in mine for a moment before he died to thank him for writing of marriage as he did in *Cass Timberlane*, thank him for dwelling on the qualities of patience, modesty, courage, and love that persists.

XI

The Poets of the World Lie Sleeping

*T*HE moment came in April of 1951 to sail away, to leave, momentarily, those things which had attached themselves to us or us to them during the two-year occupancy of our Bridgewater house. It was the ideal moment for Van Wyck to quit his study, a re-enacting of the Sabbath day of rest on a scale of ample design. But the departure was not easy. After all, we were bidding farewell to a part of ourselves become familiar and reassuring as the sturdy maples along our village street. But to be stabbed vividly awake in the course of discovering a new path is one of man's prerogatives, and I thought of a phrase of Thomas Mann: "Habituation is a falling asleep or fatiguing of the sense of time. . . ."

On the first morning at sea aboard the *Britannic,* a Sunday morning, I awoke as a gentle sense of nostalgia invaded my heart. For a few brief moments I dwelt then on the scene at home in Bridgewater, where bells rang out into the blue sky beyond the two church steeples and above our magnolias just now opening their flowers. Acolytes and choir, like small earnest bright angels in their scarlet cassocks and white surplices, gathered on the green below the church entrance waiting to enter and sing the opening lines of the processional hymn. Were I there I would join in the "angelic song," composing myself then for a temporary removal into that world of simple goodness and faith called by men the Kingdom of Heaven. I had come to enjoy this re-established pursuit of mine, a pursuit in depth following a long lapse, the joining of hands with the community, a neighborly sharing within the Episcopal service, an age-old ritual which survived in beauty.

Through the porthole I could see a patch of ocean in circular shape as it held our ship aloft, a pleasant ship and well staffed. Van Wyck, on the day of embarkation watching the stewards in cabin and on deck, seeing their immense absorption and apparent pleasure in the job to hand, said: "The English have a fine sense of pageantry, of histrionics. They play their role with an ardor that other nationals don't have." This was true. Who else, from the length of the deck, tea tray borne high, could achieve the grand gesture of courtesy as the tray was placed across each lap, a tribute especially ordained?

Van Wyck and I scarcely slept on the night before our landing at Cobh for the vast excitement of reaching the shores of Europe. We took turns looking through the porthole for signs of land. The stars were brilliant, and we told each other we should have a fine day for the landing. Once we saw a lighthouse flashing its signal. At 5:00 A.M. the steward called us, and we hastened to the deck. There were few passengers about in the bitter cold. One, a thin man with melancholy eyes and a face of stone, wore a ten-gallon cowboy's hat. We had noticed him during the voyage, always motionless and alone, as though posing for a photograph, at the ship's rail. Now, Van Wyck spoke to him in the intimacy of our pre-dawn meeting, and we found he was no masquerader, but the owner of a ranch in Wyoming. Born in Cork, he was returning to the old country for the first time in thirty-five years, traveling with an invalid wife and a magnificent Packard car. The sunrise was soon upon us, a round red disc of fanning pink clouds, and with the growing light came a renewal of those impressions stored in childhood: that virginal shock which is the first sight of land as the ship pulls slowly toward the shore. All about us were the cries of greeting gulls, the smell of northern freshness, the quiet, hanging like a spread sheet stretched across meadows, low hillsides divided into punctilious squares and oblongs holding motionless sheep and cattle between the hedgerows and, wherever man had not laid his hand or guided his plow, there were the wild flowering things, gorse clumped in yellow, the pale pink of hawthorn, the cowslips and violets. One felt almost stricken with the beauty of the scene in the newness of early morning under a static, cloudless sky.

On board the tender taking us ashore at Cobh were many disembarked tourist passengers returning briefly from their jobs in the United States to visit the old folk in Ireland. Almost any among the young women might have been seen in New York or Boston dressed in neat black serving luncheon at Schrafft's. Today they were glamorous in new attire from Macy's or Filene's. The cowboy was with us, his wife in her wheel chair, and the Packard, which had taken many minutes to lower to the deck. They were indeed to make an impression on the inhabitants of Cork. There was time between our landing and the departure of the Dublin train to have "a bit of a walk" about the town of Cobh. This was suggested to us by our porter, as friendly and eagerly cooperative as were the Irish everywhere during our stay. They seemed more ingenuous, more content than the Irish of our cities at home.

We set out, Baedeker in hand, for the Cathedral at the summit of the town. Van Wyck and I supplemented one another, more or less, as we traveled. He became absorbed in the major points of interest, refreshing himself on the history of the place, studying maps, leading me to important buildings and the galleries. I stared at the people, their faces and clothes, peeking between the curtains of windows as we passed, looking at the plants growing in gardens, prodding my husband in the direction of landscape. His addiction to Baedeker, and mine to a lesser degree, had begun in childhood; and on our shelves at Bridgewater were thirty or more of these red-bound books, inscribed with the names of his parents or with that of Miss Eliza Kenyon, a great-aunt of Eleanor Brooks and cultural directress, in her era, of the city of Plainfield. Several of these were to go with us on our travels, no matter what their date, for the newer guides seemed to Van Wyck inadequate. "Europe remains Europe," he would say, "with few changes, and Baedeker knew it better than anyone else." Now and then there was a lapse in up-to-date information, as when once we drove from Waterloo Station in London to the hotel where, as a young man, Van Wyck's father had spent some time. We had not engaged a room in advance, merely telling the taxi driver to proceed to that address. On our arrival we were confronted by a fenced-in crater made by a bomb in the Second World War. Again, Van Wyck had, not long since, lent a Baedeker on Greece to a friend who planned a trip to Athens. She presently returned it saying that in the foreword, among "practical hints," it was suggested to the visitor he bring his own bed coverings because the rugs presented him for bedclothes in most of the hotels "were almost always full of vermin." Also, because of the presence of bandits, travelers were "strongly urged to pitch their tents within the bounds of the Acropolis." This copy of Baedeker proved to be the edition of 1904.

On the five-hour train journey to Dublin we were gently drawn through meadows of moist green that fell on one side to the sea and rose on the other to distant hills. High above valleys we saw the gray stone ruins of mediaeval fortresses, skeletal fingers pointing to the past; belonging to the present, little new lambs tugged at their mothers' teats while agile black cattle wandered grazing and men ploughed the damp earth. In the chinks of retaining walls, as we flew past, tender-hued primroses were growing, and creeping phlox, English daisies, and candytuft required no care from the hand of man.

The arrival at Dublin in afternoon was a cheerful business. We found the station porter sympathetic in spite of our fourteen pieces of hand luggage, and the taxi man drove a leisurely roundabout course to the hotel in his pride at pointing out the monuments to Van Wyck, who appeared to know so much about them. We descended at the Shelbourne Hotel, become a part of Irish history, and our room proved to be what we had pictured and hoped for: large and comfortable, furnished in chintz and mahogany, with a broad round center table for writing and for our books. And it faced on St. Stephen's Green, that lovely park lying softly below and bound by its iron grille. Looking out, I saw stretches of green grass and flower beds, and I perceived a mother duck conducting her thirteen ducklings on their early-evening outing down the stream. Along various benches young girls sat intently reading, and it seemed wonderful that they preferred this to the movies. Striding past, long-legged men in raincoats walked home from work. In the street, bicycles were everywhere, forming a major part of the traffic, winding with assurance between buses and the tiny private cars that darted from many angles.

Our stay in Dublin was interrupted on the second day by the arrival from the north of Van Wyck's stepsister, Dorothy Whyte, and her son John. They had come the long way from County Down to carry us back for a protracted weekend at Rostrevor. The car was chauffeured by an Orangeman, a young man of narrow head and tight, thin lips. A dour, grim race of beings, I decided. We were taken through country noticeably less lush and expansive than that of the south and through towns occupied with industry, among them Drogheda, where Cromwell had slaughtered many among the population after his victory there. He seemed no longer to be the god we were taught to revere in our youthful studies of history.

Rostrevor, situated on Carlingford Lough, is a town of villas and inns, and the Whytes' house, built of stucco and similar to those on the Mediterranean, was ornamented with balconies intended for occupancy beneath a hot sun. During our stay, however, the thermometer remained at forty-five degrees and a wet wind blew from the north, while the house, in the manner of all the others, was heated merely by coal fires in the two living rooms. I was warm only at the moments of standing before one of these fires, skirt pulled high, and I soon found the reason for the British addiction to steaming tea. The late-afternoon parties to which we were invited during this visit were as agreeable as possible when, seated before the fire about wide, linen-clothed tables spread with quantities of hot buns and buttered bread and cakes, we drank our four or five cups apiece.

Like all people under the current English system, Dorothy Whyte had been taxed into something close to poverty. She was a widow, generous and self-abnegating, with two children to guide. Her young daughter, Ursula, was at a convent school. John was a graduate of Oxford, a clever young man who hoped to teach history when his army service was at an end. Van Wyck said that John's profile was very like that of the youthful Cardinal Newman.

To meet us on the day after our arrival Dorothy had invited the county in for cocktails, an unusual form of entertainment for that spot. It was very gay. People came in force, not the brogue-speaking Irish of the south, but differing somewhat from their English cousins in their instant approachability and friendliness, their ready humor. One old lady of ninety-four, upright, gay, direct, had walked the mile to Dorothy's house in order to be present at the first cocktail party of her life. She wanted to learn what one was like before it was too late, she said. Dorothy had primed everyone on the subject of Van Wyck's writing, and they all gathered about him to pamper and to spoil. His cheeks, as he attempted to fend off these agreeable attacks, were the color of a setting sun in a tropical land.

We bade good-bye to Dorothy and John and to their bulky, bundled little maid, built rather like a black Kerry bullock, at eight o'clock on a chilly morning, and, seated in the train for Dublin, looking back over the days at Rostrevor and its environs, I realized how many were the gathered impressions: the penetrating cold, almost a personality in itself; the smell of coal smoke in the damp, heavy-hanging air; the early-morning crackling of the fire in the living-room grate; church bells tolling; the delicious healing warmth suddenly bestowed by the glass of the Whyte greenhouse, where the sun's strength was cumulatively stored; the gaunt gray stone of the Rostrevor Hotel, with its tall windows opening on Carlingford Lough and its starched, white-capped waitresses, servants of another generation, standing at attention within. I had enjoyed my bicycle rides with John, one in the rain to market and back, another on a Sunday afternoon along the edge of the water past row after row of neat villa gardens. Also, our evenings with Dorothy, cross-legged for added warmth in her deep chair, darning and stitching, courageous and competent, while she and Van Wyck dwelt on a past they had shared when they were young and touched on a future too amorphous to be securely outlined.

Back in Dublin and well established at our hotel, we saw plays on two successive evenings, an unusual occurrence for us, who rarely managed to go to the theater at home. The first, at the Gate Theatre, put on by the company of Lord Longford, was a revival of the *School for Scandal*. It was well acted and for me the lines were doubly delightful because of Van Wyck's pleasure in them: an old friend come to communicate with him once again. The playhouse itself was rather shabby and very cold and the seats uncomfortable, but we preferred it to the overstressed luxury of our own theaters, where so much is done for the body and so little for the mind in the way of nourishment. Lord Longford stood in the lobby background between the acts that evening, a Falstaffian figure of a man with a red carnation in his buttonhole. It turned out that he was a good deal of a scholar, maintaining his company of actors as an outlet for his own and his wife's plays as well as for the classic repertory they performed so well. On the second evening, at the famed Abbey Theatre, we saw a revival of a play about contemporary Ireland by Lennox Robinson. We had excellent seats, bought only the day before, third row center and costing five shillings each, and yet the house was full. A new experience to be thus entertained at so little cost and on the spur of the moment. Soon after, we were to meet Ria Mooney, directress of the Abbey during many successful years, and we at once became admirers of her talent and her ingenuous simplicity.

To the letters of introduction we had brought from the Colums we had many replies. For Padraic is well beloved in his native Ireland. Among the first to greet us were Francis MacManus, a novelist, and the poet Robert Farren. They took us to lunch at the Gresham Hotel in the heart of Dublin on the great thoroughfare O'Connell Street, where motor traffic and bicycles were entwined in profusion, a vivid crowded scene which reminded me of a Brueghel gone modern. MacManus told us that the Gresham had been the setting for a part of Joyce's beautiful story "The Dead." We were much drawn to MacManus, whose wife had recently died of cancer and whose ten-year-old son was at that moment dying of an incurable heart ailment. I asked if I might send the boy a book or a toy. "Oh, he's outgrown toys," MacManus answered, "and he reads a book a day. He's all right. He's a happy boy. He knows he's not long for this world but he's glad for having grasped so much of life at his age." Before lunch ended, Farren asked Van Wyck to go on the air, the local Radio Eireann, modeled on the B.B.C., to give a fifteen-minute reminiscence of J. B. Yeats. Although well nigh a novice in the art of broadcasting, Van Wyck accepted the invitation in order to repay a little of the kindness showered upon us each day, and to an ever-increasing degree. Besides, he had been very fond of Mr. Yeats.

Another Dubliner whom we were several times to meet was Thomas McGreevy, director of the National Gallery. He was suave, articulate, witty, and a nabob within his sphere as well as a devotee of the Church. Within the right context my husband was all for Catholic abundance, particularly when it kept the great cathedrals alive and functioning. This was not the case with the two oldest churches of Dublin—both fixtures, for the last three hundred years, within the Church of England and chilly for lack of sufficient worshipers. One of these was St. Patrick's, where the great Swift had been dean and in which his bones lie alongside those of his Stella. It seemed to me remarkable that a vested clergyman of the Protestant faith should have desired and been permitted to bury his lady beneath the pavement of the transept of a church from which he guided his flock, and later, when his work was done, be placed at her side. On a brass plaque set into the pavement we were told that she was buried at midnight. How dramatic a scene in that magnificent somber edifice, the bleak, black night and the towering vaults lit by flickering candles, and Swift's grief, wider, deeper than all the rest.

It behooved us, because of Van Wyck's early connections with the Yeats family, to go out to call on the painter John Yeats, at the Portobello Nursing Home on the southerly outskirts of the city. At seven o'clock of a lovely evening we boarded a bus, our preferred manner of transportation in Europe, and climbed to the upper deck, from which we had a fine view of the city as we went. The nursing home faced the Grand Canal, and from Mr. Yeats's room we presently beheld it as the falling sunlight brought a glow to the wings of a pair of white swans slowly swimming. At our back a coal fire burned in the chimney, and each of us held a glass of Irish whiskey. A grand moment. Yeats was a distinguished man in appearance, with courtly manners and a kindly, tolerant point of view. As a good, but possibly not remarkable, painter he had been overshadowed by his famous brother, but his reputation had steadily grown and his pictures were then selling as fast as he painted them. At seventy-six, and not strong, he had recently entered his third period of painting and planned soon to open an exhibit in New York. His talk with Van Wyck was principally about his father, old J. B. Van Wyck spoke of his courage in going to America to live at the age of seventy, making a new life for himself there, and Jack Yeats answered: "You speak of courage. What of this? Once my father's eyes gave out momentarily and he believed he was going blind. He said nothing about it but he called for my sister, Lily, and began dictating a novel to her. If he was no longer to be able to paint he would turn himself into a writer, and the sooner the better."

At the end of an hour, when a pretty nurse opened the door, we said good-bye, reluctantly, as one does if one knows the person will not be seen again on earth, and I brought away the memory of a tall, lean man whose bravery equaled his father's.

The Poets of the World Lie Sleeping

A luncheon took place at University College, the Catholic college founded by Cardinal Newman. It was situated on St. Stephen's Green within two beautiful Palladian houses built as private dwellings in the eighteenth century. We were guided through abysmal cold to a room on the ground floor where, before a bright coal fire, three men awaited us. One was the university president, Dr. Tierney; the second was the chaplain, an exceedingly knowing and charming man; the third was our old friend MacManus. Lunch was served at a small table immediately in front of the fire, and this very pleasant occasion did not break up until four o'clock. Much of the talk had to do with the Irish at home and abroad, including a comparison of the Boston Irish with the Boston Brahmins. A sister of Mrs. Tierney who lived in Cambridge, Massachusetts, was married to an exchange professor at Harvard and, while seeing a good deal of the James family and their friends there, people whom she enjoyed, she wrote that in secret her heart was with the "unregenerate Irish." Following lunch we were taken on a tour of the houses, lovely and unspoiled by years of academic application: lofty, graceful rooms with mantels of tender-colored marble, ceilings whereon angels and cherubs floated, curved niches holding delicate, dedicated statuettes. From the walls of the salon sprang figures in high relief, muses and graces, charming creatures contrived, we were told, with the love and pride in their craft by artisans imported from Italy at the moment when these superb houses were building. We hoped that nothing would arise to do them harm.

On a day of chill winds and sharp sunlight Van Wyck and I went by train from Dublin to Navan to lunch with the William Walshes, who lived on an estate named Bective, the birthplace of our friend James Stern. The big house in which he was born belonged then to Boston friends of ours, but the smaller house held William Walsh, overseer of the property, and his wife, Mary Lavin, writer of short stories, many of which I had read in the *New Yorker*. Van Wyck had had an enthusiastic but rather haphazard correspondence with Mary Lavin, several of her letters going astray to be replaced by others full of apology. Now, as we left the train at eleven in the morning, Walsh handed Van Wyck still another note from his wife, which explained a recent illness of hers and the fact that she was still kept in bed.

"Why didn't you put us off?" we exclaimed in unison.

"For nothing in the world would we be doing that," he said quickly. "We'll go up to my wife's room straight away. And by lunchtime she'll be getting dressed. I'm certain of that. It would be too much of a disappointment to her not to be seeing you."

We waited briefly in the Walsh living room, with its ancient oak beams and white-plastered walls, its great pots of primulas and beech boughs of tender green. Wide windows gave us a view of the River Boyne and a ruined abbey beyond it. Soon we were invited upstairs into Mary Lavin's bedroom, and there we made the acquaintance of the young woman whose stories were rated among the best in modern-day Ireland. She looked very appealing as she sat in bed against a pile of pillows, her Irish black hair making a fine contrast to the background and her large eyes compelling us by their direct look of sympathy. Papers were spread about the bed, and we saw that she was at work on her writing. But she seemed happy to be interrupted, to take Van Wyck's hand in hers —a genuine admiration—and she begged us to draw our chairs beside the bed while the obliging William brewed tea from a kettle on the hob before the fire.

Things turned out as he had predicted. After a walk about the fine grounds of Bective and a stroll along the Boyne, that stream of bloodshed and romance, Van Wyck and I sat down to lunch with both Walshes at a table in the living-room window. Mary Lavin told us that as early docent for her work she was chiefly in debt to Lord Dunsany. His house was close by, and formerly they had been much together. At present he was living in England, having turned his place over to his son in order to escape the inheritance tax. Their friendship, therefore, his and hers, had to be maintained by correspondence. "A sad pity," said Mary Lavin. She said also that the Ascendency bigwigs of the neighborhood, with their beautiful houses and their equable manner of life, their taking of the good things for granted, "had much to teach us poor Irish, so long the underdogs." I wondered about the truth of this, listening to her lovely, lilting tongue, seeing the beech leaves, pale in their green, against the high white wall, thinking of her writing that so moved the heart.

The days became ever more crowded with people who sought friendship with Van Wyck. At home in his study, the Venetian blind drawn down along the window that faced the front door, a signal was continually abroad that protected his working hours. Here in Dublin, no signal was possible, nor was any sustained work on Van Wyck's part. But the interlude, though fatiguing, was agreeable, chiefly because the people we met seemed each one to have read Van Wyck's books and to have taken pleasure in them. Moreover, there was gratitude everywhere not only for his work but also for the discovery of his personality: for his modesty and his impulsive generosity.

Most recent among our acquaintance were the Monk Gibbons. Through them we were to meet the Protestant world of Trinity College. Monk Gibbon, a scholar and a poet and the father of six children, lived in a house at Dalkey, near to the sea, with a large, roughly stuccoed living room. It was a well-bred bohemia. His pretty wife carried the appearance of fatigue, but her smile was brave. I went with her into her kitchen while the men were talking one Sunday afternoon, to help her with the tea tray. Here were a huge copper kettle on the boil, several platters of Irish bread, and, over all, like a shower of blossoms, a bevy of bright-colored children's socks hanging from a clothesline. We were joined at tea by Lord Moyne, an attractive man who was the reigning head of the Guinness brewing family, himself "a bit of a poet." He drove us back to the Shelbourne later and invited us to inspect the brewery, largest in the world, during the following week.

On a Sunday of the Whitsun holiday we were driven out into the lovely Wicklow Hills by C. P. Curran and his daughter; he was the great authority on Georgian architecture as well as an expert on Irish history. The sun was out to bless the day, and entire families were spending the hours digging peat from the hillsides, to stack it in small oblong blocks for drying. On the next Sunday, we were told, they would return with their carts to carry the blocks home to heat their houses. At Glendalough, the Currans showed us the Seven Churches, that much-visited group dating from the sixth, seventh, and eighth centuries, and we saw the retreat of St. Kevin: "a high name over the sea-wave, chaste and fair," as the ancient bards sang of him. His retreat, a cave giving on the lake, had been discovered by a shepherd of the hermit's day, and from that moment people flocked to hear him preach, "clothed in coarsest garments and living on herbs while a crowd of tame birds sang on his shoulders and hands." We were to be with the Currans again at an evening party given in the long-enduring Irish twilight at their Georgian house of brick in Dublin, which reminded me of the houses at home in Washington Square. There were present Lennox Robinson, whose play we had seen, a painter, a publisher, a politician, and the widow of John McCormack, the tenor, now become a papal countess, a lady of cheerful affluence. At ten o'clock Miss Curran served tea and cakes, the Irish custom that plunged us backward into the world of Maria Edgeworth, and that I found so agreeable in the chill Irish climate.

A half-day we spent at the Guinness Brewery and with the family of Lord Moyne. This held a feudal splendor that began when we were called for at the Shelbourne by the brewery car and its punctilious chauffeur. Lord Moyne, who received us on our arrival, was a handsome man with a gentle smile, who ruled his tremendous empire of stout and porter in a somewhat apologetic way. We were ushered into a chill anteroom where three meticulously dressed gentlemen, members of the controlling board, awaited us. On a table were whiskey and sherry and a silver pitcher which held a hot extract of malted yeast, a by-product of beermaking. We drank this with considerable pleasure, a cupful each, flavored with sherry. It tasted like a glamorous sort of bouillon, a life-giving essence. In an adjacent room, the immense round dining table used by the board of directors had been covered with a white cloth, and was laid for lunch. The sideboards surrounding it held platters of food of such quantity, so varied, and so tempting that we were hard put to it to make our choice: cold lobster, galantine of veal, chicken mousse, sweetbreads in wine sauce, braised celery, and huge joints of beef and mutton. A vivid coal fire burned at my willing back as, finally, I was led to my place at table, and I faced the cool marble busts of departed Guinnesses.

With the end of the meal and our grateful farewells we were put in the charge of a brewery attendant in uniform and visored cap, a sprightly, white-haired little man who during the next two hours escorted us through the plant, up and down metal stairways from roof to cellar. He was one of a corps of guides, trained in this profession, who dealt with several hundred visitors a day. We passed the gigantic vats in which the malt painfully fought a losing battle with the yeast. The concentrated odor of escaping gases here was overwhelming, or would have been had we leaned over the vats for more than an instant. "If you lost your wits with the aroma you'd fall in and that'd be the end of you," said the guide. "But sure and it'd be a beautiful death." The great repair shop in outside yards looked to us like one more painting by Brueghel: men swung monstrous mallets, flames darted upward, boys braced their feet against the pull of curving barrel staves. Yet everywhere the absence of bustle and tension astonished our American eyes. Beginning with the elegantly composed gentlemen at the top and descending to the washers, vat-tenders, and loaders, all seemed leisure and quiet security. Our guide told us that he was to retire on a pension at sixty-five and that during all the years at the plant, ever since his boyhood, he, along with every other employee, had received his three daily glasses of porter. "The workingman's drink," he named it. "Stout is the drink of the upper classes," he explained in a manner to make all seem fair and right.

The end of the tour brought us once again to Lord Moyne, who awaited us outside the plant at the wheel of his Ford station wagon, which had been built with a special outsized body to make room, he said, for his wife and nine children—two by a previous marriage—when they went off touring together with the goat that gave them the milk for their tea. We were driven through Phoenix Park, scene of eighteenth-century Irish history, past the stone shaft upholding the phoenix erected by Lord Chesterfield when he was viceroy of Ireland. Here, on the greensward, we were able to re-create Le Fanu's brocaded, bewigged noblemen strolling in elegance or fighting their duels in that distant day. At Lord Moyne's house, not far beyond, it became at once apparent that this establishment was fully of the present. A pram stood on the lawn near the front door and a doll lay on her face beneath an overturned child's express wagon. Lady Moyne came out to greet us, her skin glowing, her eyes violet, and her dark hair gently curling. It seemed not possible that with her youth and relaxed detachment she could be the mother of seven children. This I understood rather better when, just before our leaving, the children's nanny, Miss Brush, appeared—a capable, middle-aged woman with a firm handshake and wearing a spruce gray flannel suit.

We had our tea in a white-walled dining room where French windows curtained in pale-blue damask opened on the sun-drenched lawn. The table held one more feast: bread of every hue, cakes, meringues, pots of honey and jams, pitchers of orange and lemon crush, great jugs of milk, and tea from a magnificent silver set. Four of the children sat about the table. They were beautiful small creatures with shining hair and vivid cheeks, and when we took our places, they looked intently at Van Wyck, whose cheeks were as pink as theirs, drawn to him as children always were. Later he said the scene was like a Thomas Lawrence canvas come to life. Tea ended, we went into the garden, Lady Moyne carrying the baby in her arms. We walked beneath a double row of flowering cherry trees along the path of a spring garden edged with the blue of forget-me-nots. The birds sang, the children laughed and ran, our hosts smiled: an idyll of spring described by the poets of an earlier time.

That evening after dinner, in the soft northern twilight, Van

Wyck and I had a stroll in St. Stephen's Green. We watched the mother duck and her little ones as they took their evening swim, and we told each other how beautiful it all was and how pleasant the trip had been and how happy we should be at home again in our own land.

Monk Gibbon, that fine, intelligent man who combined executive capabilities with sustained kindness, took us to call on Mrs. William Butler Yeats, George, widow of the poet. We were not at first drawn to her, aloof and impassive as she seemed on answering our ring at the door front, while we stood, hesitant, on the brownstone stoop without. Van Wyck was shier than usual; for he needed, always, to be drawn out, set at ease, and her unresponsive, somber face did not compel. Gradually, however, during the hour of our stay, in the way that a person constrained by encircling animosities warms to the one who releases him, she showed her pleasure in being with a man so undemanding and so well able to reconstitute for her a happier past. She seemed moved not alone by Van Wyck's reminiscences of the Yeats family but also by his unspoken concern for her lonely state, his perception showing him how complete this was.

We were presently served coffee in a small, dim back study where hung the large self-portrait of J. B. Yeats, so familiar to Van Wyck, on which the old painter had been working in New York at the time of his death. Then we were taken into the poet's library at the front of the house. Here were books, a collection of Blake engravings, and, spread across a broad table, the letters and papers which currently related to him. It was evident that a significant part of Mrs. Yeats's existence was her present correspondence with the literary world, and her determination that no portion of her husband's work should fall into limbo. She questioned Van Wyck, now, as to the whereabouts of a portrait painted by John Sloan of old Mr. Yeats and his friends gathered about his perennial table at the Petitpas restaurant in West Twenty-ninth Street. She remembered, she said, that Van Wyck had been one among the others. It was all touched with sadness, this haunting residue of a great man's life, and we were not sorry to leave the chill dark house and emerge into the sunlight of a flower-edged street.

Another encounter, again under the aegis of Monk Gibbon, brought us nothing but pleasure. This was a meeting with Maud Gonne, whom Yeats in his youth had so much loved, and who was the inspiration for many of his poems. We were set down in the twilight at a bus stop in the village of Dundrum, where Maud Gonne lived with her son, Sean MacBride, in a house marked off from the street by a high iron grille and placed in a garden. The front door, indifferently painted, had been deeply gouged by the paws of dogs, and I saw at once that the place belonged to people too casual or too busy to care for the meticulous. We were let in by young MacBride, the grandson, who briefly explained that he must leave us after introducing us to his grandmother. We had been told that Sean MacBride, Minister of Foreign Affairs, was currently up for re-election and we supposed that his son was due at some important political meeting. He opened the door of a large room lit by a coal fire and a lamp with battered shade of rakish angle. It stood on a table behind a low chair which held an old lady wrapped in a shawl. She was reading in the uncertain light, and was not at first aware of our presence. Her face was deeply lined but her eyes and forehead were fine, reminders of the days when her beauty had brought her fame, and her soft blond-gray hair, caught up casually with combs, seemed as live as when people had turned in the street to stare at its gleaming red loveliness. An instantly compelling person.

She greeted us with a charming elegance of manner in that shabby room, thanking us for having troubled ourselves to come the long way from Dublin to see her, and she explained with a smile that there would be only one of us at a time with whom she could speak. "A tiresome old woman with bad hearing," she said. Monk Gibbon, the first to talk to her and in worshipful mood, as were we all, asked whether she realized that she had been the inspiration of the greatest love poetry in the modern world.

"Oh, you mean Willie," she answered gaily, as though Willie's poetry had been a kind of youthful prank played on her. And later when someone mentioned Yeats she said: "Willie and I were like brother and sister, you know." It was clear that she wished the relationship to be understood in this way.

She told us she was finishing her book of memoirs and she spoke of the difficulty in dealing with the story of her marriage to Mac-Bride: "For I am able to present my version of its failure while my husband is no longer here to present his." Her beautifully cadenced voice, her frankness, mingling with restraint, served further to enchant us.

The subject on which Maud Gonne entirely let herself go, however, was that of Ireland, the passion of her being. As the fire glowed and we sat encircling her, she gave us the story of her youth, her upbringing. Her mother had died when she was four, and her father then made her his constant companion; she had adored him. Side by side, on horseback, they rode about the country owned by Ascendency circles, where the contrasts between the great estates and the peasant hovels had early saddened her. She had been horrified at watching the eviction of peasants, the burning of their houses for non-payment of rent, and she was continually grieved by their chronic state of hunger. After her eighteenth birthday she announced to her father that she intended to set to work in order to remedy matters. He not only gave her his approval but also resigned his commission in the British army so that he might come to her aid.

"But he did not live to carry out this plan, for within a fortnight of our talk he was dead."

A long silence followed this part of her story, and she stared at the burning coals as though they were a link with the fire of those other days. Watching her, I saw the empty spaces about her now, the solitude, that seemed almost as great as the one holding the widow George, back there in Dublin City. And I was conscious of the shadows that grew and increased in the corners of the room and, beyond the tall windows, of the wan stretch of lawn where no soul walked in the waning light.

"My father had taken me to see my mother on her deathbed," she continued now, "and he said to me: 'Never fear anything, not even death.' So I've not feared physical danger. But I did not see how life was to be faced when he died."

Her guardians had attempted to hold her in England, she told us, to make a fashionable young woman of her, curtail her work for the Irish peasants. They did not succeed. She came, she labored, she conquered.

"I believe that my life has been of some use," she said, smiling up at us with a touch of the defiance so necessary in her youth. "Today, no one in Ireland need starve."

Mrs. Monk Gibbon leaned forward, then, to remind Maud Gonne of the High Mass held not long ago in the Pro-Cathedral Church of Dublin, celebrating the twenty-five years of Irish independence, to remind her of the ovation she had received on leaving the church, an ovation greater than that given to any other soul.

"I was there," she answered in a ringing tone, and drew her head high as a soldier on parade.

Two days in Galway, following this visit, brought our Irish stay to an end. We were much looked after here, as elsewhere, by the kind Irish, who responded with remarkable alacrity to the various introductions given us. We were taken deep into Galway City, with its relics of Spanish architecture derived from the days of sea commerce with that land. We were shown the Romanesque Church of St. Nicholas, informal, haphazard, charming, which is known as that where Columbus knelt to pray before setting out for the New World. We hung over the stone bridge that crosses the Galway River, its moldings rubbed low and shiny by the pressure of men's arms leaning along its length as they watched the salmon below, the big fish ranged side by side neat and immobile as sardines in a box, before making their way upriver to breed and spawn. We spent an evening with Monsignor Brown, reigning head of the great Catholic University, who possessed a formidable reputation for his learning, his wit, his worldly acumen; he was the sort of person who has ever flourished within the arms of the Roman Catholic hierarchy. An immensely tall man with a long, immobile face whose dwelling was that of a scholar and patron of music: books everywhere about the walls and a grand piano athwart windows giving on a grassy court which held lofty and ancient oaks.

On a warm fair day we were driven about nearby County Clare, that land of lime and primitive dolmens and ring forts and delicate little wild flowers that constitute a botanist's dream. Here, at Ballylee, we entered the Norman tower of stone which the poet Yeats, on a visit to his patron, Lady Gregory, had first seen as a young man when "there was a mill with an old miller and ash trees throwing green shadows upon a little river." Eventually Yeats bought the tower for the sum of thirty-five pounds. He had it restored for occupancy with his young wife: "four great rooms, one above the other, wide stone fireplaces and mullioned windows." It stood before us then, on the little river, wrapped in sunshine and emphatic still, but the mill had gone, the ash trees had been cut, and the entrance door flapped in the breeze. A plaque set into the tower wall was engraved with an inscription:

> I, the poet William Yeats,
> With old mill boards and sea-green slates
>   And smithy work from the Gort forge,
> Restored this tower for my wife George;
>   And may these characters remain
>   When all is ruin once again.

Van Wyck and I spoke to each other unhappily now of Yeats's wife, of life's unpredictability and its vagaries, of the transient quality of strongholds, even though made of stone.

There came, in Galway City, a rainy, blustery morning of no engagements, no specific plans. It was at the end of our stay, and Van Wyck suggested that we board a bus for Connemara, a romantic country we had not seen. The very sound of the word, Van Wyck said, filled the imagination, brought half-remembered scenes from the written past of those who had known it. We were seated, before long, on a forward bench of the bus from where the view of the countryside was unimpeded, rumbling on at a slow pace, and our reward, presently, was entire. For the sun at eleven o'clock scattered the clouds and brought a belated glory to the scene, to the sea below us, to stretches of sand and to mountains that rose jagged and austere above the humps and hollows of bogland beside the road. We drove through cobblestoned villages, stopping to gather up passengers: women with shopping bags of woven twine, young girls in search of beaux at the next town, peasant women with wind-worn faces, their shawls lying untied about their shoulders in the new warmth. Out before us as we moved, bands of silly sheep leaped meadow walls to clutter the road, hogs were guided by their owners' wands, and stubborn, small, rough-coated cattle grazed undisturbed at roadside borders in spite of the bus driver's horn.

We descended at Clifden to eat our lunch and to walk about the pleasant town. Coming on the local bookshop, much like one of our own in Greenwich Village in New York, we found the owner to be a lady in slacks with a blithe, birdlike voice. She looked intently at Van Wyck and asked: "Are you a writer? You look like a writer. Are you famous? You look famous." As soon as might be, a flustered Van Wyck extricated himself, buying a few post cards from the inquiring lady, and soon we were en route by taxi to the nearby castle, Ballynahinch, which I had wished to see ever since reading an account by Maria Edgeworth of her enforced stay there with a family of vast landowners named Martin. It was the story of a disastrous drive with friends through the then-untamed land which we had that morning traveled, when their coach horses became mired in a series of yawning bogs and the passengers had been obliged to seek refuge at Ballynahinch, remaining on for several weeks because of an illness which attacked one of the party. In a letter to her brother, Miss Edgeworth described the day of their arrival, the devastating illness of her friend, the impromptu journey of one of the postboys who was sent running "with the speed of light" in a torrential downpour, leaping from bog to bog all the long way from Ballynahinch Castle to Oughterard in search of a doctor. A moving story.

Ballynahinch was at present run as an inn, the bleak austere atmosphere of Miss Edgeworth's day softened by modern comfort, its terraces and shrubberies lovely to look upon. After our tea in the drawing room, from where we could see the broad lake below, Van Wyck and I strolled hand in hand along a path deep in blossoming azaleas as far as the castle gate and thence out to the highroad where our bus driver of the morning had told us to await his return to Galway. We sat in the warm sun on a little bridge, our legs hanging over a brook. I sniffed the delicious odor of a wild rose cut for me by my husband from a neighboring bush, and we listened to the song of a cuckoo. Contentedly, Van Wyck murmured: "One can wrap one's mind about Ireland," and each of us gave thanks to the fair country which soon we should have to leave. Ireland, held by its contradictions, by its love of the land and the stars, by the sounds of the spoken voice and the singing harp.

> 'Tis time at length for me to foot it homeward.
> For the poets of the world lie sleeping.

XII

Several Times Farewell

E journeyed next to England, to visit the Nigel Laws, who lived in Buckinghamshire. Nigel I had known well during the years of the First World War when I had lived in Washington in an accommodating house with my husband, John Saltonstall— absent much of the time on duties connected with the navy—and three young children. At that moment Nigel was youthful secretary to the British ambassador and an intimate of Tom Spring-Rice, the ambassador's nephew, with whom I often made music, he being an accomplished pianist. Lean, long-legged, black-moustached, Nigel possessed the humor made classic by Edward Lear. Together we strode happily across the meadows adjacent to Rock Creek Park, and our talk ranged from profundities to the absurd. Toward the war's end, as if to celebrate victory, we had attended a memorable "Alice in Wonderland" party given by an enterprising dowager, when Nigel became the March Hare and I was Alice. He had returned to England at the end of the war, and we had rarely met since, although we maintained a correspondence in which promises to visit him and his wife in England became a continuous part.

On that renewed meeting in June, 1951, at the Marylebone Station in London we found, fortunately, that we were still recognizable to each other and that the surface changes in appearance were forgotten in the talk and laughter which came forth as naturally as in the days of our youthful effervescence. Van Wyck and Nigel at once liked each other, and after our arrival at the house in Chalfont St. Peter, where we were met by Nastia, Nigel's Russian wife, we became a well-established foursome. The sympathy that grew between us was increased by an accident that occurred soon after our arrival, when Van Wyck and I inadvertently managed to let an immense bathtub overflow, thereby causing Nigel and the butler, trousers uprolled, to mop up the water inundating the hallway. Somehow, with the Laws' fine manners and magnanimity, the episode became a joke, and we were strangers no longer.

Nastia had been a famous beauty married, previously, to a high-ranking member of the British Foreign Office, and much on the international scene. At present she and Nigel had allowed worldly preoccupations to slip while they concerned themselves with growing plants, finding these an excellent substitute for receptions and dinner parties. Their property was of considerable consequence, the garden extensive and varied and beautiful, and although two gardeners and a "boy" were on the outdoor payroll, the Laws themselves spent mornings and afternoons in the legendary rock garden, many of whose plants had been gathered by them in the French Alps and the Dolomites. Also requiring special care were a number of exotic shrubs sprung from the Himalayas or more temperate zones. As for the roses, they bloomed as flowers bloom in paintings by the Italian primitives, each blossom as perfect as those at the feet of Virgin and Child. What pleasure, as I was to find on early mornings, to examine and to gather these dew-drenched objects of loveliness while birds sang in the branches of surrounding beeches and lindens. Inside the house were the multitudinous collections sprung from the background of the two owners: portraits of ancestors, carved ivory and shell *bibelots,* delicate miniatures, diamond encrusted, a superb group of early celadon vases from China, books in tooled bindings, silver ornaments inherited by Nigel from his father along with an engraved likeness of the Bishop of Bath and Wells, a most agreeable-appearing forebear of euphonious title whose countenance especially appealed to Van Wyck. There were also Nastia's snuffboxes of amber, tortoise, and gold, and signed photographs of Russian royalty.

For our entertainment during the week of our stay—a routine which suited Van Wyck, who was left to himself at a desk in a small upstairs study from breakfast until lunch—we were driven during the afternoon about the countryside to spots of interest. With Nigel's long legs beneath the wheel of his tiny Austin, we swept along country lanes between high hedgerows, stopping to visit such places as the cottage where Milton sought refuge from the London plague to work on *Paradise Lost*; the churchyard at Stoke Poges which was the inspiration for Gray's *Elegy*; the plain-faced, ancient Quaker Meeting House, background for the grave of William Penn. As we found our way home at evening we drove through Elizabethan villages where, after tea under the tranquil aura of great Tudor houses, with their octagonal lodges, men and women worked in tidy flower beds, leaving cottage doors open to the evening air, while below us the valleys of Buckinghamshire flowed away into the slow twilight of England.

A friendship destined to grow into rewarding permanence we established at this moment with Chiang Yee, Chinese painter-writer. He had been for some years engaged on a series of books to which he had given the name of "Silent Traveller," and a year earlier he had written from Oxford, where he lived, to ask Van Wyck if he would consider writing an introduction to a forth-coming book: *The Silent Traveller in New York*. Van Wyck accepted, contrary to his usual habit, because of the book's ingenuous and entirely personal quality. After its publication, following a series of letters between the two men, we met the author for the first time in the lobby of Brown's Hotel in London. He bowed low as he greeted us on our arrival, thus making us aware of that ingrained oriental courtesy which was a major part of his tradition. We were then taken to the theater, to Chinese restaurants, to museums, while Chiang Yee's character unrolled before us like some meticulously ornamented Chinese scroll displaying both the wisdom of the ancients and the fresh naïveté of a child. There came the moment, nonetheless, when it was borne in on us that we could not indefinitely accept kindness and hospitality on any such scale, a debt increasing with each agreeable day. We decided, then, to withdraw, to quit London, to make our farewells to Chiang Yee in the hope that he would later come to visit us at Bridgewater, and we fled away on an afternoon of permeating sunlight to Waterloo Station, where, more or less on the spur of the moment, we bought tickets for Salisbury.

Our arrival in the ancient town was a memorable one. From the train window the cathedral spire seemed the mark of man's abiding faith in a power beyond his earth-bound vision. And this clinging sense, intangible, amorphous, remained to haunt us during the days to come. At the White Hart Inn, a simple place of provincial English origin, we engaged our room and drank our tea with other guests in the hospitable entrance hall. Then we set forth to examine the cathedral close. The sun as it neared the horizon grew in intensity, bringing a glow to the weathered arch of stone which was the entrance to the close. We walked beneath it, passing house fronts carefully disposed along a narrow, cobblestoned street, until of a sudden, all barriers gone, there was spread before us a vast green lawn, tableland for the mighty structure planted upon it like a portion of some lofty forest, magnificent in its solitude and the austerity of its self-containment. In position at a suitable distance, like an orderly aggregation of people who watch the crowning of royalty, were the buildings that bordered the close, houses of brick, their façades heavy with climbing roses. Indeed, the air was filled with the scent of roses, proclaiming thus their portion of that fair world.

Back at the White Hart a poster in the main hall announced a performance of Shakespeare's *Winter's Tale* that evening at seven o'clock in a neighboring garden. The hands of the lobby clock pointed to a quarter before seven, but Van Wyck was eager to see the play even though it meant going without dinner. An amiable porter suggested that he order a cold supper to await us in the dining room on our return from the play, and we went off on foot to find the festival garden at the rear of a house edging the river. Here we sat on a lawn facing the garden wall, which served as backdrop for a cast of both amateurs and professionals. They moved to and fro along the pebbled paths, speaking the lovely running lines and dancing to the music that issued from a recorder hidden in the shrubbery. Returning arm in arm as darkness fell over the long-drawn English twilight, happy and tired, we found a minor banquet spread in the solitude of the hotel dining room. The scene reminded me of Goldilocks and the Three Bears. Indeed, all afternoon and evening we seemed to have been caught in a kind of enchantment. "How civilized these English are!" said Van Wyck, his eyes shining with pleasure. "I'm afraid I'd succumb to them entirely if I stayed here long enough."

At Stonehenge, near to Salisbury, on the moment of confronting those anonymous blocks of stone upended with persistent finality against the sweep of sky, my thoughts flew to the tales of fairies, and goblins and gnomes encountered in childhood, to the early impressions of magic which persist as long as life lasts, and that stark and simple plan, that mysterious gesture made by venerating man so long ago, wrapped me in a sense of timelessness. On the drive back, Van Wyck told me of the essay written by Emerson after a walk to Stonehenge in the company of Carlyle. And I remembered the sad and beautiful story of Hardy's Tess, who had chosen to lie upon one of these tranquil stones while black clouds drove across the moon on the night before she bade farewell to her love and to her life.

In company with Tania and Jimmy Stern, who had exchanged their New York flat for a house in Dorset, we spent an afternoon in the Hardy country, and Van Wyck stood leaning on his walking stick for some minutes studying the statue of the writer in his native town of Dorchester. "England remembers her great literary men," he said rather unhappily. "In America they're forgotten by the next generation." From Dorchester we drove to the village of Chaldon Herring, to see Van Wyck's old friend Alyse Gregory, with whom he had carried on an episodic written correspondence since the death of her husband, Llewelyn Powys, a member of the gifted family of writers, whom Van Wyck had known as a young man. At that time Llewelyn made his neighborly calls on foot to the Brooks's house in Westport, avoiding the highway, and bearing in his hand a posy of field flowers. He had succumbed at the early age of fifty-five to tuberculosis. The story of his rare gifts, his accomplishments, I had read with pleasure in Van Wyck's essay on him printed in *Chilmark Miscellany*.

Arrived at the village, we were told by an "ancient" that the Powys ladies lived "up yonder." "You'll have to be walking," he told us. We left the car and began the climb upward along a winding path that led through downlands thick with sheep; as we went, the view below us became ever more striking, the country above us more wild. Van Wyck and James Stern exchanged anecdotes along the way, a verbal encounter which slowed our progress so that no harm came to my husband from the sharp physical exertion. As the color of the downs went from green to purple in the fading afternoon light we perceived a small fenced-in house, and emerging from it a figure moving rapidly toward us. It was Mrs. Powys, or Miss Gregory, as she preferred to be known, a short, somewhat bent woman with gray hair who wore a long-skirted black dress with a white ruff about the neck. She resembled, I decided, the nurse in *Romeo and Juliet*. She was delighted to see us and led us through the dooryard garden, high with red poppies, to her dwelling, one single room above another and attached to a somewhat larger wing where lived her sisters-in-law. Glancing back at the poppies before I entered, I wondered if these had perhaps become her companions along with the birds on the branch of a wind-blown ash, taking the place of the human beings with whom most of us fill our lives.

A charming, gentle, and swiftly responsive person, Alyse gave us tea and slices of "American cake" of which she was very proud. It had been sent her by a friend from New York. We learned presently how seldom supplies reached her, and we feared she might be depriving herself in offering it to us. "The grocer drives up with his wagon once a year," she informed us, "but my sisters-in-law take turns with me in walking down to the village several times a week to gather up the mail and the smaller necessities. We also have our vegetable garden." It was with real sadness that we bade good-bye to so brave a creature, whose manner of life caused Van Wyck to say on the way back to civilization that in her company he felt himself "a rank Philistine." We hoped that her husband's grave, marked by a block of Portland stone on a cliff edge nearby, above the channel, might serve as an enduring presence.

In Paris, in July, toward the end of the European journey, the balcony of our hotel room on the Left Bank looked out over the Seine toward the Sacré-Coeur. Each morning at an early hour Van Wyck drew back the heavy window curtains that I might see the light of the rising sun slanting on the river below. When the day was warm we sat on the balcony to eat our breakfast. Later, we went to wander slowly about the narrow old streets surrounding us, and Van Wyck's comments brought a fine summary to the things I had found there during other Paris days, those of my girlhood and young marriage. Indeed, he had an unobtrusive and unstudied power to set in order the values of all that had gone before. Thus, by example and without pedantry, he taught me to pause, to select, to ponder, and to study. We walked the length of the Rue Saint-Jacques, the street which had seen the start of the long, holy pilgrimages to Jerusalem, and we lingered in the dim corridors of the Musée de Cluny, with its often tragic story of mediaeval Paris. On the Ile Saint-Louis and the Ile de la Cité, those two islands of ancient habitation, so charmingly enclosed by the arms of the Seine, Van Wyck was profoundly happy to find, as we strolled along the river banks, the names of the writers who once had lived there applied in permanence to the fronts of those houses

Portrait of Van Wyck Brooks
by John Butler Yeats, 1909

Portrait of Gladys Brooks, at fourteen,
by Florence Wyman

Portraits of Van Wyck and Gladys Brooks
by John Carroll, 1946

(*Preceding page*)
Van Wyck Brooks in Bridgewater, Connecticut
Photograph by Robert Gumpper

Van Wyck Brooks
in Carmel, California, 1911

Van Wyck Brooks at Martha's
Vineyard, 1950

Van Wyck Brooks at work, 1953

Miss Okamura, Gladys and Van Wyck Brooks
Dr. Suzuki, Dr. Hisamatsu, Chiang Yee
in Cambridge, Massachusetts, 1958

Van Wyck Brooks's study
in Bridgewater, Connecticut
Photograph by Robert Gumpper

The Bridgewater house
Photograph by Robert Gumpper

John Hall Wheelock,
Van Wyck Brooks, Tania Stern,
Julius Teller, Phyllis Wheelock
in the garden
at Bridgewater, 1955

Julius Teller, Gladys and Van Wyck
Brooks, Chiang Yee in the
Bridgewater garden, 1960

Van Wyck Brooks in the Bridgewater garden
with his grandson Peter Brooks, Gladys Brooks,
and Julius Teller, 1960

Portrait of Van Wyck Brooks
by D. G. Whyte, 1957

Van Wyck Brooks being interviewed
for television, 1956
Photograph by J. R. Mayers

Van Wyck Brooks with William McFee
on the latter's eightieth birthday

Van Wyck and Gladys Brooks with her daughter
Jean and son-in-law O. W. Haussermann, Jr.,
at Bridgewater

At the party given by
the American Academy of
Arts and Letters on Van
Wyck Brooks's
seventy-fifth birthday

Van Wyck Brooks, Lewis
Mumford, George Biddle,
Mark Van Doren

Van Wyck Brooks,
Pearl Buck,
Matthew Josephson

Van Wyck
and Gladys Brooks, 1961
Photograph by Robert Gumpper

Van Wyck Brooks
in California, 1956
Photograph by J. R. Mayers

(Following page)
Gladys Brooks, 1967

which had contained them and their work. Together, on a warm afternoon, we visited the Place des Vosges, that dignified square of freestone and brick built by Henry IV, its steep-roofed pink houses still intact in their uniform rows. I permitted myself to imagine a possible stay of longer duration at Van Wyck's side, the two of us come to dwell here following the enlightened example of such previous tenants as Richelieu, Madame de Sévigné, the great actress Rachel, and Victor Hugo. We should be securely enclosed, shut away from the tumult of traffic, and our outlook would be the rounded tops of arcaded roofs and the clipped trees bordering them.

"Why not rent one of these sweet houses for a while?" I asked him. "What a good time we'd have!"

"Rather a long distance from my study and the post office in Bridgewater," he answered with a smile.

At night we continued our wanderings on foot and we delighted in the beauty of the Paris monuments illumined by floodlight and extinguished in contrasting shadow. Van Wyck preferred this method of free maneuver to the restrictions of café seats which confined us to a view of our fellow men, of whom, he said, ninety per cent failed to compel one.

A notable occurrence during the Paris visit was the presentation of a mystery play in the square in front of Notre-Dame, with the cathedral as backdrop: *Le Vray Mistère de la Passion,* written in the fifteenth century "in honor of God and for the instruction of the unfortunate." An audience of ten thousand watched from improvised stands that mounted toward the sunset sky. They sat in silence as the moving story of Christ's sacrifice was enacted below, the aura of that far-gone century recaptured in its essence even to the yawning pit of flame wherein the wicked perished. Most moving was the sight of the great Rose window of Notre-Dame lit, when night fell, from within. Murmurs of "Ah," a long-released breath, swept softly through the crowd as that magical circle of colored glass appeared like a bouquet of roses becalmed, to transfix us all. When the play ended, men and women went slowly off in the darkness to dream of Paradise and the golden song of angels.

My youngest daughter, Jean, and her husband, Benjamin Bradlee, and their three-year-old son, Benny, had arrived in Paris a few days before us. Ben had been assigned a post in our embassy there, and they were searching for an apartment as well as for a maid with whom, occasionally, to leave their boy. Van Wyck possessed an enviable talent with children, whom he treated as equals, and, becoming aware of his innate shyness, they were drawn to him in sympathy. This was the case with small Benny. We were many times called upon, in consequence, and our trips to the Louvre and to other picture galleries were now cut short in favor of our outings with him. After a while an apartment was discovered in the ancient Rue de Vaugirard and a *bonne-à-tout-faire*—that wonderful French institution which combines intensive labor and self-sacrifice and acumen in the person of one female—was engaged to help Jean function within the new setting. The woman spoke no English, but on her arrival for an interview with the Bradlees, a sober, middle-aged person sent by the hotel porter, she handed them a slip of paper which read: "I am honest."

We were now free to accept an invitation from Jo and Florence Davidson to spend a week with them at Bêcheron, their manor house in the district of the Loire at Saché. Van Wyck was not entirely sorry to leave Paris, a limitless and fatiguing extent of history and monuments never to be grasped in full. And, in the day-to-day exchange with taxi drivers, waiters, hotel porters, he had been thwarted by his lack of spoken French, a continual reminder of failure. So he was relieved to reach Bêcheron. This consisted of a long low building of stone and stucco with moss-grown roof and ancient chimneys reminding one of elderly caretakers. Four great lime trees and a twelfth-century dovecote marked the entrance to a walled enclosure of smooth green grass, a kind of Eden seizing upon the sensibilities of those who entered, drawing them from the everyday world. At noon and at teatime we lingered here in conversation, while at evening, when the sun had gone, we ate from a long refectory table in the dining room.

Bêcheron was a center for several great châteaux of Touraine and was situated only a few kilometers from Azay-le-Rideau, one of the most delicately contrived and perfect among them. When I was a child I had heard this place described by my mother. She and my father had toured the châteaux in romantic fashion, riding a bicycle built for two, and I remembered her appearance as she dismounted on her return—wide-cut bloomers, blouse with high-boned collar, boater hat worn down over her eyes—and her delight in the purity of Azay-le-Rideau, the white swans swimming in the water-filled moat. Now, with Van Wyck at my side, I was to discover its loveliness for myself, and to visit it a second time before leaving Bêcheron, when I borrowed the cook's bicycle and became a solitary pilgrim in the silence and the glow of early evening.

At Chinon, with its turrets and dungeons and deep window embrasures of stone, I thought of Tristan and Isolde, of the timid Mélisande, prisoner in her far tower, of Jeanne d'Arc awaiting in a black pit the verdict of the monarch of France. We drove presently about the town where Rabelais had lived on a narrow cobblestoned street above the banks of the Vienne, and Van Wyck was enthralled with the spot. "I could write a book here," he exclaimed, reluctant to turn his back on so much serenity, so large a slice of history.

At Tours, following our visit to the elegant eighteenth-century buildings one associates with Louis XIV, *le Roi Soleil,* we went to sit at a table in the shabby Café de l'Univers. This was the tree-shaded place on the main square where Balzac had rested and drunk his early-morning café-au-lait following the arduous overnight journey by coach from Paris and before he set out on the fifteen-kilometer walk to the Château de Saché, the small castle belonging to his mother's friends, the Margonne family. Later that day Jo Davidson took us to visit this spot where the writer had lived and worked intermittently during several years. The building was of stone, uncompromising in its blunt mass, clumsy, yet not without distinction. It made me think of the gawky country cousin of an elegant city-bred family, devoid as it was of ornament save for the crude carving above the twelfth-century doorway. We climbed to the little third-story room which had been Balzac's, with its curtained bed against the wall, the room in which he wrote *Le Père Goriot* and *Le Lys dans la Vallée*. We stood beside his worktable, which held a small brass lamp with pink glass shade, and we saw his quill pen lying, perhaps, just as he had left it, and we looked out on the River Indre lazying among the reeds and the wild flowers of the valley which he had so loved. His spirit, his force, his courage were everywhere about us, and I felt an instinctive kinship with this man whose uncounted hours of labor bore a likeness to those of my husband.

Conversation during meals at Bêcheron was always vehement when Jo and Van Wyck were together. Jo pounded the table, his great bulk making it tremble, his flow of words uttered at top speed through a heavy beard. At these moments Van Wyck's vitality blossomed afresh, his interest in the subjects discussed seeming never to flag. They talked of Israel, which Jo and Florence were soon to visit, and Jo's staunch belief in the pertinence of the recently established state, and the manner of its governing, became an infectious thing. This outpouring of energy and good will Jo eventually bestowed on Israel itself when, established there for several months, he modeled the heads of innumerable toilers and patriots, men he met in the streets or on jeep excursions throughout the countryside. His high enthusiasm led eventually to his death, for on his return to the autumn winds blowing about Bêcheron, exhausted by his efforts, he was to develop pneumonia and to die in the hospital at Tours.

A subject which brought us pleasure during that July at Saché was the story of a trip to Italy the Davidsons had undertaken earlier in the year with Helen Keller and Polly Thomson. Through the auspices of the Italian scholar Gaetano Salvemini, ardent anti-fascist and anticlerical professor at Florence and occasionally at Harvard, who had had a close escape from death at the hands of Mussolini's Black Shirts, arrangements were made for Helen Keller to visit the Medici tombs and the David of Michelangelo under circumstances especially suited to her. With scaffoldings built for close approach to these monuments she had been enabled to explore with her fingers a past hitherto unavailable to her. She followed the contours and surfaces with slow, loving hands, her face shining, we were told, like the fairest of angels.

"Michelangelo's power came through as never before," cried Jo, "as I watched that extraordinary woman's sure touch. Her fingers seemed to be doing the original modeling. Marvelous! Superb!"

On leaving Bêcheron, when Jo bade us farewell—forever, as it was to happen—he presented Van Wyck with a drawing he had made of Salvemini when they were in Florence together. We sailed for home at the end of July on board the *Mauretania,* and to our surprise and pleasure found that Dr. Salvemini was on board. He was bound for Cambridge and the Harvard Widener Library, to work on material he needed for his current book. He expected also to visit Ruth Draper at Dark Harbor, Maine. The two were old friends and had shared a similar experience in tragedy, Ruth having lost her lover in a plane accident when he attempted to scatter antifascist leaflets over Rome, Salvemini having lost his wife and children in the Messina earthquake.

Van Wyck introduced himself to Salvemini, and showed him Jo's drawing as an added reference. There began, then, the conversations which during the voyage brought the two men much pleasure. On our first evening together, Salvemini, a fine man nearing eighty, with a white pointed beard, a vivid smile, and quick, intense gestures, told us that in the district of Apulia, where he was born, the term *"salvemini,"* was used as a blessing when the fishing boats set out to sea. "God preserve you," it meant. In their final talk, leaning against the rail on a day of torrid heat as we overlooked the slow tugging into port of our great ship, Van Wyck turned impulsively to Salvemini.

"Do you like Santayana?" he asked.

"No! With enthusiasm," was Salvemini's reply. And Van Wyck nodded his approval.

XIII

Makers and Finders

*T*HE months moved on, bringing a dense pattern of work for us both, bringing human beings at home and afield, bringing intermittent rest. Along the streets of our serene Connecticut village, where, each afternoon, Van Wyck and I had our stroll, we were protected in summer by the great maples lining our house front and by the privacy of our garden at the rear, where the three magnolias on their way to the hundred mark cast their shade over the lawn as birds drank at the pool, and we sipped our evening Manhattan cocktail. In winter, when fewer people sought us out and Van Wyck begged off from the daily walk, while the quiet sun found its way inward to warm us and to bring us tranquillity, there were hours of reading and writing for me as well as for Van Wyck. At that moment I was reorganizing a book begun long ago as a novel but become, little by little, a memoir of my childhood, while Van Wyck in that year of 1952 was working on *The Writer in America,* which was to be, he believed, not only an answer to his critics taken on as a body but also a definition of his purpose in writing the history of American literature. Also, it would become a statement of his credo, a summons to purpose and faith. But first he must take his soundings in uncharted waters, a task both difficult and dangerous.

Meanwhile, on January 5, a day for rejoicing, came the publication of *The Confident Years,* the fifth and last of the series *Makers and Finders,* so-named from a phrase of Whitman. Begun twenty years back, as Van Wyck emerged from a protracted, difficult, and saddening illness, it stood at last as a fact. Later, in 1963, after Van Wyck's death, I was to come on a letter which might conceivably have had a bearing on the inception of a plan for the various studies of writers and their work, a letter from Edmund Wilson written to my husband in May of 1921:

Could you possibly do an article for the "New Republic" [Wilson asked]. It seems to me that there is a great need for some American to do for our own Victorian Age what Strachey has done for the English. You have certainly made a magnificent beginning in Mark Twain, but I should think some of the minor figures would be worth doing,— Thomas Bailey Aldrich or John Hay, for example. I wish you could do a few portraits of this kind for us.

Fifteen years after the date of this letter there was published *The Flowering of New England,* dealing with an epoch earlier than that suggested by Wilson, and a book that had been a long while in the making. But may not the term "minor figures" have lodged dormant in Van Wyck's thought during his breakdown, that unhappy time when neither confidence nor serenity nor the labor of the mind were his to possess? And then, a flowering.

In his New York *Herald Tribune* review of *Confident Years,* Malcolm Cowley wrote:

Judged as a whole, "Makers and Finders" is the most impressive work undertaken and carried through by any single American scholar of our time. Most works conceived on this scale have been collaborations, like the three volume "Literary History of the United States," which had fifty-five contributors and seven editors and associates. Even when scholarly books of more than average length are published as the work of one author, they usually acknowledge the help of advisers, assistants, colleagues, students, researchers, librarians and secretaries. . . . Mr. Brooks doesn't follow this custom. . . . He works alone. In this age of corporations and collaborations he is one of the few remaining handicraftsmen, independent and unmechanized. There are more than 2500 American authors mentioned by name in his five volumes. He read all their important works himself, rising at six o'clock on winter mornings; he couldn't accept reports from other readers. All the notes are made in his own angular hand. . . . His first drafts are written, not dictated, and he reads his own proofs, always with a sharp eye for errors. The result of this handicraftsmanship is that "Makers and Finders" has a personal tone, a consistency of judgment and a unity of effect that is lacking in even the best collaborations. It gives us the story of the literary life in America as reflected through a single broadly sympathetic mind. . . . It is his recovery of the American tradition that is important for the world today, his recovery of the tradition in volume after volume: it is his proof that in literature this country has long possessed a usable past. It is, beyond this, his love of letters as an art and his integrity as a lonely scholar. We are always much too slow to recognize a great achievement. Let us not make that mistake in the case of "Makers and Finders" which will be remembered long after our time.

I had on that day gone alone to New York by train and at the Danbury station bought the *Times* and *Tribune,* finding photographs of Van Wyck on the book-review pages of both, and next, in Grand Central, picking up the *Saturday Review of Literature* I was again greeted by his face, this time on the cover. When the newsman handed it to me I exclaimed: "That's my husband!" The man smiled, and I felt very happy. The book's appearance had synchronized with the hundredth anniversary of the founding of E. P. Dutton, Van Wyck's long-time publisher, and on the evening of this day Elliott Macrae and his wife, Marjorie, drove out bringing champagne, to celebrate the event with us. We dined beneath the downward gaze of Van Wyck's ancestors hanging from the walls, and Van Wyck, his cheeks flaming, was able to let himself go in the presence of his publisher and friend, so that his eyes showed his bright pleasure, the vehemence of his feeling released for the moment, although, as always, it was the others whom he encouraged to talk. All evening the telephone rang, bringing congratulations, and it was not easy, later, to drop to the obscurity of our inner selves, to blot out the tangents of public life. We settled, however, to our game of Chinese checkers and, gradually, we were back in our private world.

One other coincidence, this a sad one and not to be outlived, was the news of Jo Davidson's death at Tours. His recent letters to Van Wyck, from Israel, had been full of a wild pleasure. "Such people! Terrific!" But for Jo there had not been the strength, the stamina, to withstand the excitement, the overriding vitality he had put into his labors there. A splendid end, Van Wyck felt, perhaps tragic, but on the grand plan which had ever been his. So, in the New York *Times* on that memorable day, Van Wyck Brooks and his dear friend Jo Davidson appeared together in print and in photographs, one in life, the other in death.

A birthday party for my husband, his sixty-sixth, was attended by our faithful Julius Teller and by Charlie, Kenyon, and Kappo. The talk revolved about Charlie's wife, Inez, whose increasing illness of mind and spirit had meant, recently, that she be placed in a sanitorium. This was deeply disturbing to Van Wyck, tender of heart as he was, and unhappily conversant with life inside mental hospitals. Was he not later to write in his chapter "A Season in Hell," from *Days of the Phoenix,* of the "purgatorial mists" which for long had wrapped him, the acedia or melancholy suffered by the mediaeval monks in their monasteries? But he realized now, thinking of Peter and his unfortunate mother, that when the new scheme of things had been permanently established, the boy would become more and more a part of our lives and Bridgewater his base when he was not away at school. This additional security would help him to grow. We talked also on that day of a request to Van Wyck that he take part in a summer seminar at the University of Montana, at Missoula. The invitation was similar to others of its kind received over the years, characteristically declined, but now he decided to accept. With his history completed and the current book well in process, there was leeway for this sort of distraction, and he felt also that a meeting with the dynamic spirit of the roundup region would fertilize his imagination and enliven the work in hand. He was encouraged in this decision by his two sons, and it was suggested that Peter go with us into western spaces.

Another birthday, Peter's twelfth, in June, brought a group of his young friends to our house. They ate their lunch outdoors around a table on the long piazza in the cool, quiet air, while from the garden came the complex and lovely odors of honeysuckle, peonies, roses, and mint. Van Wyck hovered about the table filled with content, loving this boy as he did and able, at last, to show an affectionate interest in all that happened, a power more or less thwarted in the days when his sons were young. Then, his own life had been a thing of jagged edges torn by the urgencies of family existence, family survival, as these competed with his career, the struggle for a place in the world of literature. Watching them all on that tender June day beneath a soft blue sky I was reminded of Carl Sandburg's lines "blue as the dew on cornflowers in any of the summer months," words that seemed to evoke a promise of tranquil continuity.

At June's end Van Wyck was given the degree of Doctor of Letters by Northeastern University. In the vast Boston Arena I listened, one among eight thousand others, to the citation, which was simple and moving and spoken with authority. I sat beside my son, John, and wished that Van Wyck's sons might have been there to share an impressive moment which was, after all, a reward for labor, a kind of consecration ex post facto, a benediction. For me it was an exhilarating occasion. I had not before been initiated into the rites attending academic honors, had hitherto come no closer to these than to place in attic camphor the hoods previously bestowed on my husband.

The skies of Montana at night in July were crowded with stars, the "heavenly bodies" of which, when I was a child, my grandmother spoke with awe and with pleasure, and we could see them spread far in their devastating splendor along the unimpeded skies. By day, Missoula seemed small and without purpose, its one modern structure in skyscraper image being the hotel we inhabited for two weeks. The city was dominated by the university, which overlooked it from a distant height. Here, each day, Van Wyck took his place at the seminars and panel discussions with students who were come to attend the "Rocky Mountain Roundup of the Arts." A few of these were young, many were older, some were professional writers. A discussion which arose during the proceedings, providing more than routine excitement, was one between Leslie Fiedler and Van Wyck. It took place toward the end of the session, and the contradictory standpoints of the two men stirred acute feeling among those who heard them. The subject concerned human values and their ability to endure. Van Wyck maintained that a feeling for values was omnipresent in the mind and heart of man, continuous from one age to the next. Fiedler said that values were relative, that science and the views of Freud as well as the stresses governing men's ideas beneath the urgencies of war had stultified, if not destroyed, the moral code. Van Wyck's answer to this was an unequivocal "no," and the crowd followed him with high determination. A score on the side of the angels.

The Regional Roundup at an end, we gathered up Peter Brooks from the ranch where we had temporarily placed him and where he had had the good fortune to share quarters with the youthful wrangler, delightedly helping him with the chores. We were carried off, then, the three of us, on a week's motor trip to Glacier Park. Our hosts were young friends from the East, the Richard Ormsbees; he was a biochemist who worked on tularemia and allied diseases of the northwest at the Rocky Mountain Laboratory. We crossed Logan Pass, the highest point yet attained by the automobile, becoming a brief part of the magnificence about us: the mighty summits of mountains, the green glimpses of downward tumbling valleys, the alpine flowers, a multitude of blossoms flowering pell-mell at these heights, their faces close to heaven and washed by the clarity of the sun. Peter best summed up our feeling, perhaps, when on an instant granted us by the gods of this high world we emerged from the clouds that wrapped us to see it in its entirety. "Boy! This is classy!" he said.

On the return trip we came on a herd of buffalo, ninety or more, survivors from the past, grazing within the enclosure set apart by the government, and we visited the cherry orchards along Flathead Lake, mile upon mile. The ripe fruit was on sale to passers-by at five cents per pound to him who picked his own, and it amused us to see Van Wyck holding a filled paper bag in one hand, diving in with the other, like an adolescent freed from all restraint and at his favorite pursuit. From a distance we watched the jagged-topped Mission Mountains, a running accompaniment to our passage north and south, where grizzly bear bred and roamed, and we spent a night in one of the mammoth hotels open during the summer months and designed to resemble an inordinate Swiss chalet with mile-high gabled ceilings, interior balconies ornamented with the heads of mountain goat, mountain sheep, moose, and deer, and fireplaces burning ponderosa pine of acid hue and pungent smell. We passed the long-spread mountain lakes McDonald and Swift-current, limpid and fresh, olive-green at sunset, sharply blue at noon, inhabited by wild geese and duck and the finicky blue heron, with its fastidious manners, that charmed Van Wyck. And, on foot, one perfect afternoon, we found the small oval of Lake Grinnell lying secret and beautiful at the base of its glacier. Lastly there was the little town of Big Fork, a curiously luxuriant oasis with large trees, tidy gardens, and white-painted houses, almost a New England village. It was here that we spent our final night in a small hotel which might have been a provincial inn of the British Isles, its respectable bar tended by a middle-aged barmaid, its speckless, lace-curtained parlor ornamented with painted china and plumed reeds. The landlord, a spruce, white-haired man, was a humorist who informed us, when we asked his nationality, that he was French and went by the name of O'Brian. It turned out that he was Boston Irish and had left his native city for Big Fork when a lad.

We told him, in return, that recently, in Ireland, we had met O'Brians who pronounced the name, "O'Breeong," French fashion, and we had a gentle laugh together over this. I liked him, and on leaving gave him my little bouquet of alpine flowers to place on his polished office desk: a symbolic gesture of farewell to Montana.

In Bridgewater once more, at summer's end we sat in the garden, where, book in hand, motionless, the old high-crowned Panama on his head, Van Wyck seemed so essentially a part of the scene that he might have been one of the major, the more deeply rooted trees. We left, after a few weeks in place, for a weekend with Jack and Phyllis Wheelock at East Hampton, Long Island; two softly gleaming days wherein the pull of the recent summer seemed stronger than that of the winter to come. The prospect of again leaving home had become possible because of our affection for the Wheelocks and for their house, one not easy of access to our car on the day of arrival, the narrow dirt entrance road deep in puddles from recent rains. Coming on it at the pace of a pedestrian, we beheld it in the dignity of that earlier era when its owners stopped a pair of bays and surrey at the brick walk leading upward to the entrance door. Nothing had changed. The house flowed along an elm-crowned hill, a weathered mass of gray shingle entangled in vines and shrubs, to enforce our awareness of that long-past moment when leisure was a valued way of life. Here were holly and juniper like those in Chinese pictures, chamaecyparis from the Carolinas, beeches from England, and limes that drew the bees in spring. All were interwoven, and their aspect of undisturbed acceptance magnified the attribute of repose which the place possessed. Broad grass paths at the back of the house led to benches placed here and there against some wide-backed tree, and wild flowers played their unobtrusive part in embroidering the scene. A quiet, gentle spot where quiet, gentle people had lived and set their stamp.

Indoors, the quality of the house was the same: walls of white plaster dimmed by the years, beams and doors of brown cedar casting shadows, and everywhere, in massive repose, chests, highboys, and dressers. Upstairs, ancient lanterns hung from pegs of wood and washstand sets of sprigged china filled bedroom corners. Bookshelves held the same heterogeneous and happy mixture as in the garden without, and over all hung the clarity and essential cleanliness brought by sand and sea. Not a dark or gloomy passage anywhere, or one that glared, divested of secrets. Jack had put into verse the spirit of this spot where he had lived for sixty-odd years, grateful as he was to his father's conception of it, to his labors. In a poem entitled "The Gardener," he wrote:

> These woodland ways, with your heart's labor bought,
> Trees that you nurtured, gardens that you planned,
> Surround me here, mute symbols of your thought.
>
> Your meaning beckons me on every hand,
> Grave aisles and vistas, in their silence, speak
> A language that I now can understand.

And in a poem called "House in Bonac" he described:

> . . . and the great hall downstairs,
> With its wide fireplace and its oil lamp hung
> From a girder over the table where they gathered
> To talk or read aloud through warm evenings
> While the cricket plucked his harp and the shrill, prolonged
> Stridulation of grasshoppers flooded the summer night . . .

On one of the days of our visit, Van Wyck drove me along East Hampton's village street past the classic wooden windmill and the duck pond and the green, institutions of my own childhood, and so on out Hunting Lane, which my sister and brother and I had so often traveled on our bicycles. Finally we came to the high, wind-blown hilltop on Hither Lane where our family house had stood, built of stucco in the image of a Normandy farmhouse, overlooking the sea three meadows away. How well I remembered the soft, salt damp of the breeze blowing my hair and the feel of daisies against my bare legs as I walked through the meadows under the moon on a fair night, making my solitary way to the beach beyond. And the cherry tree at the foot of the drive that wound upward to the house, bringing shade to us hot, tired children as we paused beneath it before climbing the hill, bringing shelter, also, for our bicycles, tossed to the ground beneath it. The house had burned, so I could not show it to Van Wyck, nor could I share with him the sea's breath from that spot because of a massive growth of trees that crowded, now, the hill's high crown. The cherry was there in place, though shrunken and aloof, and I was glad to recapture this slanting bit of the past, along with a vague nostalgia for far-gone things. Sorrow it was not, as long as Van Wyck was at my side, he who had driven sorrow forever away.

During the autumn at Bridgewater in that year of 1952, we had a three-day visit from Chiang Yee, our Chinese "Silent Traveller," who with his classic generosity offered to illustrate that portion of my journal which dealt with Ireland, should this be presently published. George and Hélène Biddle came also, to tell us of their winter in Rome; and, most moving to us both, was the visit of Florence Davidson, who spent the hours talking of Jo and who put into Van Wyck's hands the ivory-knobbed walking stick carried always by this vital, generous man.

Our Christmas brought all the Brookses, save Peter's mother, while our tree, soon to hold real candles for burning, was cut by the boy and his father from a hillside above the Housatonic. Early on Christmas morning, at breakfast, Van Wyck presented me with a small jeweler's box withheld from other offerings beneath the tree. It contained two small charms to hang from the delicate chain bracelet I wore about my wrist, one an amethyst heart, the other a bit of carved green jade. I knew, in my pleasure, that I should keep these pretty bits in close proximity for many years to come. Later that morning, after presents had been opened and while we waited for our turkey, Van Wyck read aloud to us from his book in progress, the opening pages of the first volume of his autobiography, which concerned his boyhood in Plainfield. These dealt in part with Miss Eliza Kenyon, Eleanor Brooks's great-aunt, distinguished administrator of the seminary there. We listened with pleasure to the story of that extraordinary woman who for years had illumined the cultural center of this town, drawing to the seminary such distinguished people as John Fisk, Julia Ward Howe, and Madame Ruttkay, sister of the Hungarian patriot Louis Kossuth. Miss Kenyon's diary and much of her correspondence were at that moment in Van Wyck's possession, and he was therefore able to reconstruct her life in some detail, including her "soul-friendship" with the Mr. Blake who was Thoreau's confident and executor. Together, once, on the birthday of Elizabeth Barrett Browning, this pair had placed a nosegay of violets beneath her portrait and read aloud portions of her *Sonnets from the Portuguese.*

A single sad event fell into the cheerful, closely knit community which was our holiday world. This was the arrival on Christmas morning of William McFee, Van Wyck's old friend, who entered our midst like some great broken-winged sea gull dropping to the sands where a flock of shore birds twittered. He had come to tell us of the death of his wife, Bea, at five o'clock that morning. On the day before, Van Wyck and I had gone to visit her at the nursing home where she lay, taking her a few blossoms to hold in her fingers. The illness setting its hand upon her had then run all but its final course. Van Wyck repeated once again words I had not liked to hear because of their haunting finality: "The last years of life are irreparably sad." I began, then, to believe that he might be right.

XIV

Hope, Fear, Time

$\mathcal{A}$ SMALL walk-up flat in New York's Greenwich Village became ours for a month at the beginning of January, 1953. It belonged to Matthew Huxley, son of Aldous and Maria, whom I had encountered years back when they lived near me briefly at Rhinebeck, New York. I had not forgotten the lovely Maria's ingenuous ways of prescience wherein, guided by the plaster-smeared palm of her subject's hand, she was enabled to become a connoisseur of character, nor could I forget the unheralded, spontaneous display of learning that Aldous exhibited during our meetings. When first he came to tea at my house on a raw day of April he had turned away from the people about him to concentrate his pleasure on a small species of tulip ornamenting the tea tray, *Tulipa clusiana,* from the Mediterranean, which he at once identified and called by its generic name. And later, driving across country to California, he had, I was told, learned with ease to know and categorize each plant that grew in the wide desert. An admirable power, it seemed to me. Now we were to occupy the flat of his son Matthew and the latter's capable, boyish-bobbed, blue-jeaned wife while they, in turn, went off to visit the family on the West Coast. Three flights up from the entrance, the front windows looked out rather sadly across Sullivan Street on the old Mills Hotel, nightly refuge for male tramps. From our bedroom windows we had the more pleasant view of the Sullivan-MacDougal Street gardens. It was in this room each morning that Van Wyck spread his papers along a card-table top for the daily labor.

Meanwhile at home, before leaving, by contrast with things to come, the New Year had arrived undemonstratively after an evening of solitude for Van Wyck and me in our living room. A beagle, inheritance from the Charles Brookses, lay at our feet, the fire blazed in the chimney, and our reading was pleasantly interrupted by the music issuing from a record player: Berlioz's "Harold in Italy," Mozart's Serenades, Haydn's Harpsichord and Oboe Concerto. Outside, a light snow fell against the black columns of trees along the green, and a massive vehicle with huge red winking eye, the town's snowplow, moved to and fro sweeping accumulation from surrounding roads—a kind of Cyclops and guardian angel combined, protecting symbol of village life. At ten o'clock, the usual hour for bed, we turned out the lights blazing all over the house in honor of the new year's breaking, we put the beagle in his cellar chair, we shared a big yellow apple in lieu of champagne, and we welcomed the future with an embrace given each to each.

The initial party launching us into the world of New York was one in charge of the P. E. N. Club. The program was concerned with the writing of history under existing methods and, incidentally, with its current lack of literary style, its taint of journalism. I listened intently and I thought of Malcolm Cowley's article about Van Wyck's attitude toward these things while a professor of history at Yale was on the platform. A large, bulky man sure of his direction, he described his enterprise in hand, a compilation in six immense volumes of a history of the universe which was to have contributors from all over the world. By contrast, Van Wyck appeared an almost ephemeral creature and most gentle when he arose to speak of differences in viewpoint. And his method, as he described it, seemed less a method than the emanation of his own mind and being. A challenge to battle, to a bitter-end fight, was then proclaimed by Dorothy Thompson, tempestuous and highly articulate journalist of her day, and I was not sorry when the chairman brought the meeting to its close.

Kenyon and Kappo, established just then in a cold-water flat in the East Sixties, invited us to dine. We were amused at their ingenious use of the allotted space, free, as it was, from all but essentials in furnishing. The chief ornament was a dead tree that went from floor to ceiling, brought from the Bridgewater woods, its trunk and limbs divested of twigs and bark and possessing a soft gray sheen pleasant to see. Around this upward-rising shaft, Kenyon had constructed two circular shelves whereon a pair of cats, also transported from the country, cavorted in graceful ways, their tails and an occasional forepaw hanging downward to bring a touch of the jungle to the scene, which might well have been designed by Salvador Dali.

In the February city, a move away from the Huxley flat lightened our hearts, or, in modern parlance, our "sense of guilt." This for the reason of being bound about, as we had been, by those unhappy homeless creatures who walked the streets by day and sought communal shelter by night. To see one of these men, coat collar up against the rain, motionless beneath the dripping rafters of the Mills Hotel as he awaited the opening of the doors, was a saddening occurrence, and little there was that we could do save hand out an occasional quarter to a broken figure mumbling his plea as he pursued us along the street. The deciding episode for us took place in our house before dinner one evening when a man called from the lower hallway asking if Van Wyck, whose name he apparently knew, would favor him with an interview. A man of literate background, he proved to be, who made it a habit to accost writers, telling them of a money-making scheme which would enable them to live and do their work in security: a confidence game of the first order. Van Wyck, hanging over the banister in conversation, seemed much intrigued by this interview with the lower regions and unable to bring it to an end, to send the man away. I feared he might be invited to dine with us, but a solution was at last effected when I produced a five-dollar bill. "Poor fellow!" my husband more than once said as the evening wore on. "I might so easily have been in his place." It was then that I remembered hearing of Van Wyck's predilection for tramps, one acquired young, when several of his Harvard classmates had shared with him a horror of the "Bitch Goddess Success" and a fascination with the world of the slums: a veritable *nostalgie de la boue.* And I thought of those pages in the *Confident Years* that dealt with Josiah Flynt, an inventive and versatile man. Nephew of Frances Willard, who had founded the Women's Temperance Union, he had escaped from a reform school and become a hobo, joining the tramps and crooks of the land, their hangouts the woods and haystacks along the roads, the boxcars of trains. He was able to contrive moving stories to get a meal, an actor as well as a bum, who "could change his whole manner, his vocabulary and his accent in a moment." A romantic, haunting world.

Because of our proximity to harrowing scenes of this sort, it seemed best that we exchange our background for something more commonplace. We engaged a small suite, therefore, at the old-fashioned Hotel Earle, on Waverly Place, where at once we breathed a freer air. Here, the largest, sunniest room was the kitchen, and here, ten minutes after our move, Van Wyck had established himself, pre-empting the table with white-enameled top. "We shan't be doing much cooking here," he said by way of explanation as he took up his pen on the first morning, the breakfast dishes pushed to one side.

One of Van Wyck's encounters with the rewards and the terrors derived from public engagement took place at Union College, in Schenectady, where in February, 1953, he received an honorary degree. The citation was as moving as that at Northeastern University, and again I was proud and happy. Only, I said to myself, it's a pity I cannot hang copies of words such as these

about my husband's neck in the way that the sign of his status is
fastened to a blind man, in order to proclaim his achievement to
the uninformed. This idea came to me in the train that carried us
back to New York. I sat snug against the window, my husband at
my side, and I read *Bleak House,* biting into it as though I were
consuming a great loaf of homemade bread, and I told myself once
again that Dickens had known human character, human motives,
just as Van Wyck also knew these things. Dickens's writing, for
example, of Mr. Skimpole graciously accepting bed and board from
his old school friend, Jarndyce:

He was a bright little creature with rather a large head; but a delicate
face and a sweet voice, and there was a perfect charm in him. All he
said was so free from effort and spontaneous, and was said with such
a captivating gaiety, that it was fascinating to hear him talk.

With this as springboard, my mind flew to various among Van
Wyck's portrayals of character, of Emily Dickinson:

. . . She rolled up the months in mothballs and laid them away, as
she had swept up the heart and put away love; and she saw hope, fear,
time, future and past as persons to rally, welcome, play with, flee or
tease.

Soon after the return to New York we spent an evening with the
Colums. Side by side, these two had led concentrated, consecrated
lives within the world of literature. Padraic wrote poetry, Molly
read poetry and recited it: " 'Tis poems by the ream I know," she
told me, a flame that leapt through the flesh and bypassed the
outer marks of time. As for Padraic, with his attributes of the
saint, his orientation toward good will and mercy, he was a wise
man who followed his guiding star. It was a pleasure to be in the
company of two souls who compromised with neither the world
nor the devil. They surrounded Van Wyck with admiring affection,
and he responded with a glow that lit his eyes as he talked on
and on with the freedom based on years of attachment.

Letters reflecting the influence of *The Writer in America* were
arriving in quantity. Many of these came from young men be-

wildered by the problems of writing in a world of turmoil, fluidity, and scattered choices of action. A dam had apparently been released by the reading of this book, and the letters held a torrent of self-explanation and avowal. Inevitably, there were enclosures of written work, published or in progress, with requests for a critical analysis. Impossible for Van Wyck to deal at length with these eager and confused aspirants, but he managed some sort of reply to show his good will and his faith in the future.

The setting for the bestowal of the Doctor of Letters degree on Van Wyck by the University of Pennsylvania in June, 1953, was a wider and less intimate one than that of Union College, and our entertainment was on a rather more magnificent scale. On the evening before the exercises we were driven at a decorous rate in a large, black limousine to Germantown, where we were to dine with Mr. Robert McCracken, chairman of the board of trustees of the university. A hot wind, aftermath of a tornado in the South, swept the trees that ornamented the splendid houses of the vicinity, blowing peony petals, bending the stems of delphinium, bringing us the sudden scent of roses mixed with the tar of roadways, a disquieting, oppressive atmosphere. Van Wyck and I were greeted by our host and drawn away from other guests into the comparative quiet of a lovely garden of cool green. Here, Justice Owen J. Roberts was introduced to us, an immense man who exuded calm and forbearance and tolerance flavored with humor, all necessary appurtenances to his profession, I thought, and some possibly cultivated toward this end. At dinner I sat next Mr. McCracken, who quoted poetry over the dessert and seemed pleasantly familiar with my husband's work. A cultivated man. On the other side was a Mr. Hopkinson who talked modestly of his garden and the tools he used in working it. I later was told that his ancestors had contributed much to our American Revolution, one Hopkinson having designed the American flag, another having written "Hail Columbia, Happy Land."

Next morning, the car driving us to the university exercises held Miss Edith Hamilton. This was an especial pleasure for Van Wyck.

He was happy to know that she, also, was to receive a degree, in honor of her several books on classical Greece and Rome, books that he admired. A slim, frail old lady who possessed an underlying determination and sense of personal direction, she had remained away from the McCracken dinner party of the night before because of her deafness and her dislike of large parties. Her companion and I, on arrival at the university, went to sit in the bright sunshine to watch several hundred young graduates receive their diplomas. Van Wyck and Miss Hamilton, motionless and correct on the stage above us, looked to be imitations of themselves in their mortarboards and gowns, as wax figures are imitations of the original, and I wondered how their inner being fared on display in this conspicuous glass case. Finally, the citations for the chosen candidates were read, the honorable hoods thrown about their shoulders, and we were summoned to lunch, following an address by Milton Eisenhower, brother of the President. That afternoon, we left Philadelphia for Swarthmore to spend a night with Professor and Mrs. Robert Spiller, he whose efforts were to lead, eventually, to the placing of Van Wyck's papers in the University of Pennsylvania Library.

On the return to Bridgewater, we stopped off for a half-hour conversation at Princeton with Ashley Montagu and his delightful wife. He was an English anthropologist teaching at Rutgers who lectured and wrote on the important doctrine of human love, and he and Van Wyck had recently been in correspondence, sharing a belief, as they did, in the natural goodness of man. Both of them felt an aversion for the doctrine of original sin, so much in favor at the moment. Montagu's recent book, *The Natural Superiority of Women,* had been handed me with a wry smile by my husband at Christmas. We were unable on that afternoon to remain for tea with the Montagus because we counted on reaching Bridgewater before dark, and we set out presently to urge our car across the Jersey flats. Once upon a time, Van Wyck told me ("Van Wyck who knew everything," as Julius Teller had remarked), this far-reaching expanse, the site of meadows cut by natural streams, went by the lovely name of the "Hoboken Dells," where spring violets and trailing arbutus grew in the sweet air. Now, the meadows were colored in saffron, the stultified waters were tinged with oil, and the air was heavy with chemical fumes. Row after row of circular tanks and relentless chimneys were in action, and beyond the windshield of our car spurts of flame mounted to the sky like the fiery breath of some dragon. By contrast, the crimson sphere of the setting sun was a gentle thing. Of grace, in this arid land, I could find but one sign: a series of delicately molded metal towers bound one to the other by ephemeral wires hanging all silvery in the evening mist.

The Biddles invited us to spend a few days of August with them in Truro, on Cape Cod. Their household was composed of three artist bohemians, father, mother, and son, Michael, who led unpampered yet highly sophisticated lives based on talents of a wide order. George, a painter-craftsman, played the flute, wrote books, strode the moors, plunged through great waves breaking along the sandy floor. Always in action, he permitted himself repose only at the brief moments when, his long, bare-boned frame lying prone, almost lifeless, on bed or couch or sand, he gathered impetus for contests ahead. Hélène Sardeau Biddle, Belgian born, was a skilled sculptress. When not in her tree-shaded studio, she undertook the duties of housekeeper-cook, preparing the meals of a chef, or, as musician, she joined the sounds of George's flute and my violin on her small organ. Michael, a talented youth, upright and narrow as a sapling, reminded me of Picasso's "Portrait of a Boy" in the so-called Blue Period. He was active in the manner of his father, overcoming the surf's mighty power with a fine abandon, and he inherited from both parents a remarkable manual dexterity. Between Van Wyck and George there existed a strong bond born in the early Harvard days, and I marveled at the extent and duration and depth of their conversations, self-perpetuating, self-nourished, self-sufficient as a mountain freshet. Now and then, during our stay, when Van Wyck took up his book, signal for the need of solitude, George invited me for walks across the Cape Cod moors thick in sweet fern and bearberry, that low-growing ground cover of tiny shining leaf which, years ago at the Arnold Arboretum, I had come to know under the name *Arctostaphylos uva-ursi,* a name as difficult to pronounce as was its intricately woven texture to tread upon. We walked swiftly, George pressing the cover with his bare feet, neither of us conscious of the sharp, steep hills as we moved into the sunset whose flaming power seemed to subdue the waters on the horizon. A pleasure derived from the visit to the Biddles was my coming on a book about Cape Cod by Henry Beston, *The Outermost House.* Beston, a friend of Van Wyck, who regarded this book with delight, calling it a minor classic, wrote of the year he spent in a small house he had built himself on a forward dune overlooking the sea at Eastham. Living alone as he did, Beston was able minutely to watch and record the rhythm of a wave's progress to the shore, a bird's webbed feet marking the sands, the autumn hegira of butterflies, the slow approach of the Coast Guard's lantern swinging from an invisible hand at night. Serene, sober words.

During our month on the Vineyard, that summer, our stay at the Silo was brief. In August, we turned it over to the Saltonstalls, always much at home there with their small children, and we moved for ten days to a carriage house converted into a duplex apartment at Windy Gates, the Baldwin acres. This they lent to their friends, the rent being requested in the form of companionship. Roger, a will-o'-the-wisp with a social conscience, could be found on the place here and there at any hour of daylight, while at nighttime, when the flicker of his torch passed our open door, he seemed an ally of the fireflies. In his variety of tastes he was comparable to Thomas Jefferson, caring alike for the rights of man and for the proper growth of his trees. Among his delights were the walks he took alone through the woods, spotting the birds whose songs he imitated with a fine skill. He stopped by, one quiet evening, to alert us to the call of a Carolina wren who had surprised him by coming so far north. The pattern of her refrain went from low to high, from high to low, and I asked him if both notes issued from the same throat. Roger chuckled at the question and said that this method of song was a part of the wren's equipment. Listening, I thought of the themes of Brahms, often so cleverly reversed, and I wondered whether the great man might have learned from this small, inconspicuous creature. In one of the haylofts on the big rambling place, Roger had fashioned a shelter for barn owls, who returned year after year to nest there and, despite clawings and scratchings, he managed to band the newly hatched fledglings. He was assiduous, also, in collecting the children who happened to be about; these, on the morning we left the island, included the small Saltonstalls, who arrived to take part in the annual rite. Roger guided them, one after another, up the rickety ladder to peer through the opening into the dark haven high above where the mother owl fed her brood. Another of Roger's attributes was that of musician. On a summer night, after his prowl about Windy Gates, his lantern hung in the corn patch to keep away the deer, he returned to the house to play Bach and Mozart, the limpid notes becoming a part of the surf and the stars. Van Wyck called Roger Baldwin "the last member of the old New England tradition," and he attempted to persuade him to take up his pen on his retirement from the Civil Liberties Union and set down the notable story of his life.

In October, Van Wyck received the Theodore Roosevelt Medal at a dinner given by the Association in the house at 28 East Twentieth Street where the former President was born. The medal was presented each year to two men distinguished in their respective fields. William Beebe, the naturalist, was the other recipient. The dinner was a protracted one of about a hundred people on a very warm evening, and I wondered how Van Wyck, invariably appalled by the onus of public speaking, would surmount the ordeal when the moment came for the speech requested of him. Archibald Roosevelt, son of Theodore, sat next me, and he distracted me somewhat, as the minutes went slowly past, by asking me whether I had suffered from being married to a man in the public eye. "You and I shine in reflected glory," he said. "I've done nothing all my life but

176

shine in reflected glory." Bringing an end to this conversation, Van Wyck's speech, when finally the moment came, went very well. I need not have feared for my husband. He seemed much at home, and it pleased the Roosevelt relatives and admirers to hear an anecdote about the late President, who had come to Harvard when Van Wyck was an undergraduate editor of the *Advocate* to attend a party at that office. Among other guests that day, Van Wyck said, had been an obscure English writer. When he was introduced to the guest of honor he, as well as the company present, had been astounded to find that Roosevelt was familiar not alone with the titles of this writer's books but with their contents also, and was able thus to exhibit to one and all his famous photographic memory. The core of Van Wyck's speech, however, was a plea for the writing of history as literature in contrast to the current reliance on mere reportage, a subject much in his mind and presented here with force and distinction.

Our Thanksgiving we spent with Peter Brooks at the North Country School, in Lake Placid. Walter Clark, the headmaster, was a person of great understanding and generosity, and the feast, as planned by him and his wife, was the most thankful among those I had known. The school building, situated in a cluster of fir trees which shielded it from the widths of the Adirondack country, was on that day drowned in a sun that pressed its warmth through broad glass windows as we sat at table before a great fire glowing in the chimney. At the outset of the meal the company stood while Walter Clark arose, a tall, lean, perennially upright man who resembled the figure of one of the saints carved in the portal of Chartres Cathedral. Into the silence he spoke, asking each of us to think of ways in which we could be grateful for the benefits vouchsafed us. A long meditation followed, broken at length by the sound of children's voices singing in the distance a chorale of Bach. A fairy tale with a happy ending, one that might have issued from the pen of the Grimm Brothers, who were themselves products of the north. I could see, glancing at Van Wyck, that he was as moved as I was, standing silent on the opposite side of the long board.

We were weary that night on arriving home, but the recollection of the hours spent at North Country School remained quietly in our minds as we turned off the lights on a far-reaching day.

XV

Wit and Wisdom

*W*INTER in our village brought waves of snow and gales
and ice, with the thermometer oftentimes at zero, when all life
save that of the birds who fed at our station sought shelter and retirement. A blessed time of year, for our hearth was very much our
own and each of our household belongings appeared to renew its
significance. In Van Wyck's study, dropping deep into the chair
opposite his own, I dropped deep, also, into myself, permitting the
essence to flow between us that is born of silence. At noon, eating
our lunch, playing checkers in the broad south window of the
dining room, we were enfolded in sunshine, while our tea we drank
by the fire in the easterly corner of the living room, beneath the
Yeats portrait of Van Wyck, as the winter afternoon fled away in
a torrent of scarlet across the western sky.

None but the voices of dissent arising from the world of politics
at Washington disturbed our serenity. It was the moment in 1954
when Senator Joseph McCarthy, in the name of righteousness,
persecuted men of conscience who strove to defend the country and

their own actions from insinuations of evil, when "Patriotism" as defined by the senator from Wisconsin was a thing to be demolished, and the term "subversive" struck from the current vocabulary. Repercussions of the battle reached our small town, where some among innocent and credulous voters believed that the menace of Communism, as preached by McCarthy, would, in his hands, be choked at the source.

More important than distant political battles to most village inhabitants were the minor disagreements spread for airing at the local church-supper meetings. On a January evening some sixty of us gathered in the basement of our Episcopal parish house to eat turkey and sweet potatoes and gingerbread. Van Wyck and I shared a table with a retired clergyman, nearing ninety, long-time rector of our parish, and the Hammonds, Agnes and Dan, both of whom played a major role in our lives, she a valiant and unerring housekeeper, he a consultant-caretaker of our premises. I sat between the rector and Dan Hammond, one as deeply entrenched in the spiritual as was the other in the manual. Dan was an excellent carpenter-cabinetmaker, and his eyes shone when he spoke of his tools and the objects they were capable of turning out. At the end of the meal, while the men stood about smoking, we women gathered in the small kitchen to wash the dishes, a job making for much solidarity as each attempted to relieve the other, working at top speed in order to attend the meeting which was to follow. This lasted, as it turned out, for two hours, and I feared that Van Wyck would weary as he heard one report after another on the needs and the labors of the church. Later he told me that he had been impressed, touched by so great a display of duty mingled with apparent pleasure. Indeed, the proverbial heart of stone could not have withstood the pride and satisfaction of the parish lady who had recently embroidered the emblem of the cross in white and gold along a brocade stole to be worn by the rector on special church days. "When I'm too old to do anything else but sew," she said, "I hope to spend my time embroidering vestments for the church. It makes a person feel so peaceful."

We went to town at the beginning of February to greet advance copies of *Scenes and Portraits,* just off the press. During the hour needed by Van Wyck for inscribing copies for friends, I went to lower Fifth Avenue to hunt for hotel rooms where we might spend a week or so strolling about the Greenwich Village streets which so compelled and relaxed my husband, attending a few plays, hearing one or two concerts, seeing our friends. A short break from winter rigors was due Van Wyck, who, after all, had been warned by his doctor against cold winds and exertion. It was difficult to remember this, for he mentioned the pain almost never. But walking in the cold at too swift a pace he would now and then come to a halt and remove from his pocket the tiny gilt box which held pellets of nitroglycerine. To circumvent attacks of this sort we had, that winter, intended to go south, to St. Augustine or Savannah. But when the moment arose for settling on a date we felt somehow impotent, unable to proceed, thrusting the idea from us. Finally, on a Bridgewater morning when sunshine flooded our freshly painted kitchen, plants on window ledges were alive with well-being, birds cascaded at the feeder beyond, I interrupted Van Wyck, sitting tranquil at his study table, in the warmth and the silence, to inquire why we had decided to leave this haven of ours for so protracted an absence.

"Why not give the trip up and stay home?" I asked.

"Why not?" Van Wyck echoed, glancing from his work, pen in mid-air.

"But your heart?"

"I can stay indoors on the bad days. You know how much I like to be indoors." This was one of our regular jokes.

I danced a jig of joy, and Van Wyck smiled a quick smile of pleasure, lowered his pen, and went back to work. It was settled, and the small apartment we were to occupy at the Fifth Avenue Hotel was our compromise, rooms of wide windows on the top floor of the tall structure, where we looked into the open sky about us and to the world of the city far below.

On our way from Danbury by train to New York, we perceived

a tiny ladybug lying motionless on the seat opposite. It had been carried by one of us on bag or overcoat from our house, which harbored a colony of these little creatures of good omen. It lay defenseless now on the wide seat, inadvertently separated from its fellows, and it seemed preposterous that we abandon it to fate. As Van Wyck said, "If one gives one's imagination full scope one can become identified with the most insignificant forms of life." I made a gesture as if to gather it into my brief case, but Van Wyck stopped me. "It will be crushed to death there," he said. And, after all, we left it where it lay.

The New York weeks were broken in their line by a sudden flight to Paris, which I undertook from sympathy for my daughter Jean, who had been ill. This was the first time since our marriage that I had been separated from my husband for more than a night or two, and I might have been girding myself for an eleventh-century crusade. Van Wyck decided to return to Bridgewater during the time I was to be away, and Margaret Cobb agreed to stay with him there. All seemed well arranged, simple and easy. But on our parting at Idlewild, as I watched him move away in his loose gray Burberry, the rough, lightweight coat which he wore even on the coldest days because it had become a part of himself, seeing him doff his Homburg hat in farewell, as he went through the exit, I knew that that staunch compact figure, aloof yet compliant, determined yet vulnerable, had become the pivot of my life.

The journey successfully accomplished and Jean well recovered, I landed at Idlewild on a day of torrential rain to perceive my husband, a readily discernible figure, waiting to meet me: a splendid moment, canceling that of my departure two weeks earlier. Soon, he and I were driving off in a downpour which had no power to deter us, driving homeward, safe and together. We talked at random: I at full speed, joyfully, telling him of myself, my feelings, thought, behavior, during the days of our separation; Van Wyck, characteristically speaking less of himself than of another, of Margaret Cobb, his companion at Bridgewater, whose forthcoming book on her mother, Harriet Hubbard Ayer, he had

much on his mind, hoping for its success. He went on to tell me
of a film recently completed, a documentary on Helen Keller put
together by Katharine Cornell and her friend Nancy Hamilton.
It was to be privately shown at a New York theater during the
coming week; the showing would take place at midnight and was
intended largely for stage professionals, who could thus view it
after the conclusion of their own performances. "A difficult thing
to do," Van Wyck said of the film, "to catch Helen's spirit, to com-
bine the story of her childhood, the period of her training, with the
present."

When the evening arrived, we were asked by Polly Thomson to
meet Helen and her at the Cosmopolitan Club, that we might have
a drink and some conversation before the performance. As we sat
beside Helen, she reminded me of a good child who has been got
ready by her nurse and told be still until the party begins. Her
smile was quick and candid as ever but her vivacity was subdued,
and I wondered if she disliked the idea of being on view, as
presently she was to be, her life spread wide for all to see. In the
theater lobby were many notables of that world come to watch the
story of a life, unlike theirs, spent in darkness. The picture was
very moving, the difficulties feared by Van Wyck seemingly over-
come, as it blended the early photographs of Helen with her later
achievement. We saw her as a lovely girl attentive to the teaching
of Anne Sullivan, of Thomas Edison, of Alexander Graham Bell,
one of her first admirers. We saw her many years later as she
addressed the Sorbonne at Paris on the hundredth anniversary of
the death of Louis Braille, designer of books for the blind, and we
followed her through hospital wards where her groping fingers,
touching the blind, brought them fresh courage. We watched while
she dealt in patience and perennial dignity with the vast crowds
flocking about her on her far journeys of good will, and finally we
became a part of her present life within the house at Arcan Ridge,
at Westport, the daily rite of dressing, of solitary morning walks in
the garden along the rail guideline, the dishwashing with Polly in
the kitchen, where Helen did the drying. We watched her alone in

her study surrounded by her Braille books, typing her letters as she smiled her charming smile at the thought of some friend, and we saw her in bed, ready for the night as Polly, tucking her in, discovered a big Braille book hid beneath the blankets, a touching joke. Last, we saw the serenity pervading Helen's face while, unconscious of the camera's proximity, she let her head fall back against the pillows to prepare for sleep. At the sudden darkening of the screen and before the house lights went on, one could sense, in the silence, the swelling upsurge of emotion in the hearts of the onlookers. No one moved until, quietly and alone, Eleanor Roosevelt left her seat to go to Helen, halfway back on the aisle, and to take her hand. Then came the lights and the applause, fervent and long-lasting, which mingled the homage and the affection felt for Helen and Polly both: two on the side of light.

The Limited Editions Club bestowed its medal, in 1954, on Van Wyck's work as a whole, and in order properly to accept it, he and I, with other honored recipients, were asked to a party on the Starlight Roof of the Waldorf. Several hundred dinner guests, members of the Limited Editions Club, were there, and from the dais, where we sat, we gazed down on them beneath us. I was reminded of the crowds gathered to watch the guillotine of the French Revolution. Next me was Joseph Blumenthal, owner of the Spiral Press, which turned out rare items of fine printing, and he and I were able to linger in our conversation on the compelling beauty of Cornwall, in Connecticut, where he owned a house. The principal speaker of the evening was Robert Frost. Carl Sandburg spoke also. When it came to be the turn of Van Wyck to "say a few words," on the acceptance of his award, unprepared as he was to face the multitude below, his shyness made it necessary for him to be pushed to the microphone by Fredric March, who was master of ceremonies. "A scared boy saying his piece at graduation," Freddy later said.

The weekend following this event brought the Wheelocks to stay, and they, in turn, brought Alan Paton, famous would-be emancipator, he who had for years striven to loose from bondage the black population of South Africa. His two greatly loved books, *Cry, the Beloved Country* and *Too Late the Phalarope,* had been published at Jack's instigation by Scribner's. Paton had recently been traveling over our land, and his passage was celebrated by the colored race wherever he went. It was fortunate for us that he could spare the time for a weekend at Bridgewater. I had expected a shy, large-eyed, soft-spoken dreamer. Rather, he was a sturdy small man with thin, tight-lipped mouth and eyes that pierced when, briefly, they concentrated on an object or an idea. Otherwise his eyes seemed remote and their owner noncommittal, retiring into himself, as he did, if the situation or the topic failed to summon him outward. But at the moments of his being roused, he was acute, articulate, and compassionate. The bravery on which his life depended he took for granted in a land where injustice proliferated like the mesembryanthemums of the plains. It was a necessary weapon.

The summer of 1954 brought us in August to Yaddo, at Saratoga Springs, New York, that agreeable and life-restoring colony founded by Mr. and Mrs. Spencer Trask, who had bequeathed their great mansion and grounds to writers, painters, sculptors, composers. A structure of wood and stucco in the Elizabethan manner, the house possessed towers and turrets of brownstone, a pseudo-castle of immense high-ceilinged rooms which had not escaped the touch of eccentricity. "Our local Blenheim Castle," as it was called by Van Wyck. An imposing window of Tiffany glass was at the head of the broad living-room stairway, and a minor fountain trickled above a pool at the far end. Portraits of the family, in tweeds and velvets, by Eastman Johnson hung life-sized above the heads of guests who came here to converse at evening and to sit in the massive overstuffed chairs lining the room in rigid sequences. The music room, beyond, was rowed with walnut benches resembling church pews which confronted a pair of pope's chairs and the gilded throne of a Venetian doge, seat of Katrina Trask in the days when musicians had been summoned from the city to play or sing for her and her guests. Here, at evening, we listened to the collection of records or to the work of one of the colony's composers that rang out from the concert grand piano while, in the distance, beyond the room's mullioned windows, the Green Mountains of Vermont, mist-bound, gradually lost the line of their contour in the evening light. Also on a vast scale, within the five hundred acres of woods and meadows, were terraces and pergolas and a rose garden surrounding a fountain which, in continual play as it was, attracted the sightseers from neighboring towns. There were beds of flowers for cutting, greenhouses, potting sheds, and a kitchen garden that grew our table vegetables. Woods of pine and spruce and fir made delicious walking on warm days, and here were situated many of the studio buildings used by the artists and writers, who were asked to keep to themselves, in the interest of work, until late afternoon. Lunch we ate in our rooms from workmen's pails, but the colony assembled at evening to dine in the dark-paneled dining room, where, later, various plans were made for the evening's entertainment. Van Wyck and I were given a pleasant room and bath in a house smaller, less imposing, than the mansion, and there was also provided for his work a cabin with a wood stove. We became very fond of Mrs. Elizabeth Ames, the competent directress, and of her assistant, Polly Hanson, a young poetess. Together they ruled their kingdom with equity and with tactful sympathy for the various problems of their subjects, who, one and all, were blessed, as also they were afflicted, with the pronounced ego and the raw skin of the artistic nature.

The Saratoga race track was less than a mile away, and many of us, as August unfolded, allied ourselves for the moment with the age-old, win-or-lose precepts of the gambler, each devising his own method, attempting his own salvation in betting on the horses. Within the gates of the race track all seemed to function as an oft-repeated scene in a well-rehearsed play while the tree-shaded paddocks, the sleek beauty of the horses, and the romantic appearance of the jockeys spread the elements of an old-fashioned summer romance over the scene and in our hearts. On the days we remained behind at Yaddo, the repetitious voice of the announcer from his

lookout over the course below, the swelling shouts of the onlookers, rumors of glory or tragedy, came to us on the summer air
as if grounded in eternity.

On certain afternoons Van Wyck invited me to drive with him
to the center of Saratoga. It amused him, among other attractions,
to watch the people going in and out of the spas, taking the
waters. Sometimes I myself went to lie in a warm bubbling bath
or under the weight of beneficent hot packs. At those moments my
husband waited in the lobby, book in hand, wearing an ancient
seersucker jacket, its lower pockets weighted with paraphernalia,
and he watched the clients enter and retreat, fascinated by the various types of Jews come for the annual rite of cleansing the inner
as well as the outer man, accustomed, as many had been before
the war, to the pleasures and rigors of the European spas. Among
these clients were dignified rabbis in their kaftans, long-haired,
skull-capped. One man of this race we came on accidentally as we
walked the streets, an elderly scholar who sat in the sprawling
garden of a house in a poor neighborhood, white-bearded, shoulders
bent in the attitude of perpetual homage to the heavy Talmudic
book he had before him. He might have been one of the prophets, so
great was his preoccupation with "The Law," so entirely was he
removed from earthly things. On several trips to the city we made
the detour into the street where the old man had set up his shrine
on a rickety table beneath a dying elm. Van Wyck was fascinated
by this display of becalmed application, pausing for a long moment,
walking stick hooked over his wrist, to view the scene. It seemed
to lift him to that rarer air wherein the pure and the valiant fore-
gather, seeking an evanescent truth.

We went with Jay Leyda, whose book *The Melville Log* was
about to be published, to see the house built by Melville's grandfather, where he stayed as a youth, and which was now preserved
as a monument, at Gansevoort. It was here that Melville had
placed the setting, supposedly, for his novel *Pierre*. The village of
Gansevoort was a poor, jerry-built place, and the house itself,
though set apart in a tree-shaded meadow and possessing the white

columns of the Greek revival along the façade, had little other merit to attract us. Inside, the living rooms lacked the touch of elegance and bedrooms were small and foursquare. We thought without envy of the daily scene as it had unrolled for the Gansevoort and Melville families. One small building only, at the rear of the house and in a pretty setting, enlivened our attention. This was the outhouse, necessary to the period, of wood painted white and paneled in brick, substantial, graceful, and possessing a shuttered window as well as a chimney attached to a stove within. A self-sufficing unit where men had lingered. The stamp of authority was still upon it.

Leyda, at Yaddo, spent his days in compiling one more "Log," this having to do with the life of Emily Dickinson. He invited us to an evening party not long before our departure, at which certain of the poet's posthumous letters and poems were to be read, her genius exhibited and discussed. The principal participant in the reading was young Aileen Ward, who was much involved just then in working on her life of John Keats. One of the letters, written by Emily Dickinson to her brother when she was eleven years old, was chattering and blithe as the song of a summer bird. A gay, effervescent creature she seemed at that age, before she sought the seclusion which turned many of her poems into darting shafts of despair. The evening was very pleasant, seated as we were about the fire at West House, the smaller house which we inhabited. Many of the younger aspirants sat on the floor, and above us the evergreen boughs and flowers which I had gathered that day formed a background to a poet's fair words. Van Wyck appeared as interested as the others, a quiet and attentive member of the audience. And yet I wondered. Had he not himself written a beautiful essay on Emily Dickinson, one wherein, as he described her, "a shy little childlike creature glided"? Was he not thoroughly conversant with her work? But, during the entertainment, there was no expository word from him. Rather, he appeared, modestly, to learn with the others.

"Why didn't you tell us something of your own about her?" I asked him later, back in our room.

"It didn't seem necessary," he answered, taking off his reading glasses to put them on the bed table. "They were enjoying themselves." And he reached up to turn out the light.

This was, for us, the final party at Yaddo, and soon after, we bade good-bye to our friends there, trying to thank Elizabeth Ames, who had so assiduously entered our day-to-day existence, bestowing help with self-effacing skill. Last, we said good-bye to Polly Hanson, diminutive poet-secretary, who flitted here and there, saying little, aware of all, intent on her job like a hummingbird at work on a flower.

During a trip to Yale in October, at the invitation of Alan Paton, we watched as he received a degree of Doctor of Humane Letters. The other recipients of honors were the Archbishop of Canterbury, the Bishop of the Greek Orthodox Church, an East Indian bishop, and Bishop Dibelius, the brave German churchman who had held to his post throughout the war in defiance of Hitler. Alan Paton looked small and shrunken in his academic robes, the flame born of his intensity burning bright. We could not find him when the ceremony ended, but he telephoned us that evening to say good-bye. He and Chiang Yee had become migratory birds to whom we counted on offering shelter whenever they alighted in the vicinity of Bridgewater.

Chiang Yee, on the day after Thanksgiving in that year of 1955, played the role of staunch friend when he accompanied Van Wyck by car to a New York pier where they were to gather up Van Wyck's brother-in-law, Francis Stimson, arriving by ship from Panama on the last leg of a journey from Tahiti, his home for many years. Frank Stimson, Eleanor's brother, I had not as yet met. From the various accounts concerning him I rather dreaded a visit from this unusual man, scholar and romantic in equal parts, dynamic, forceful, demanding of attention and endlessly compelling in his powers of conversation. He was on his way to the Peabody Museum in Salem, Massachusetts, where were to be stored as a permanent unit his papers relative to the Tahitian people, their folklore, customs, their several languages: a great man and egocentric, with vast powers of intellect. Great men, I reflected, are by tradition unstable in their behavior and demands: Frank possessed, in addition to these unusual indigestible morsels of genius, habits of soft living in a tropical land where ease combined with the assiduous ministrations of a native wife had established daily requirements which we, presumably, must fail to meet. Van Wyck's descriptions of Frank, of earlier visits made to the house at Westport, had not set my mind at rest. These visits had been spaced five or more years apart, and, on the last occasion, arriving as he did on a blustering February day minus overcoat and clad in tropical clothing, he came down with pneumonia soon after reaching land.

The three men appeared in Bridgewater just before lunch, and as I ran downstairs to greet them Chiang Yee was in process of carrying from the car the bags and the multilingual typewriter and the heterogeneous equipment necessary to Frank's pattern of life, a process requiring patience and fortitude from any who assisted him. At once, however, I was drawn to him as he kissed me on both cheeks to welcome me, belatedly, into the family. He was more gentle than I had been led to believe, more aware of the other person, even though his habit of monologue might lead one to think otherwise and, during his several interspaced visits to Bridgewater, I became really fond of him.

At Christmas, after we had eaten dinner, he held an audience enthralled while the afternoon waned, explaining the phonetic system of the Polynesian language, describing the constellations of that universe, the dangers from coral cuts and spirochetes, the various theories of Polynesian origins. He showed us photographs of his pure-blooded native wife, daughter of a local king, with her long, flower-decked hair and her look of steadfast character, and we saw reproductions of the tree-enclosed bungalow where he lived the years in eating, sleeping and writing, each of these pursuits as basic as another to his nature. Presently, his voice grown hoarse from the prolonged effort of conversation, he took up a pack of cards and kept us for long minutes as he demonstrated tricks of legerdemain performed with a disarming skill. A man whose vitality and day-to-day labors were commensurate with the massive bulk of his physique.

The winter meeting of the Academy, ever in a familiar pattern yet ever bringing fresh enlightenment, was presided over by Archibald MacLeish. Van Wyck read his obituary tribute to Frank Jewett Mather, erudite critic of art, and Robert Sherwood read the tribute to Eugene O'Neill. Among the Academicians present at the touching ceremony were John Hersey, who appeared far too young to be in this company, Reinhold Niebuhr, Wystan Auden, and Joseph Wood Krutch, these three recently drawn upward from the Institute. My own chief pleasure in the day was a viewing of the manuscript collection assembled by Hannah Josephson, librarian, under the heading, "The Great Decade: 1850-1860": manuscripts and paintings both. Spread within glass-covered cases were page after page written in the hand of the great men who had made that decade: Thoreau, Emerson, Whitman, Hawthorne, Melville. Whitman's lines were full of corrections and erasures, and in a child's lined copybook stood entries of nouns or short phrases, scribbled at random. Hawthorne, apparently, had made no corrections, his words flowing on, complete and full, like a quiet river well within its bounds. Emerson's beautiful letter to Walt Whitman on a first reading of *Leaves of Grass* was reproduced for us in the Academy catalogue:

I find it the most extraordinary piece of wit and wisdom that America has yet contributed. I am very happy in reading it, as great power makes us happy. . . . I give you joy of your free and brave thought. . . . I rubbed my eyes a little to see if this sunbeam were no illusion; but the solid sense of the book is a sober certainty. It has the best merits, namely, of fortifying and encouraging.

"Fortifying and encouraging," were not these the attributes celebrated beyond all by Van Wyck Brooks? I was happy that the great tradition carried on.

The Geismars, Anne and Maxwell, faithful friends who conquered winter storms in the manner of Santa Claus's reindeer, drove to Bridgewater from Harrison, New York, on a desperately difficult day, to have a December luncheon with us. As always, they were affectionate and articulate companions: Max, with his demeanor of troubled concentration, as though continually searching in retrospect for the right word or phrase where these concerned his writing, but permitting himself, now and then, a smile of sudden pleasure; Anne, valiant, downright, and inexhaustibly free with her sympathies. Max and Van Wyck saw eye to eye about much of the current writing, especially that of the "new critics," and the two men remained friends to the last. They sat on with us until after the sun had established its pattern of bright farewell along the pink wall of our living room, and I was glad, after they had gone, to see Van Wyck's look of reminiscent pleasure, the pleasure of a skier returning from an afternoon on the slopes: a lucid pleasure carrying no aftermath of penalty.

XVI

Stones in the Sea

HE New Year's Eve of 1955 we spent in a motel on the highroad between Roanoke and Bristol, Virginia, at the start of a journey to California, where we were to stay at the Huntington Hartford Foundation, another writer-artist colony, for three months, joining the Biddles there. On this particular day we had driven four hundred miles and were, that night, ready for bed without benefit of any greeting to the newly born year. The trip to the West continued for eight days, a journey in no man's land situated somewhere between boredom and fatigue but broken by short-lived delights: the passionate fling of a free-flowing sunset across the sky's great arc, the shape of a dark holly tree against a white house, sheep cropping a curving hill in lonely serenity, the dignity of pilaster and column ornamenting a county courthouse, loose-limbed colored boys sauntering homeward from work in the fields—all seen for the moment and swiftly gone into limbo.

Driving along a narrow road of descending curves on a late afternoon, we came to the Huntington Hartford Foundation buildings at the foot of a deeply gashed cut known as Rustic Canyon. At first our new abode at the canyon's rock bottom, set dimly in the woods under the light of a dying day, seemed far from the gleaming sky. The house to which we were led, a small dwelling of stone, stood on a sunless strip of lawn, and inside, the furnishing was an inadequate collection of drab, uninviting colors. Tired and numbed by travel, we began our unpacking in a routine sort of way that lacked life's pulse, and there seemed little to say as each of us dwelt inwardly on the long ten-week stretch ahead.

Presently, there was a knock on the door, and the Biddles entered. We loved them both wherever they were, but on that afternoon they became fellow conspirators, guardians of our destiny, angels of mercy. We shared the evening cocktail with them, and our spirits rose. They assured us that our small dwelling could easily be supplemented to our taste, that in the canyon each day we should have several hours of the bright California sun, that the roses on our lawn would bloom in profusion, and that the mimosa trees along the lower canyon road would become an ever-fresh pleasure. Best of all, the hours of quiet, in the pattern of the colony, would mean uninterrupted work for both of us, enabling me to make sure progress on a book I had begun, an essay on Dorothea Lynde Dix, ministrant to the insane. Indeed, as it came to pass, within a short space of time we had entirely adapted ourselves to our little stone house; the sun appeared over the canyon top at nine o'clock; roses filled a tumbler on our living-room table; and on the walks before lunch along "Mimosa Way" I found a profusion, among the many varieties of this tree, for cutting and bearing home, to the delight of my husband. The days, at first, moved past in a wonderful monotony without disturbance from friend or telephone. Although we ate our meals in the Community House, there were few people living at the foundation just then and our only steady companions were George and Hélène, veterans at Pacific Palisades, who now and then took us to call on their friends.

The first of these outings was a visit to the house in Beverly Hills of Edward G. Robinson. As we approached one more among the many instances of architectural splendor and landscaping, Van Wyck murmured: "But are these people alive, do they lead real lives?" On our being introduced to Mrs. Robinson and several lady friends in attendance, a minor royal court, a Filipino butler appeared with a tray of cocktails, mixture of whiskey and rum, with which the ladies were served before they left en masse for a three-thirty appointment. Our host then took charge of us, leading us to the galleries hung with his magnificent collection of French painting. It was in the hope of seeing this that we had come. I watched Robinson as we went, lips drawn tight, impassive, with a curiously oriental demeanor, a stamp which well fitted his habitual dramatic role of villain. But confronted with his lovely pictures, moments later, his expression livened, he ceased to be aloof, and I felt in him a tragic sense tied to tenderness, qualities which constitute the base of man's experience on earth. He lingered long over the painting of Rouault, mystical modernist, telling us that his admiration for the man was "colossal." A religion of sorts. An hour later, bidding good-bye to our curious little host, politely dressed in his Sunday best and generously sharing with us the beauty of his treasure, I wished him well and hoped that in the future there would be much of that joy he felt in the work of Rouault.

In black darkness at six in the morning on February 16, at the base of our canyon, wearing his bathrobe and red leather slippers, Van Wyck brought me my pot of tea. This was his birthday morning, and he lingered for a few moments, seated at the foot of the bed, to open the small packages I handed him. Then he went off to the big table in the kitchen, where stove and sink were concealed behind folding doors, to begin the day's work. I was glad that we were separated by only a thin partition, glad also that I had caught something of the addiction to writing from him, the ever-recurring joy of setting down one word after another in continuity and in hope. We were now thrown more often with people than we had been at first, at cocktails or dinner, but no other moment of the day or evening was as enjoyable as these early hours of mingled silence.

Mr. and Mrs. John Vincent, he a composer and present administrator of the Huntington Hartford Foundation, were assiduously hospitable, and we were several times bidden to join them and their friends at their house in Pacific Palisades. Also, there had been our first encounter with Hollywood, where Van Wyck might have been a youth at the circus, in his undeviating absorption with all that went on in this world of legend. Our host on that day was Fredric March, currently taking part in the film *The Desperate Hours.* Freddy had arranged that we should see him at work, and we were met at the studio gate by a man who bore a faint resemblance to him and served, at that moment, as his stand-in, taking Freddy's place on location whenever this became necessary. A sad sort of role, it seemed to me, if played in perpetuity, and I was happy that no such arrangement could ever be carried out in connection with my husband's work. In the studio, Freddy greeted us with kisses and explained that the director of the film was a genius of sorts, and also a great perfectionist, and we were to expect, he said, a certain monotony in the taking of shots, which were likely to be repeated many times over. This was indeed the pattern of the afternoon, and we were amazed and admiring, both, in seeing the fresh spontaneity which continued to be Freddy's as, laboriously, endlessly, one brief scene was halted and rephotographed until it satisfied the all-powerful lord of the studio. We saw with the awe of novices the men who controlled the sound track high above the floor, and the beautiful camera on its giant tripod. And I remembered an earlier day in Paris when Gloria Swanson had been shooting *Madame Sans Gêne,* and I'd seen her, in a fit of simulated rage, hurl a chair mistakenly but directly at the camera, smashing the lens. A major catastrophe. Chiefly, on that afternoon in Hollywood, Van Wyck and I were magnetized by the crews of supers, who sat apart in the dimly lit background, smoking, drinking coffee, silent, as they followed the making of the film, men and women of varying age, varying type, waiting, each of them, for the chance of a walk-on part in the course of some scene, thereby earning a coveted few dollars. They might have been the Children of Israel waiting to be led across the Red Sea. My heart went out to them, as did Van Wyck's. He felt an especial concern for an elderly ex-actor, his white moustache meticulously waxed, a carnation in his buttonhole, whose worn shoes beneath the brave attire spoke of long months of inactivity.

When the moment came for our leaving, Freddy, still at work, turned us over once again to the ubiquitous stand-in. He guided us along corridors, allowing us to have a glimpse as we passed another studio of Danny Kaye, who, in the role of mediaeval court jester, tossed a dummy baby in the air and caught it as it fell. Lingering for a moment, we saw a woman approach him and thrust her own live baby toward him. At once the dummy was discarded and the one of flesh and blood gathered into the actor's arms. A quite marvelous world of make-believe, but we were not sorry, finally, to return under the sunset haze of Los Angeles to the small stone cottage we had come to know as home, driving through that "invertebrate city," as Van Wyck called it, to the definitive boundaries of our narrow canyon.

The mail one morning brought us advance copies of Van Wyck's book on John Sloan, the book most recently finished. We discovered the package on the floor of the Community House beneath our postbox, and we left the breakfast room and hurried with it to our house to tear it apart. After admiring the book's outer aspect, its gay yellow jacket incorporating the reproduced self-portrait by Sloan, we sat on for an hour while Van Wyck turned the pages swiftly, eagerly. At moments such as these, I'd noticed, he made no verbal comment, but appeared, inescapably, to be confronting himself for fresh appraisal in the pages of his writing, on trial as he was, as he felt each time, for his life.

During the last days of January, we drove to Los Angeles to drink tea with Mrs. Edward MacDowell, widow of the composer and founder of the MacDowell Colony for artists and writers at Peterboro, New Hampshire. This had been the first colony of its kind and served as a model for the others. Indeed, Huntington Hartford might not have established the community we inhabited at Rustic Canyon if the Peterboro example had been lacking. Living now in California, Mrs. MacDowell, at the age of ninety-eight, was a remarkable old lady, slim, upright in her bearing, aware of the world, and full of humor still, although the pattern of her days had been curtailed to the extent of moving between bed and a window chair. She was glad to see Van Wyck, whose unassuming manner of simplicity endeared him to the elderly as well as to the young. They talked now of the men and women in *The Flowering of New England,* many of whom Mrs. MacDowell had known as a girl in Boston. She spoke also with affection of Molly and Padraic Colum, frequent guests at Peterboro, aware as she was of the inner character of each, able with an innate wisdom to weigh and to value. A quite perfect example of growing old, of preparing to quit the world, this seemed to us, the gradual lessening of physical strength as the mind played quietly with past and present, much as a child plays contentedly beneath an apple tree on a long summer day.

Our existence, as the weeks moved toward spring, became rather more crowded with people. Several of these were connected with the University of California at Los Angeles, that radiating center of education which so successfully combined the traditional with more recent disciplines. There was a reception given us by the University of Southern California, at which Van Wyck, in spite of himself, became a magnet for thirty or forty people, members of the English department with their wives and various graduate students. On occasions such as this, his color heightened, his hair rigorously upbrushed, he seemed to be held aloft by the concerted action of the crowd, rather as an idol is carried by the faithful —his habitual shyness, his dislike of adulation, transformed into temporary acquiescence under the pressures of the moment. An evening spent at the California Institute of Technology impressed us with the lively qualities exhibited by its undergraduates, several of whom we met: an amalgam of brains and humor and tolerance as they applied themselves to the various disciplines of science. These, it was explained to us, were so complex, their movement and changes so rapid, it was difficult to encompass the myriad ramifications with entire exactitude, so that a written equation had oftentimes to be followed by an interrogation mark. In an undergraduate magazine, shown us that evening, we were amused to find a brief contribution entitled "Epitaph" which set out to controvert any such uncertainty:

The world mourns the passing of Sir Arthur,
Whose vision stretched to Arcturus and farther.
Now he is in his individual heaven
where I/a is *exactly* 137.

Van Wyck was delighted to encounter Will Durant at a dinner party in Hollywood, to be able to tell Durant of his admiration for him as a historian. Later, when we saw Durant in his own house, when we entered his study, it was not difficult for me to see how much, in the manner of their work, the two men had in common. On a shelf in the large dark room, purposely shut away from the prevailing view, was a series of tall, ruled, office account books that held the manuscript of Durant's histories written in longhand, as was my husband's, two separate drafts for each of the volumes. And the method of preparation for his work resembled Van Wyck's in the extent of his reading. At evening, he told us, he sat often for several hours in this study after a full day's labor, listening to a program of classical music while at the same moment he read from some learned source, a book propped on a stand before him. He was a tiny man, concentrated, without airs or pretensions and with straightforward blue eyes which, along with his alert movements, belied his white hair and his seventy-odd years. He had been born in French Canada and trained for the priesthood, but a youthful reading of Spinoza put an end to this career, and he finished his education at Columbia. Durant's wife, Ariel, who collaborated with him in his work, was tiny also, and intense, a talkative, passionate woman with the fire of a battling prophet. She drew us by her invincible quality and her underlying tenderness. A united couple. They welcomed us in generous fashion and led us to their dark-paneled, high-ceilinged dining room, where the table was spread for a banquet. We were treated to ices, walnut cake, whipped cream, and kumquat jam as well as to the coffee served from a tall, encrusted silver pot. The two men had much to say to each other. Discussing the subject of original sin, so greatly in fashion as a tenet just then, Durant wondered whether its concept might not have been a holdover from pre-history, when men killed one another in order to survive, whether the memory of mass brutality in the long past had not so invaded man's collective unconscious as to persuade him he had been conceived in sin. Van Wyck agreed that this might be a possibility. He would have welcomed any plausible suggestion which would thrust aside the tenet itself, for, temperamentally, as also by conviction, he was unable to accept any such finality.

A summons from Upton Sinclair took us out to Monrovia, a small town east of Pasadena. He and Van Wyck had not met, although for years they had sent letters back and forth across the continent. Our car came to a stop, on that afternoon, halfway up a northward road leading to the mountains and in front of a stuccoed, garden-fronted house which was lacking in any mellow or graceful sophistication. We were a half-hour late, having had difficulty in finding our way, and Sinclair waited for us on the highway. I saw at once how eagerly he welcomed Van Wyck's arrival. He stood there, clad in a loose shirt that fell outside his trousers, thin, white-haired, a man in his seventies, like Will Durant, but more withdrawn and with a smile that seemed not entirely spontaneous. Rather, it appeared as if from established habit, though blended with uncertainty and touched with the spirit of homemade, evangelistic religion. The religious element, Sinclair's desire for man's "returning to God," I knew of from my recent reading of a book of his which my husband had asked me to glance at in·his stead. When the introductions were over, we were guided to the back yard, where four small buildings of corrugated iron were unlocked for our benefit with four separate keys. These were the fireproof storehouses where were kept Sinclair's books. Two held the translations into various languages, thirty or forty of them, while the other two were piled high with copies, both hard-cover and paperback, of everything that Sinclair had published, the Lanny Budd series and all the others, including a treatise on thought transference and the psychic arts, a subject, we understood, of profound interest to him.

Presently we entered the house through the kitchen, the one room where daylight was permitted. Sinclair approached the stove and took up a long-handled spoon to stir a pot of rice that boiled slowly over a flame, explaining that his wife subsisted solely on a diet of unsalted rice, being an invalid with a bad heart. They had not expected, several years back, he said, to pull her through one of her attacks. Sinclair had prayed all night on his knees and in a tone loud enough, almost, to be heard at the hospital where she lay. It seemed to have reached the ear of God, for she survived. Since that time he had become a specialist in brewing the dish, which was his staple also. He did not care to eat the food forbidden his wife, he told us. We were taken, then, into a room with drawn shades where we had a glimpse of an immense brass bedstead off in an alcove lighted only by two small lamps with opaque glass shades. Our host sat us down in this room, the parlor, furnished with an assortment of settees, stands, benches, no pieces alike save for two great wooden rockers covered in maroon plush. Such, I thought, might have been the decor of a parlor in the White House during the era of General Grant. Only the flowers on various tables, lovely fresh camellias, quantities of them, brought a sense of life to the curiously moribund atmosphere. Soon, there was a heavy grinding sound that came from the hall, and Sinclair moved toward it saying that a mechanically propelled chair attached to the stairway was in use by his wife. Mrs. Sinclair came in, and he parted the curtains so that we were able to see a tall woman with gaunt face and sleek hair pulled upward into a topknot. She wore a long cotton wrapper partly covered by a shorter one, a costume that did not conceal her emaciated frame. But her head was held high and she was full of dignity. Her husband hovered about, smiling his fixed smile, then summoned Van Wyck to a chair at the far end of the room, where his talk, Van Wyck told me later, was chiefly on the uncertain methods of publishers and the fickle attitude of the public. He was just then in the throes of that disillusion suffered by many popular writers when their vogue begins to falter. "Not a pleasant experience," said Van Wyck.

Mrs. Sinclair and I sat together on a settee. She struck me as very much of a person, while she talked of her youth on a plantation in Mississippi: "We had six or seven old-time slaves waiting on us when I was a girl. They had been freed, of course, but they didn't care to leave." She had always been a great reader, she told me, passionately attached to their large library in the plantation house. It appeared that she had read and admired Van Wyck. "Where did you get that fine style?" she asked him when he came over to talk with her. "It seems made of milk and honey." And she complimented him on his accurate knowledge of the South. We were brought beakers of fruit juice by Sinclair before our departure. He was a rabid teetotaler. "Many of my friends and relatives have been killed by alcohol," he said. Making our farewells, moving from darkness into sunlight, our hands filled with the camellias they had given us, I found that I had become attached to this unusual pair, whose lives mingled tragedy and heroism. Looking back as Van Wyck drove away, I saw Sinclair standing motionless again, an effigy in stone set up in the driveway.

Toward the end of March we left the Huntington Hartford Foundation for home by way of northern California. We had put in a most profitable time during the winter. Van Wyck was well along with his book on Helen Keller, and I had made progress on the second essay in the collection of my book *Three Wise Virgins*. Several new friendships had brought us pleasure, and the parties of farewell were very moving. Van Wyck and I were especially touched on our last morning by the final breakfast gathering brought into being by various community members. Irving Fineman, the writer, gave me a little bouquet of wild flowers to pin to my jacket, and the others seemed unhappy to have us go, including the chef, a well-educated man who became a satellite of Van Wyck soon after our arrival, trying to overtake him on his walks for a few moments of conversation and eager to give him various treasures in the form of books from an ancestor's library. Van Wyck, invariably polite and patient, continued to possess this man's heart.

We drove away on a fair morning when dooryards were adorned with roses and lilies and the blossoms of nicotiana, and in the roadside meadows the lovely, gregarious blue lupine spread its upright bloom. We reached Santa Barbara a few hours later, to be greeted by my eldest daughter, Betsy, wife of Lockwood Tower, and their children, in the spacious house set beside a garden wherein flowers seemed to have found their final haven, opulent as the stars in the night sky. Following several enjoyable days here, including a trip to the Santa Ynez Valley and its ancient mission church, we moved northward along the coast, driving through a pageant ordered on an immense scale by primeval gods. Our road cut into cliffs that mounted sheer to the blue heavens, cliffs stark and bleak, oftentimes, as those ruled by Wotan, at other times grace-laden and softened by the contagious presence of spring's wild lilac. Far below us a sun so vividly streaked the sea that the eye of man could not encompass its boundaries along the horizon, a deluge of light proclaiming eternity. Presently, at day's end, we saw "the great streaming triumph of sundown," as described by Robinson Jeffers. Jeffers lived at Carmel, which was our destination, on our way, as we were, to visit Marie Short, old friend of Van Wyck and Eleanor from the time years back when they inhabited Carmel. We found her in her pleasant flower-filled living room, and she greeted us with enthusiasm, a vivid, black-haired, black-eyed woman, quick of motion and of mind, small, alert, articulate, generous. I was much drawn to her. The pattern of her life was, I thought at once, that of a tornado, except that the path of possible devastation was curtailed by kindness. Her friends were devoted to her, and, during our two-day stay, she shared them with us.

Our first evening took us to dine with Noel Sullivan, local benefactor of the church and of the arts, and known for the abundance with which he disposed of the fortune left him by his late uncle, Senator James Phelan, of California. His house was packed with heterogeneous objects placed more or less at random. It held costly paneling of oak, valuable *bibelots,* books in quantity, dogs, cats. The dogs roamed untrammeled, sniffing the guests, begging for food; the cats leapt upon the dining table, helping themselves from the condiments placed on the huge Lazy Susan revolving at the center. On an electric grill in a dining-room corner, as we sat at table, a manservant cooked the chicken presently to be served us, and I was reminded of the story of Squire Hastings, country gentleman of the English seventeenth century, whose house and whose habits were chronicled by his contemporary the first Earl of Shaftesbury. In Hastings's great hall, we are told, where the spit turned before the fire, dogs and cats abounded, and "a little white round stick fourteen inches long lay beside his trencher that he might defend such meat as he had no mind to part with to them." Sullivan differed from Hastings in the dissimilarity of their pursuits, Hastings still riding to hounds at the age of eighty, Sullivan a patron to the musicians who came to play for him in the great music room, where, high above the two grand pianos, a symbolic transparent cross glowed under a concealed light. The cross had been designed for Sullivan by Una, wife of Robinson Jeffers. In another room stood a printing press used for the making of books written by Sullivan's friends the poets.

The principal pleasure of the evening for me was my meeting with Jeffers, "that great man," as Van Wyck spoke of him, tragic poet and tragic being. His wife had died three years earlier, and it was believed he could not continue without her. For she it was who had held him close to the living world, had blown the warm breath of life into his veins, which otherwise might have become transfixed, turned into granite like the rocks he had drawn from the sea-washed shore and carried to the promontory where now stood the house and the tower become their shelter. We talked, he and I, before dinner, during dinner, side by side, and I found it difficult to quit him. Next morning we met again, Marie Short and Van Wyck and I, at the place of his making. It possessed the quality of permanence, as it held the quality of melancholy. It was here that one came to know Jeffers, the lonely man, tall, head bent as one of the great redwood trees bends to the gale, his smile turned inward to lighten for a moment the massive burden which was his to carry even though the more tangible one of stone had long been discharged.

> Stones that rolled in the sea for a thousand years
> Have climbed the cliff and stand stiff-ranked in the house-walls;
> Hurricane may spit his lungs out they'll not be moved. . . .
> . . . I too have escaped and stand. . . .
> Out of the tide-wash . . . I must stand here
> Alone with open eyes in the clear air growing old. . . .

The day following our arrival was given over to visits as Marie Short drove us along the coast to the homes of Van Wyck's acquaintance, through a lovely land of pine and water and friendship. In the afternoon we climbed the high hill that mounts above the Big Sur, there to seek out Henry Miller, writer and idol of his many followers. We found him in a two-room house with but a few wind-swept trees between him and the sea below, which reaches to Japan. He came out to greet us, a small man, unshaved, unremarkable save for his smile, which brought an instant focus to his eyes as they dwelt on us. About his neck he wore a coarse cord tucked beneath his shirt and, for want of anything to say at first meeting, I asked him what hung from it. He drew it upward to show us a coin and explained that it was a holy medal of the Jews, and that it included words of praise for him who fosters human kindness. This, I could see as our visit progressed, Miller attempted to practice, cultivating the gift-bestowing instinct within his own nature, and thus, as William James once put it, permitting it to become a living part of him. He offered us one of his canvases, being a painter as well as a writer, but we felt we could not accept it. He appeared delighted with Van Wyck, telling him he was much nicer than he had supposed. "I thought you were a stuffy old man, but you're neither one nor the other," he said. "And you remind me of Nietzsche as well as my grandfather."

Our days in California were almost at an end. In Berkeley for two weeks we inhabited a small house leased for us by the Alexander Meiklejohns, whose own lovely house on La Loma Avenue overlooked the bay. Several small parties given by the Meiklejohns confronted Van Wyck with certain of the university professors, and we dined at sunset high above the bay with Anthony Ostroff and Miriam, he a poet and acquaintance from weeks shared at Yaddo. Van Wyck took me for several walks about the older portions of the city, and he seemed very much at home there.

"You see, I spent the winter of 1910 here," he explained when I questioned him. "I was waiting to be married at Carmel in the spring. Eleanor was in Paris, then, with her mother."

"Wasn't it rather lonely for you? What did you do with your time?"

"I read and I wrote. Chiefly an essay which I had printed, one hundred copies in the form of a pamphlet."

"What was it about? I don't remember seeing it ever."

"I called it *The Soul*. An adolescent outpouring. Not worth reading."

"Oh, but I'd like to read it. Where can I see a copy?"

"There are one or two copies in a carton in the Bridgewater attic, presumably. But I'd rather you left it alone."

"What became of the hundred copies printed?"

"I sent away thirty or forty to my friends. The rest I left on the shelf of the boardinghouse where I lived."

"Oh, Van Wyck! Let's go and see if we can find the boardinghouse. There might still be a dusty pile of them somewhere."

He laughed. But we did walk to the street he had lived in, to find that the house was no longer there. All the more urgently, I resolved to hunt up any remaining copies of *The Soul* as soon as we were home.

On that same day, in Berkeley, late in the afternoon, a young postgraduate student, a stranger, arrived by appointment to call on Van Wyck. I gave the two men tea in our small living room and I noticed that the student carried in his brief case to set it beside his chair. After tea the brief case was opened, and he took out a slim yellow pamphlet. "Do you recognize this?" he asked Van Wyck. He held it up and I saw the title:

The Soul. An essay toward a Point of View.
San Francisco 1910

I glanced at my husband, who said nothing. But I thought he was not displeased.

"You can see what the price was," the young man said, and he pointed to a figure in pencil in one corner. "It belongs to the university. A rare item. They let me have it briefly."

"I'm so glad you brought it," I said. "The first time I've seen it." I smiled and took it into my hands.

The moment was to come when I read *The Soul* carefully, slowly, as it required to be read. This was not until after my husband's death, when, at last, three copies turned up among his papers. As I finished the reading I saw in greater fullness the origin of those qualities which had endeared him to his friends, his acquaintance, to strangers: his gentleness, his lovableness, his freedom from guile. He had early become intent on the matter of the writer's conduct, on his work and the aura which must envelop it to keep it pure. After urgent deliberation, a search for verity, he thrust aside the desire to please, the need for playing a game, while his life became more than ever a sober undertaking. And I, reading his words fifty years after they were written, had found the plan, the explanation, laid down in that short essay written during the dull months when, a youth, alone, he sat in his boardinghouse room waiting for his bride.

Truly we cannot be less than tender, serious, merciful. To caress life with its little fragile offerings of light, to reject nothing but the fixed forms of half-truths, to learn without cynicism, to see through everything as one sees through a crystal, to be in solution, in perpetual readiness, to be as responsive as mercury, to have instant sympathy with everything in the very moment it comes to our attention, never to think ourselves small because the universe is large, to be conscious of ourselves only in moments of growth, to quit nothing until we have begun to see the nobility in it, to wait and hope and dream until the whole world has become vibrant with sense and the apparency of things has melted away and we see in everything a connection with everything else, meaning with meaning—surely this, or something like this, might be truth. . . .

Presently, almost without warning, we were en route early one morning for the San Joaquin Valley of growing vineyards and, thus, for Connecticut. A golden time it had been for us, as, indeed, so much in our lives seemed made of gold.

We talked as we drove, moving along hillsides that held their fruited burdens downward toward the valley, and we mentioned this past happening or that, recalling recent memories that stood brightly behind us. I spoke of Jeffers, who had won my heart and my mind. Van Wyck spoke of the letter he had just received from President Nathan M. Pusey, of Harvard, an invitation to accept the Doctor of Letters degree in June from his alma mater. This had brought him a contentment made, I could see, from the sense of labor rewarded, from loyalty to bygone days, and, even more perhaps, from the surprise of a gift unexpectedly bestowed. Indeed, the occasion lying on ahead in Cambridge, as it was presently to be encountered by my husband during the warm days of June, became a confluence of circumstances which unrolled like some well-contrived parchment in his willing hands. There were, first of all, the duties he had been asked to assume as chairman of the Phi Beta Kappa Society: the opening address from the platform of Saunders Theater, the ritual of presiding. Following this, soon after, came the ceremonies connected with the Harvard graduation and the bestowal of honorary degrees. Van Wyck was in excellent company here, surrounded as he was, among others, by Archibald MacLeish, by the young painter Andrew Wyeth, by

Harvard's ex-President James B. Conant, and by Konrad Adenauer, come from Germany to receive his citation and to make an impressive speech. "A devoted man," Van Wyck called him. But the summit of that day proved to be the glowing fact that Helen Keller also received a degree. She, the first woman whom Harvard had thus honored. In advance, because of a strictly held secrecy veiling the names of honorary candidates, we had not known that she awaited the event with Polly in Boston as we ourselves waited on the opposite shore of the Charles River in Cambridge. A great happiness to Helen and to Van Wyck when, finally, they confronted one another in this fresh guise. The two days of festivities were entirely agreeable, we were to find, situated once again within the pleasing bounds of Cambridge, where a value continued to be placed on the enhancement of the mind and where policemen used the broad "a" and were on intimate terms with Harvard professors.

Acoma, a pueblo in New Mexico established by the Tewa Indians three centuries back, we encountered on the drive home between Gallup and Santa Fe. Van Wyck was eager to see this spot because it had served as background to Willa Cather's story "The Mass at Acoma," in *Death Comes for the Archbishop*. We turned off the highway on a Saturday morning of April, striking southward for twenty miles along a crude road of packed sand until we reached the base of sandstone cliffs, rising three hundred and fifty feet toward the sky, which held the town and its two-towered seventeenth-century church. This church of Acoma we knew to be just as its Indian devotees had built it, stone upon stone, carved ceiling beam ranging parallel beam, each one carried on men's patient backs the long way across the country from far Mount Taylor and upward along the face of the cliff to the chosen spot.

The climb for us, though unencumbered, was difficult enough. Leaving our car in the valley, we began the ascent on a crude and treacherous path of stone while vast clouds gathered, darkly converging above our heads. Moments later, without warning, we were startled to perceive an Indian boy who watched our progress from behind a cleft between two rocks. He pointed to another path, a longer one and almost obliterated by drifting sand. We followed his direction, taking it slowly, making but small progress because of altitude and exertion, and we reached the summit at last to be received by a middle-aged Indian woman in a flimsy cotton dress who took us in charge. She walked us about the wind-blown streets, past row upon row of untenanted two-storied houses of stucco having narrow doorways barely negotiable to the human figure. These had belonged to the four hundred souls who had lived here at the town's inception. Today, but five families occupied it, and only on the days of high feast did a priest climb the rock to celebrate Mass in the church. It was a mournful place. Almost no one moved in it. A woman carrying a bag of groceries passed us as we entered the church. I wondered how far she had gone to buy them. She flashed a quick smile at our guide but did not glance at us. I felt we were invisible or had taken the form of ghosts. Even the children did not stare. The day grew dark, the sun almost overwhelmed by clustering clouds, and we did not linger before the church altar. I thought of the story of Friar Baltazar flung to his death here from the rock by the Indians, and a feeling of dark apprehension gripped me as we returned to the street, where the wind grew more and more turbulent. Searching Van Wyck's face, I saw that he too had a sense of foreboding. He stood still, took out some money, and paid our guide, and in silence we moved to the edge of the cliff where the downward path began. The wind was now formidable, blowing dead against us, and it was difficult to cover our faces to mitigate the sting of whirling sand. The walk back to the car was an affliction.

On the highway once again, we headed for Santa Fe. Before us, along the horizon, a pink cloud appeared to rise from the ground, and soon we discovered that it was, in reality, a whirlwind of copper-colored sand moving to encircle us. During three hours Van Wyck drove on, car windows tight shut, lights on full, a sinister glow in possession of the frantic world, groping his way along the white line that divided the road—a life-saving line it proved to be.

For this was an authentic dust storm of the West. We arrived at last in Santa Fe and entered heaven in the form of the La Fonda Hotel. An unusual greeting awaited us as, on our way to the desk, we came on a glass-covered case in which books were displayed for sale and among them were Hamilton Basso's *View from Pompey's Head* and Van Wyck Brooks's *Life of John Sloan*. Reward after labor, symbol of the familiar and of rest.

That evening we spent with Oliver La Farge and his wife and the Karl Larsons, he an accomplished craftsman in wood and metal. At the moment, Larson and La Farge were at work on a book dealing with the Indians, a subject which had absorbed La Farge during the many years he had lived in New Mexico. His origins in New York and Saunderstown, Rhode Island, and his youthful education at Groton School, had early established another sort of background from this present one, and it seemed, as he talked, that a certain dichotomy existed between the two, one difficult to bridge. Confiding in me over a nightcap he said: "I don't know what it's all about, this business they call 'leading one's own life.' I've never been able to get it straight." Van Wyck, I noticed, remained silent, his battles behind him. Had he not begun to fight them as a boy of twelve, seeking in Europe his basic direction, and was not the final assault won when he emerged, a whole man, from his years of abstinence and melancholy within sanitariums? I was sorry to leave the charming La Farge house, the beautiful Indian rugs decorating the walls, the Mexican crucifix standing among the books in Oliver's study, the exotic flowers, but I felt gratitude, once again, for the guiding purpose in our own lives, for the continuity which goes far to assuage the burdens of existence.

Palm Sunday shone quietly along the Santa Fe streets, the storm of yesterday become a hazard surmounted. Van Wyck and I walked slowly toward the Cathedral, the great church of Willa Cather's Father Latour, who had built it when he was archbishop of the far-flung diocese. He had sent to France for the young architect willing to carry out his plans, and together the two had made the simple edifice of stone, with its "golden face" which grew upward in the spirit of "good Midi Romanesque," reminding Latour of the churches of Auvergne, his place of origin. It possessed an aura of peace, and the "steep carnelian hills" at its back were an enduring protection. We spoke of this story as we walked to High Mass on that Palm Sunday morning, of the poignance of Willa Cather's writing, and I thought of Father Latour's last days here, lying in his small office close to the Cathedral on a cot covered with the nuns' fine linen, while he meditated on the past and allowed the future to do with him as it wished. The Mass would have pleased Latour, a full-blooming pageant celebrated before the altar, a "ballet," Van Wyck called it, enacted by the bishop on his throne, his assisting priests, and numerous candle-bearing, incense-swinging acolytes. Mexicans and Indians predominated in the densely occupied pews, and although the service continued for several hours, it held the unflagging, the passionate accord of each.

Leaving the comfortable Fonda, the tree-shaded spaces of Santa Fe, the becalmed presence of its Cathedral and its tales of the past, we set out once again for home. We had been invited to have lunch with Witter Bynner, poet of the Southwest and for long identified with New Mexico's cultivated inhabitants. As always after a protracted separation between Van Wyck and a writer friend, the fresh meeting brought more than surface contact and the immediate exchange. Bynner received us in his garden, where Chinese lanterns and tinkling bells swung from tree branches. He shared the house with a friend, and it was filled with superb ornaments: jade, bronze, wood-carving collected over the years. But although he was surrounded by so much luxury, Bynner's existence as a writer and lover of books held the aspect of tragedy because of the threat of coming blindness. He accepted his equivocal position with a dignity and reserve which made for understatement, even for the ignoring of personal suffering. It was impressive and touching. I was glad, before we parted, to be able to thank him for a poetical rendering he had made some time earlier of the philosophy of the great Chinese Lao-tzu, a small book become my companion during the

comparatively empty years which unrolled before my meeting with
Van Wyck:

> If the sign of life is in your face,
> He who responds to it
> Will feel secure and fit
> As when, in a friendly place,
> Sure of hearty care,
> A traveller gladly waits.

A few more days of unremarkable driving brought us once again
to our village. Not the least of my pleasure on the journey home
had been my proximity to Van Wyck, learning history from him
as we went, laughing over the jokes we shared, lamenting the
problems that beset mankind. As is usual when two are on the
road together, there were disagreements over route and direction.
At these moments I wished to make inquiries of passers-by while
Van Wyck was intent on working things out unaided and requiring, oftentimes, long minutes to do so. Apropos of the differences in time as we moved east from one zone to another, he
begged me to desist from all questioning. "No use asking anyone
at what point the clock changes," he said. "Time is eternal to all
men." Once, we were caught for several hours on a narrow road
behind a car that dragged a U-Haul trailer. The driver of this
vehicle, a young man with a family, was careful and considerate,
and if we passed him occasionally, we were invariably pleased when
again he caught up to us. "Astonishing how fond you can become
of a fellow you've barely seen and never spoken to," Van Wyck said
with a smile. Such were the pleasures of the road.

XVII

Transmutations

O N January 7, 1956, we found ourselves possessed of a stateroom with outside balcony on the *Saturnia*. Above, on one of the ship's upper decks, a table in the sun enclosure became the daily working area for Van Wyck, who was engaged in writing the second volume of his autobiography: *Days of the Phoenix*. He established himself here each morning after breakfast and became as much of a fixture as the life-saving boat in its berth beyond him. Such was his concentration that passers-by left him alone, and during the ten days of our passage he was rarely interrupted. One man, genial, large, in plaid sport shirt and checkered cap, stopped at the end of several rounds of walking to say: "I guess I know what you're up to. You're writing an article or maybe a story. Which is it?" Glancing shyly upward, Van Wyck said it was to be a book. "Will it be a best seller and what's the title?" "I've not given it a title yet," Van Wyck answered, "and I doubt if it will be a best seller."

"Oh, don't you never give up hope," the stranger said encouragingly, and patted Van Wyck on the shoulder before walking away.

The *Saturnia* made two ports of call before setting us down at Naples. At Lisbon, from a sight-seeing bus, we had a view of the city, of its charmingly uniform eighteenth-century houses, their façades a soft blue, pink, or green, and we were attracted by the facile uses of Moorish tile and the flourishing state of semi-tropical verdure. The stop at Palermo enabled us to see the Cathedral of Monreale wherein the interior of mosaic, pliable as velvet in appearance, was full of the grace of angels floating in golden beauty. By contrast, isolated, somber, a head of Christ was woven into the apse: substance and solemnity in the midst of splendor. Standing beneath, we were brought to earth by the murmuring voice of a shabby little man, a guide, worn coat collar upturned against the chill of early morning and persistent damp. Aware, doubtless, of some possible sympathy in the person of my husband, he told us that he had lived for many years in the city of Boston. "There's no place like the land of liberty," he said with melancholy, hand outstretched to receive the soiled hundred-lira notes Van Wyck offered him.

Our parting, at Naples, from passengers aboard ship included that from a young relative of Van Wyck, Edith Brooks, a great-granddaughter of the Brooks cotton merchant whose portrait hung in our dining room at Bridgewater. Her husband, Oliver Brooks, was not congenitally a part of the family. By a pleasant coincidence, the two were on their way to spend the winter at the Hotel Flora in Rome. They must come often to the Academy on the Janiculum to see us, we said. Van Wyck had not known them before this meeting and I had been somewhat startled during the first days at sea when a beautiful young woman approached my husband to place her arms about his neck, saying: "I'm your cousin, you know." We became very good friends.

After we had visited Pompeii and Paestum a brief period of time remained before we were due at the Academy in Rome. Van Wyck was eager to see Amalfi and Ravello again, having visited them as a boy. So we set forth. Leaving the bus after the spectacular drive between Salerno and Amalfi, we descended into the square and were at once encircled by porters, taxi drivers, and the general public, all striving to be heard. Van Wyck left the situation to me, and in my halting Italian I uttered the words: *"Ravello, vettura."* I believed I had asked for a car, but a light carriage drove up a few moments later, pulled by a horse with nodding plume. Our bags were grabbed by the youthful driver and stowed beneath his legs, while from inertia and inability to enter the conversation about us, we found ourselves established on the gently swaying seat. A long, slow climb was before us, Ravello not even in sight, and the road wound relentlessly upward. After ten minutes in the *vettura,* while the horse strained to keep the pull at the required pace, I got out. The driver assured me that this was not necessary, but I walked beside the carriage all the way, about four miles, while Van Wyck, knowing that the climb was forbidden him, remained where he was. Feeling more and more lively beneath the brilliant sun, I essayed a conversation with the driver and learned that he was twenty-two years old, that his marriage was contracted for, that he would take his bride to the altar in two years, and expected to have ten children. I glanced at Van Wyck and saw that he was amused at what was taking place. He looked very grand in Homburg and Burberry, upright in solitary splendor with his menials below. *"Questo signore e un re,"* I announced to the driver, and he jumped in pleased surprise, turning to stare at my husband. I was obliged to explain that Van Wyck was not, in reality, a king, that he merely had the air of one. Presently, I began to pity the horse, who had been granted no respite, and I asked the driver to pull up for a moment. In answer, he shook his finger at me. *"E molto forte,"* he said, and went on to tell me that the animal ate plentiful meals of spaghetti accompanied by wine. "Does he really drink wine?" I asked. "Very much wine, especially vermouth," the boy answered. Hearing the words *cavallo, spaghetti, vermouth,* Van Wyck called down from his throne that he and the horse shared similar tastes.

We immensely enjoyed the three-day stay. Our room overlooked the Bay of Salerno, with terraces of trees and flowers immediately below and the blue mountains beyond, deep as lapis lazuli. Over our liqueurs at evening, Van Wyck had some converse with the elegant and cultivated landlord, who told us that one had but to dig with a spade anywhere in the vicinity in order to turn up archeological treasure, and he arranged to have a seldom-visited church across the street opened that we might see the multi-colored mosaic pulpit, more lovely, he said, than the famous one of the cathedral. Our return to Amalfi, finally, was by car, through the kindness of John Aldridge, the writer, and his wife, whom we had encountered for the first time in the Cathedral Square and who, at that moment, were living at Ravello. In Amalfi, Van Wyck had chosen to go to the Hotel Luna, an old Franciscan monastery visited by St. Francis himself, situated on the sea, close to the town. This, in lieu of the more modern hotel on the hill above, for the reason that he had been at the Luna with his mother, brother, and grandmother during that productive trip when he was twelve. Later, as I read his boyhood journal, which I'd not been permitted to see when we were together, I found a reference to his stay: "Ames and I went to Ravello on donkey back. We saw the fine pulpit." At the Luna Van Wyck and I were placed in rooms barely wide enough to hold a bed. His written comment as a boy had been: "The old cloisters are very interesting and we slept in the monks' cells." He was indeed re-creating a slice of his past, in 1956. On leaving next morning we were shown the room, a large one at the corner of the building, where Ibsen had stayed when writing *A Doll's House*. Van Wyck was much moved at the sight: the round center table, chair drawn close, the scant surroundings, the persisting aura of St. Francis, and the gray sea on a cloudy morning out beyond the casement.

The arrival at Rome was made easy by the Academy, which sent its car and competent chauffeur to meet us. The car seemed to me, as we drove from the station toward the Janiculum, the one stable object in the city, such was the sense of dislocation made by a first sight of Rome's monuments. Every period of history appeared and disappeared as we flew by: broken arches, crumbling statues, fallen stones, a small and lovely ancient temple caught in the midst of motor traffic and set irrevocably apart from any of its kind, its origin. These unallied elements, these pressures of disorder were to become in time familiar, even alluring, but they were at first difficult to assimilate as an ill-chosen meal. Of Rome, in her book *Rome and a Villa,* Eleanor Clark was to say:

The city has its own language in time, its own vocabulary for the eye, for which nothing else was preparation: no other place was so difficult, performed under the slow action of your eyes such transmutations. . . .

At the Academy on the hill, with these transmutations far below us, we were received by the Mason Hammonds, who took the place, just then, of the director, Lawrance Roberts, and his wife, absent in New York. The Hammonds, of whom we saw much, continued to be kind and helpful, as was the Princess Marguerite Rospigliosi, the Academy secretary, a spinster of ancient lineage obliged, untraditionally, to supplement her slender income. Our apartment, a large one, was situated in the Villa Aurelia, a spot tied to Roman history by Garibaldi, who had occupied it during the 1849 revolution against the French for the freedom of Italy. Our living room of lofty ceiling and marble floor held a small wood-burning fireplace, and adjacent were a bedroom, bath, and kitchen. From the terrace one looked down over Rome, and here tables and chairs set beneath clipped trees seemed to promise long hours of happy converse with friends. Our initial glimpse on a day of warmth delighted us but did not prepare us for the rigors of the coming months, did not inform us that we should rarely be able to sit out of doors. Attached to the apartment was a capable but wholly domineering servant, Assunta, a middle-aged woman of bulk and character, wife of Giuseppe, the porter at the lodge. He it was who swung back the gates when we arrived by car, bowing low as if to greet eminence, an act convincing enough to turn our heads, mine rather more than Van Wyck's. As the weeks wore on, Giuseppe and my husband, although unable to communicate linguistically, became friends, and it amused Van Wyck to come on Giuseppe in a chair on the lee side of the lodge reading a translation of Mickey Spillane, which in pride he exhibited as being his favorite author. Assunta, meanwhile, took charge of our breakfast and our dinner, refusing to use our kitchen, which she said was *"molto brutto,"* carrying the food on a lengthy open-air trip, shawl-wrapped, like a swaddling babe, in her arms. Luncheon, when we were not in the restaurants of Rome, we ate with our fellows in the main building of the Academy. We were to make special friends there with Louise Talma, composer, at work on the score for an opera whose libretto was written by Thornton Wilder; with the Ralph Ellisons, he the author of *The Invisible Man,* and with the various members of the Classics department. This department was then headed by Professor William Dinsmore, of Columbia and Athens, expert in Greek archeology. Among the other fellows of that winter were Miss Gisella Richter, attached to the Metropolitan Museum, and Miss Marti, a slim lady from Switzerland whose learning and enthusiasm drew the younger scientists to her small apartment, where they sat about the floor in never-ending confraternity.

Not long after our arrival a plague of sorts afflicted various occupants of the Academy, a form of bronchial pneumonia, serious in its impact. At a lecture on the temples of Greece given by Professor Dinsmore during a dark afternoon and attended by a bevy of holy nuns, upright and decorous in the front row beneath their coifs, he was obliged to make the sad announcement of the death from pneumonia of Gisella Richter's sister, her intimate, her alter-ego. I thought of the mediaeval rites bestowed on the dead by nuns resembling these. Their presence seemed grimly opportune. A lesser victim, incapacitated, nonetheless, for several weeks, was Mason Hammond. Our Assunta also had a severe attack, while Van Wyck and I succumbed for a week apiece. Van Wyck's cough had a sepulchral sound but he recovered with speed in the way that he had. Because the fireplace of our elegant apartment functioned poorly, smoking when the wind blew, I had borrowed several electric heaters from an American friend, recently gone home, and one of these we placed beneath my husband's knees when he sat writing, wrapped about with a steamer rug. The others were continually in use for the reason that this winter in Rome was the coldest, we were told, that the inhabitants had known in fifty years. Icy winds swept downward from Siberian wastes, the tramontane, and snow fell over the Janiculum. The poor sought shelter on the lee side of the Roman walls, and my heart went out, as well, to the large population of priests whose tradition did not permit the wearing of overcoats.

Our sight-seeing was curtailed by the cold and also by Van Wyck's working hours. He was unwilling to forfeit the morning routine, and after lunch, according to meridional custom, museums and churches were closed during the siesta, reopening at the chill dark hour of four, when it was best to be at home. On the more propitious days we went forth to view the grandeur of Roman monuments, stopping in to warm ourselves at the Caffè Greco, traditional haunt of artists and writers, where, seated on a worn leather bench before a small marble-topped table, we drank cups of their *cappuccini,* a mixture of coffee and hot milk beaten to a froth. Here, Van Wyck quickly became a part of the background and he studied with interest the portraits of former patrons descending the years, unforgotten, many of them, through their books and their painting. Another spot of our liking, on a larger scale, was the Trastevere and its small cafés, to which we returned often, these in the ancient Jewish quarter just below the Janiculum. Here, the streets were overrun with human beings because of the dampness and cold within the buildings, and ground-level doors stood open on the rough cobbles, the shops of tailors, shoemakers, woodworkers. Above, women hung out clothes along balconies while children were everywhere, playing with an intensity which helped to keep them warm. A major portion, for us, of this Roman winter was the recurrent pity we felt for *"il popolo,"* the poor of the Eternal City. Symbolizing pity, a dream of mine one night, its background the Trastevere, concerned a small boy who sat on a curbstone in passionate grief. As I watched him, wondering, a little girl, his friend, explained that his cat had died. "Yes," said the boy, looking up, "she died yesterday and I buried her. They die each one after another and I must bury them all." The Piazza di Spagna and the famous steps leading down to it were poignant in another way because of the small house at the foot of the steps where Keats had died in his narrow bed in a little top-floor room beneath a ceiling of blue and gold while a fitful flame threw its shadow along the surface of the stone floor. Even the bright flowers of the market below the house, the anemones, boughs of almond, lilacs, could not obliterate the memory of that death, that life. "He died of a broken heart," Van Wyck murmured, "his work unrewarded." And we went together to do homage, standing hand in hand beside the poet's gravestone, on a hillside of the beautiful English cemetery at the borders of Rome. There was also the visit we made to the Pantheon, where Van Wyck became morose before Raphael's sarcophagus, muttering: "Dust and bones, dust and bones . . ." until I drew him out into the sunshine. Here, he was distracted and charmed by the battalion of cats sleeping and fraternizing among the hollows and passages along the outer walls of the building. A tradition of many generations.

From the Janiculum we were apt to approach the heart of Rome by bus. These were much crowded, but the crowd we found to be courteous and helpful in directing us on our way. I was always given a seat by some polite man, and once a woman stood in order to allow Van Wyck to sit beside me. This, he could, of course, not accept, and there was a byplay of bows and the doffing of my husband's hat. Something in Van Wyck's countenance drew people to him: first, the rather startling combination of black hair, white moustache, and high color. There was also the effect of his personality, his essence, a compound of the unassuming, of heedful manners with a freedom from guile that approached the ingenuous. The one untoward happening of that winter took place shortly before our leaving Rome for Tuscany, when my husband's wallet was removed from the breast pocket of the jacket he wore beneath his overcoat. We went often to the restaurants of the city, a continual lure, but it was difficult for Van Wyck to restrain himself from eating more than the prescribed daily amount. His passion was spaghetti, and a single order of this dish, as served in Italy, went far beyond the requirements of one person. He persisted, nonetheless, enjoying himself entirely, making up in outer warmth and inner padding for the long hours of chill work in our apartment. At the Restaurant Ulpia, built into the Forum ruins, when, one day, Van Wyck placed the usual order, he was roundly reprimanded by the waiter, a commanding person: "Why you Americans order spaghetti, spaghetti? The same ev-er-y day. Ever the same. This is but one of the many pasta we serve you. Why not order to be brought a *cannelloni* or a *tagliatini* or a *lasagne*? Then you learn something." In terror at the possibility of an argument, Van Wyck acceded and ate his *cannelloni* as a small boy would eat the spinach set before him by his mother. We did not return to the Ulpia.

One afternoon, in a snowstorm turning to rain, we slopped in galoshes through the space intervening between the Villa Aurelia and Louise Talma's studio, to meet Thornton Wilder, who had come to Rome in order to hear the score that Louise was currently composing. They hoped, between them, that the opera might be performed during the year following, in Germany, where Wilder's work was much in demand. The studio, an inviting place, held a Steinway grand piano, stacks of music books, and a group of chairs about the open fire. A small party had come together, and with the aid of Martini cocktails mixed by Wilder, we were very gay. In company as he was with sympathetic friends, Thornton's darting phrases of wisdom tied to humor vibrated like the wings of a hummingbird in a summer garden. Louise played some of the score, and we felt ourselves very much in the modern stream. At parting, Wilder kissed me on both cheeks, Roman fashion, and he promised Van Wyck, who had earlier requested this of him, that he would write a tribute to the memory of Thomas Mann, who had died during the year, to be read at the autumn meeting of the Academy of Arts and Letters. He had hoped to avoid spending the time on it, he said, but Van Wyck's masterly letter of request had won him over. He went on to speak of the method used by Van Wyck in writing his book *Scenes and Portraits—Memories of My Youth,* the first published volume of his autobiography, saying that Van Wyck's aversion to drawing attention to himself had placed the subject of the book largely in the background. "There's no arrogance like modesty," Wilder said, a phrase I enjoyed because of its drawing my husband down, momentarily, to the plane of the ordinary mortal whose self-love is more openly apparent.

Van Wyck's seventieth birthday we celebrated with flowers and friends and their fanciful offerings. From the Wheelocks in New York, at early morning, there arrived a box of roses, conveyed through the auspices of Phyllis's Roman cousin, and in the mail at noonday he found the words sent by Chiang Yee, written in the beautiful script that Chinese tradition had taught him:

Confucius said that at 40, he had no more perplexities. At 50, he knew what was the bidding of Heaven. At 60, nothing he heard disturbed him. At 70, he could follow the dictates of his own heart.

In late afternoon, with the help of Florence Hammond and Assunta, magnificent in pearl earrings and a black dress, we managed a surprise party for Van Wyck around our hearth when twelve or fifteen of us sat before the well-stoked fire sipping brandy and eating birthday cake. The young Brookses were among the others, having driven through the lodge gates in their Thunderbird, to Giuseppe's joy, and bringing generous offerings of fruit from Sicily and the Strega liqueur which Van Wyck so much enjoyed.

In early March the Calders turned up for Sandy's exhibition in the little Obolisco gallery of the Via Sistina. We attended the opening, so crowded with humanity that Van Wyck said he felt as if he were riding in one of Rome's buses, where, a few weeks back, his pocket had been picked. The mobiles, small, delicate, hung from above us in rainbow colors like so many sprightly young fairies with magic wands. The Calders themselves, in contrast, stood stolid and impassive below, Sandy with crimson cheeks, tousled white hair, and expansive girth, an undisturbed entity; Louisa like some Roman matron in a mantle of regal red, aloof, handsome, unsmiling, as in dignity she received the adulation of the company. We afterwards learned that because of the success of the exhibit, Sandy was followed about the streets of the quarter by a crowd of admirers with their cameras. Before their departure for Saché in Touraine—an established base for them now that their elder daughter had married Jean Davidson, son of Jo—we met the Calders at noon one day in the apartment they had borrowed from friends. Here, the furnishings most apparent to the eye were the coils of Sandy's metal wire with the pliers and other tools he used to manipulate it, and the huge basket of varicolored wools required by Louisa in crocheting her magnificent rugs. We had been invited to lunch at Sandy's favorite restaurant in the Trastevere. Its owner was an enthusiast for art, and the walls were hung with modern pictures, a kind of gallery in extension. Here, Sandy was very much at home, and the smiling waiters hovered about him laughing at his floundering bursts of Italian, his speech becoming less and less comprehensible as the contents of a big, wicker-covered bottle of Chianti gradually disappeared.

In the course of a visit made us by Dorothy Whyte, Van Wyck's stepsister and a Catholic, we received tickets for one of the large audiences with Pope Pius XII. When we arrived in the great Hall of Benediction, the places nearest the papal throne were already taken and there was little to be done save to stand immobile in the crowd, while from the rear we were pressed by the men and women and children who continued to arrive. Immediately surrounding us was a German-Swiss contingent, broad, lusty people and solid as so many bars of iron. Several of these, arriving late, wishing to join their comrades, thrust themselves forward in determined fashion to stand immediately in front of us and to block any possible view of the throne. It reminded me of a story told me

in my childhood by my mother, who, as a girl in Germany with her
invalid father, on their way to Schwalbach for the cure, had been
rudely pushed from the steps of a crowded train by a German,
who unconcernedly mounted in her place. I was pressed close
against the high-mounting figure of a man who would not move
when I made a sign, and he suddenly seemed intolerable. With a
few whispered words to my husband I turned away and managed
to make a path toward the back of the hall and well out of the line
of vision. Here, I joined three priests who stood reading their
breviaries in a quiet corner, an oasis. I set down my overcoat and
bag, from which I removed a book, and leaning against the wall, I
began to read. The book was Henry Dwight Sedgwick's *Marcus
Aurelius,* a study of the great Stoic and, although the god I encountered here was a Pagan while that of the others in that vast
assembly was a Christian, I felt the spirit of each to be the same,
a spirit concerned with self-abnegation and the betterment of the
soul. Presently, I heard cries of *"Il Papa!"* and from my corner
I saw a man of circumspect gesture, small white cap on the back
of his head, gesticulating in his high-borne litter, just as the photographs had told me he would appear. He went to sit on his
throne, and I back to my book while, during the hour that followed,
his voice intoned a speech delivered in four different languages. I
could not distinguish the words and so remained engaged with
that far pre-Christian era in which the Stoics had laid down their
tenets, the four cardinal virtues: *prudentia, temperamentia, forti-
tudo, justitia.*

We set forth on a day in late March, one of the rare days of
benign sun, to drive to Florence, where in Settignano we had been
invited to stay at his villa, "I Tatti," with Bernard Berenson, the
scholar and art collector who when a young man had helped Mrs.
Jack Gardner in the choice of her collection at Fenway Court in
Boston. Berenson was now ninety-one years old, and during several
years he and Van Wyck had been in friendly correspondence, for
he was a philosopher as well as an art expert and his mind was
remarkably clear and true. The two men's tastes and sympathies

were similar, and both, I believed, looked forward to this meeting. To provide us with transportation on the trip we hired a small Fiat, and driving, on the morning of our departure, through the involved traffic of Rome and so on out into the countryside beyond, we might have been slum dwellers joyfully spilled into the unusual luxury of trees and meadows. Among the towns we visited on our way was Assisi, where in the church of the Franciscan Convent a young priest became our guide to the frescoes of Giotto. He seemed no more than a boy—come from Illinois, he told us—a slim figure in his black cassock, skirt swinging as he strode, head held high in a kind of defiant determination. He seemed imbued with the spirit of St. Francis, holding to an inner vision that made his eyes two burning emblems of faith, and his voice rang in a kind of triumph when he pointed to a garment of gray wool, glass-encased, saying: "That is the robe worn by St. Francis on his pilgrimages."

At Perugia I chiefly remember the impression made on us at dusk when, after a day's study of the town's great painters, Perugino, Raphael, Pisano, we set out on foot through dark tortuous streets to discover the whereabouts of the Oratory of San Bernadino. Descending a long hill, slipping, sliding in a downfall of rain, we came in semidarkness on the church, its polychrome façade by Duccio lovely in its rainbow tones. We stood for a long moment, marveling at Duccio's skill, when to the sound of dripping rain was added that of singing voices from within the church. We entered to perceive a gold-brocaded priest at the altar, acolyte in attendance, while below on choir benches ten small boys sang the vespers to the accompaniment of a harmonium. They were in kneeling position, wearing jackets that seemed pitifully short and thin in the permeating dampness of a wet evening in the empty church. It was perhaps their singing that kept them warm, for their voices went to the heart. Van Wyck and I forgot our own chilled state in the joy of listening to sounds fresh and true that rose in purity to the glory of God and the angels. We lingered there until the end of the service and the departure of the small saints, scuffling, running, forgetful of angelic strains.

Our way to Florence was resumed next morning, and as we passed a sign on the road pointing to Cortona, on a hill above us, Van Wyck exclaimed: "'The Muse of Cortona,' the only Etruscan easel picture. I wonder if it could be here." I turned the car, and we took the long curving way upward, on a quiet Sunday, toward one of Tuscany's lovely hill towns, to come, presently, on a high world where the air seemed purer, the sunshine brighter. We parked our car in the public square beside a group of boys spinning their tops beneath a stone balustrade that held them in from all eternity: sharply descending slopes of olive and grape plantations reaching to the plain far below. People in the streets were returning from Mass, and, with that sense of elation born of the idea that few of our countrymen had preceded us here, we mingled with the crowd on our way to the Etruscan Museum. Arrived at the head of an arduous flight of granite steps, we reached the entrance to find the girl in charge entertaining her young man at the open door, a warmer spot beneath the sun than any within. We entered, braving the chill unheated rooms, and immediately we were rewarded: for, confronting us on its easel stood the renowned picture which we sought, the "Polymnian Muse." Van Wyck informed me that the portrait had been delineated in encaustic, and I stood before it wondering. It was vibrant and telling, as though recently painted, the face of a woman who possessed a handsome and reflective countenance of balanced composure, eyes widely spaced, a lock of her dark hair falling over a shoulder, and her small high breasts through the gauze of her dress sensuously suggestive, deeply appealing. Van Wyck was delighted with her beauty and pleased with new discovery; the keeper of the museum was delighted also because of the knowledge displayed by *"il signor Americano."*

Several days were spent in Florence at a hotel on the Arno within walking distance of the Palazzo Vecchio before we drove, finally, to Bernard Berenson's I Tatti, arriving one afternoon at teatime. Immediately, there began a pleasant pampering of our persons, a concern for our possessions, which, in retrospect, has been as difficult to forget as, at that moment, it was impossible to withstand. Our small Fiat was taken from us, to reappear washed and polished, our clothes were unpacked and pressed, shoes polished, and, in our rooms, two bedrooms and a sitting room centrally heated, the blinds were closed at evening and fresh flowers were brought us each morning. Breakfast we ate in our little sitting room beneath walls hung with gold brocade and holding small treasures of painting by Nattier and Longhi, the Venetian. Servants were assiduous, silent, skillful, and quickly responsive to our conversation.

The arrival at 5:20 that afternoon had given us exactly ten minutes in which to wash our hands and appear, according to request, in the living room at 5:30 for tea. We were to find during our stay that the hours for meals, for walks, for saying good night were fixed and that it behooved us to be accurately conscious of them. At tea, on our introduction to I Tatti, we found ourselves alone, at first, with Miss Mariano, Nicky, hostess and long-time companion to Berenson, whose outgoing, all-inclusive ways were immediately appealing. We were irresistibly drawn to her, as we had been told we should be. There appeared, presently, a heavy, dark man in navy-blue corduroy, an Italian painter who had made the official portrait of the young Queen Elizabeth not long after her accession. He was engaged just now on a drawing of Berenson. Then, suddenly, noiselessly but inevitably, as a shadow moves along a wall, Bernard Berenson entered the room. And a shadow he remained, slim, diminutive, lacking any corporeal dimension but marked by the authority of his presence and the sharp focus of his eyes. He greeted us and went to sit in a high-backed upholstered chair while the butler carefully wrapped his legs in a steamer rug. Several young people came in, Americans who were spending the winter in Florence. They gathered about B. B., as he was called by his intimates, in affectionate conversation, and they drank the tea handed them by Nicky. When they had gone, Berenson signaled me to a sofa corner beside his chair and to Van Wyck he indicated a chair on the other side. This was to be our formation during the hours we spent together, for, along with his advanced age, Berenson had become rather deaf and it was necessary to speak clearly and deliberately in order to make oneself heard. At 7:30 he stood, unwrapped the rug, and without a word left, not to reappear until the hour of dinner, eight o'clock, in dinner jacket and black tie. His pattern of arrival and departure was always thus, except that before going to bed he bade us good night.

On the next morning we were taken to the library, which was situated in a separate wing and as extensive as though it belonged to a college. Radiators placed below the bookshelves kept off the damp in these pleasant, well-lighted rooms of many windows where a corps of young women labored at sorting and cataloguing. Their taskmaster was the Baroness Alda Aurep, Nicky's sister, a persevering, yet gay and informal lady, plump, handsome, even passionate at times, I suspected. She was altogether without the traditional aura of desiccation that hangs over many a librarian's desk. In fact, I found a resemblance in those two sisters to the characters of Chekhov, their background in part, as it was, the Baltic provinces. This feeling was substantiated at an evening party in the house of the Baroness, nearby, when after dinner I entered with Nicky and came on the servants playing with a cageful of exotic birds, the soiled dinner plates and linen lying about untouched while, abovestairs, their mistress and her friends argued the merits and demerits of the Pope, an interminable battle of words carried on in the manner of the Russian story writers.

The library at I Tatti, with its important collection of works of art, was, in those years, the core of Berenson's life. He felt, he said, that it might serve to justify his existence. Van Wyck was less interested in the assemblage of fine books than in the exchange of ideas. He and Berenson had much to say to each other out of the varying experience of their lives, the burden of their thought. One of my husband's beliefs was that human beings made of the same basic stuff, of the same intensity or involvement with ideas, would almost certainly come together, without effort or plan during their lifetime, drawn by some invisible magnet. This had happened to these two men, and as the brief days passed they sat side by side unaware of the rest of us, who came and went, embroidering outer boundaries with needles pliably held. Only on politics did they now and then disagree, Van Wyck being the greater liberal of the two.

The mornings we had to ourselves. Nicky was much engaged with household duties, plans for guests, with her voluminous correspondence. People came often for lunch or dinner, and the visits of house guests were carefully apportioned. B. B. himself lay in bed to a late hour working on his catalogue of Italian painters, an all-encompassing task which he was intent on bringing to a close before being overtaken by any possible illness. At a quarter to twelve each day, however, we were summoned by Berenson's valet, who asked us to meet his master in the lower front hall in order to join him on his morning walk. Outside, an ancient Ford station wagon waited, in the charge of a receptive and knowing chauffeur, and presently the three of us entered to be driven to some point designated by B. B. We descended, then, the two men, canes in hand, on either side of me, to walk briskly at Berenson's pace for half an hour before returning to the house for lunch. Among the several walks, I remember one that brought us to a great gaunt quarry above a still pool of sinister aspect, a setting for Dante's Inferno. This, said Berenson, was the quarry used by Donatello and several other sculptors of the Renaissance, and it seemed to me, standing there under lowering skies, that I was face to face with the inscrutable source of nature from which man must ever carve his way to order and symmetry. Not far from the pond a small lodge had been built for holiday occupancy by Queen Victoria when she came now and then to Italy. She had enjoyed, evidently, being confronted with the essence of things.

Meanwhile, as background to all the rest, Van Wyck and I were steeped in the beauty of Berenson's possessions at I Tatti, surrounded as we were by Italian primitives, Chinese bronzes,

Egyptian sculpture. The pictures were hung along living- and dining-room walls and in hallways, while the sculptured pieces rested on table tops placed in casual fashion, as the average householder decorates his table surfaces with photographs and cigarette boxes. In one large unheated gallery were kept the chief treasures among Berenson's paintings that they might remain in the best condition for posterity, namely Harvard University, which was to be the beneficiary. The grounds were also a part of our pleasure, a diversified spread of green tended by gardeners engaged in clipping hedges, pruning olive trees, piling debris into a cart drawn by a pair of white oxen.

We departed one morning from this world of perfection, entering, first, our host's bedroom to give him our thanks in farewell. With Nicky in attendance, he sat propped against a density of pillows, writing his journal in the widely spaced, almost ephemeral hand that was his, and, although he was frail as a seared leaf, prey of any wind, his staying power seemed not to falter. An extraordinary man, we told each other, my husband and I, driving off into the ordinary world of everyday.

Arrived back in Rome, we found that several of our fellow members on the Janiculum had gone to Greece for the Easter holiday and the population of the Academy was thus sadly diminished. But Louise Talma was there to greet us, and under her knowledgeable guidance we attended the pre-Easter services in churches of several denominations: the great and mighty Sant' Giovanni in Laterano, where we watched the ceremony, primitive and traditional—the blessing of the oil. At the church of San Anselmo we saw Christ's symbolic washing of Simon Peter's feet, while the music accompanying this rite poured out in the beautiful Gregorian mode, sung *a cappella*. The service in a small Greek-Catholic church resembled one in a private chapel attended by family and retainers: parents and children tossed jonquils and lilies and violets on a candlelit canopied catafalque which resembled a doll's house, and the brocaded priest officiated from behind a grille, partially concealed by curtains of purple velvet. Our devotional participation, in which the music was a major part, ended on Easter evening when we were taken to the large Russian-Orthodox church by our painter-neighbor from Connecticut, Henry Schnackenberg. Here, beneath soaring vaults lit only by candles burning in the mists of incense before the great ikons, we listened to the singing of the male choir, and I thought of the many who had prostrated themselves here in joy or grief.

We set forth one day, again in the hands of Schnackenberg, to spend several hours in the workshop of the Italian Bureau of Arts, where damaged frescoes and paintings from various churches were sent to be repaired. Sometimes the repairs were minor, the filling of cracks, the washing away of layers of damp. More often a major reconstruction was necessary, as in the case of the Mantegna frescoes from Padua, almost demolished in the war under the impact of American bombs. In baskets beneath work-benches and in cartons on table tops were gathered myriads of tiny irregularly shaped pieces that waited to be fitted back into the painter's original scheme: a jigsaw puzzle on a mammoth scale. In one room, hanging alone in a kind of triumphant glory, were three Van Dycks, large and splendid. They had come from Palermo and were soon to be returned, the work of restoration at an end. Difficult for the untrained eye to detect the patching, the repaint-ing in these apparently pristine canvases—fresh, they seemed, from the hand of their maker. We lingered in a room given over to a group of small panels of Duccio belonging in the Cathedral Mu-seum at Siena. Wonderful it was to be so close to these lovely things, naïf in feeling, complex in detail, to see the tender colors under a light that illumined their value in full. Leaving the build-ing, finally, I found myself giving thanks, as one does in quitting a hospital where a grave illness has been cured, for the magnitude of the healing processes we had witnessed.

At Number 32 Botteghe Oscure, Van Wyck and I drank tea in the Palazzo Caetani, ancient Roman palace inhabited by the present prince of that name. His wife was an American, a half-sister of Katherine Biddle, the poet. The Princess Marguerite Caetani had for years been a patron of poets and had established a magazine which she named *Botteghe Oscure,* publishing the work of the moderns, oftentimes as obscure as the arcade-hidden shops for which the street was called. The outer aspect of the palace, as we approached on that afternoon, we found to be as forbidding as a fortress, the courtyard dark and unornamented. We were accompanied by a porter to the interior lift, which set us down on the third floor, to be guided through a handsome great room filled with paintings, books, flowers, and so on to a little winding staircase of one flight upward, where our hostess awaited us. A quiet gray-haired woman with charming smile and intelligent eyes, she led us into a narrow book-lined room that gave out on a terrace overlooking the countless domes that marked the churches of Rome. Lovely to see them thus rising in solemn sobriety above an immediate foreground of blossoming azaleas and oleanders ornamenting the Caetani terrace. Presently, as we drank our *apéritif,* a tall, dark-haired young woman entered followed by a heavily built man of impressive bearing. These were the poet Theodore Roethke and his wife, who were just then staying at the Palazzo Caetani. Roethke was in Italy on a Fulbright grant, having arrived from the University of Washington, where he taught. The *Botteghe Oscure* published his work, Marguerite Caetani being a patron and admirer of his. Van Wyck also admired Roethke, but this was their initial meeting.

Three of the current Italian writers were introduced to Van Wyck during our stay. Ignazio Silone we met at the house of our cultural attaché. My husband liked and respected Silone, but any exploration of the other's mind was made impossible by the lack of a language in common. He was a withdrawn, silent man, even more so than my husband, and, in appearance, sad. Had he not, after all, in his book *Bread and Wine* been irrevocably bound with the tragedies of the Italian peasantry? A writer with whom there was no difficulty in communication was Mario Praz, who spoke fluent English. We were with him more than once, first at tea in his apartment in a former palace on the Via Giulia among a network of streets close to the east bank of the Tevere. It was a vast apartment dimly lit and crowded with consoles, paintings, bric-a-brac, settees, tall armoires, books. The richness of the scene in the semidarkness and the sense of seclusion brought an emanation of the Middle Ages, when men were persuaded into occult practices and strove to transform base metal into gold. Praz, a tiny man with flexible gestures and quick conversational exchange, possessed a compelling personality. By reputation he was Italy's best and most revered critic and he gave the impression of being rarely at rest, the deeper part of his being concealed beneath the facile. The third writer to be introduced to Van Wyck was Alberto Moravia. They lunched together, and Van Wyck went afterwards to Moravia's apartment, where, he later told me, Moravia had appeared an urbane man with a well-assimilated sense of enterprise and success. We were to be with Theodore Roethke again before quitting Rome. He had had a part in a series of lectures on literary topics arranged by the Fulbright program for an audience made largely of young Italians, and held in a magnificent old palace where Leopardi had lived when in Rome. Van Wyck spoke at one of these meetings, as did Arthur Mizener, while Roethke read from his works and those of other modern American poets. Following this, the Roethkes came for a drink at the Villa Aurelia. A huge bulk of a man, free-speaking, free-acting, he enfolded the world in his embrace, yet turned away in his work, from the facile, the complaisant. A true poet.

> In this last place of light, he dares to live
> Who stops being a bird, yet beats his wings
> Against the immense, immeasurable emptiness of things.

We made several excursions with friends to neighboring cities: Tarquinia, Viterbo, Orvieto, Palestrina. But it was our chief pleasure, here as elsewhere, to walk slowly about the streets without benefit of company. The Janiculum hill, our starting point, was captivating enough to hold us there on many a lovely afternoon of the lengthening, softening, days of spring. We stopped first to look down on the fair prospect of Rome, singling out those monuments familiar to us. Then we gave our attention to Garibaldi, mounted high on his fine horse of bronze in the Janiculum Square, at the side of his beloved Anita eternally charging the foe, pistol in one hand, babe held with the other close against her heart. Moving on down the hill we came to the little church of San Onofrio belonging to the charitable order of Franciscans whose monks inhabited the spaces above a sun-filled cloister. Here it was, some three hundred and fifty years ago, that Tasso died, driving from the city below to be wrapped in quiet among the gentle brothers during his last days. And the tree outside, beyond the gates at the foot of a small Greek theater, was still known as "Tasso's Oak." We went often to sit beneath it as the poet had done before us.

Our final awakening in the city of Rome brought the sun to shine on leaf tips, and the lovely warmth of the day that followed erased, almost, the memory of long dark weeks of rain and chill. We left at almost the same moment as did the Dinsmores, and, at a party given by the Department of Classics, we bade farewell to fellows and friends, those whom proximity and a shared experience had woven into our hearts. Our very special farewell went to the Robertses, the Hammonds, and Marguerite Rospigliosi, and presently we were seated once again in the Academy car bound for the railroad station and for Naples. Arrived at this, our port of embarkation, we spent a few days at the Hotel Lucia overlooking the bay, and Van Wyck was particularly engrossed each morning after sunrise in watching from our balcony the small fishing boats moored in docility, the white steamers slim, self-contained, slipping out to sea, while, at the docks, the cumbrous freighters, their water line of red along black hulls, awaited the lengthy business of loading.

With a letter of introduction from Mario Praz, we went into the ancient portion of Naples to visit the house of Benedetto Croce, adjacent to the Institute of Historical Studies, founded in his name for the benefit of scholars. We were guided through the door leading to Croce's house and received by his daughter, who led us from one book-lined room to another, a treasure of first editions and rarities of the past. Thence, we followed her to Croce's study, where the great man had labored at the height of his powers, a place of gloomy aspect furnished overpoweringly with an immense writing table. Near to this was a smaller room to which he had moved when he was older, one wherein a tile stove, mounting high, warmed him on the days of winter. Finally, we entered a tiny room with space only for a bed and table, the setting for Croce's last years. "To work without pause was Croce's necessity," said his daughter, telling us that he wrote and read continuously save for a brief afternoon walk and that he slept only between the hours of 1:00 and 6:00 A.M. I thought of Charles Doughty, author of *Travels in Arabia Deserta,* and his tremendous epic poem in six volumes: *The Dawn in Britain.* Doughty had gone Croce one better, interrupting his work only for one hour on Sunday afternoons, when in company with his daughter he bicycled along the Dorset lanes surrounding his house. My own husband, I reflected, was not far behind these two men in the temper of his work, his devotion. We descended now, he and I, and took our slow way through the noontime crowds thronging the Via Mariano Semmola, a street of fine old palaces become tenements. Here, we paused to look in the windows of bookshops while Van Wyck indulged his fondness both for slums and for books.

Thus we came to the moment of leaving Italy, embarking for home on the liner *Andrea Doria,* her final voyage but one, before she collided with another and sank to the bottom of the sea.

XVIII

Clear and Free

*T*O Gladys with love on our ninth wedding day."

Such was the inscription written on June 2, 1956, along the flyleaf of a new copybook given me by Van Wyck, a copybook intended for use as a journal, a continuing account of our life together. We celebrated the anniversary in Bridgewater with the Wheelocks, the first of our guests to arrive after the return from Rome. At dinner, with the few neighbors we had gathered in, we sat long at table over our chicken in casserole and the festive bottles of champagne, in discussion of politics, ethics, art. Occasionally the talk rose in fervor to reach stridencies such as occur when at heart the verbal combatants are in harmony, and it made me happy to see Van Wyck's animated countenance, his mounting color. At such moments the outer and visible man receded to the background: the orderly presence in neat blue suit, the whitest of collars, tie of Italian silk, the quiet grace of manner, all this forgotten in the power of his eyes, their vibration like that of the evening star fixed in space on a clear night of August. Then, his talk became exuberant, dominating, often interrupting that of the others, an entrance into the arena which was like the tearing asunder of a piece of silk, sharply letting in the light.

Following our first return we were, as always after a time away, surrounded by our numerous family. The Towers arrived from Santa Barbara with three of their children, and they were joined by Jean and her small Benny, my Jeannie, whose marriage to Benjamin Bradlee had most sadly become a thing of the past. But we had many joyous moments together. These included Van Wyck, who joined us in the games we played at evening, and Jean wrote me later that Benny "had been absolutely enthralled in watching Van Wyck when he laughed."

With the departure of my children it became the turn of the Brookses. In New York, we visited Kenyon, lying in a hospital, ill with hepatitis and very much alone, for his wife was traveling in Europe. We stood beside his bed, attempting to draw him out and beyond the all-encompassing pressures of illness, to help retrieve, somehow, a little of the vitality lost along the way, urging him to come to us at Bridgewater for his convalescence. But he made no promises, and it was not difficult to see that he preferred his own habits of solitude, relying, as always, on the inner man. Our attention went next to young Peter Brooks, at Putney School, in Vermont. We found him on our arrival to be much excited over the possibilities of purchasing a seventy-five-dollar Model A Ford, a car with a past. "She's beautiful!" he said. "You can't pass up a chance like this. She's fabulous!" The car was duly bought by the boy with funds extracted from the savings bank, and it remained in our company at Bridgewater and elsewhere during many years of benign discomfort. On the Putney evening, the real occasion for our visit, we watched Peter play the role of policeman in Molnár's *Liliom,* a performance of dignity and feeling.

From Putney we motored to Salem to call on Frank Stimson, who had spent the winter there in rooms above an antique shop. The owners had acceded to Frank's needs, to the setting necessary for his labors, and we were amused to see how entirely his great girth had been built in behind the table which held dictionaries and reference books as well as the Gargantuan typewriter able to transmit through its adaptable keys the tongues of all Babel. Frank had been compiling his dictionary on the Tuomatuan language used in the South Seas, going each day to the Peabody Institute, where his papers were being collected and organized. Also, he continued to be assiduous in tightening the slackened bonds between himself and the rather more strait-laced Stimson family, who were, at present, ready to forgive his escape to the Garden of Eden. A return of the prodigal. We bade Frank good-bye at the moment of his entering the hospital to undergo a major operation. With no close relative beside him at the moment of the ordeal we commended him for his courage. He replied that he had made his peace with the world and had nothing to fear. A heroic nature wearing the garb of an innocent.

To tea in our garden on the return home came our poetess friend Ruth Stephan and her young son: golden, slim, upright, both, after the pattern of their Viking ancestors, a handsome pair of second- and third-generation Swedes. With them was Marguerite Young, whom we had met when she and Truman Capote were at the Tates' several years back. She was now making one of her lengthy visits to the Stephans' ample house in Greenwich, where in a room at the top, protected as it was from invasion, she could add word upon word to the long-spread book, her novel in progress, *Miss MacIntosh, My Darling,* now in the tenth year of its writing. A substantial person with short-cut, straight-hanging hair, she wore a compelling smile and antique rings of semi-precious stones. We talked of the students in her writing class at the University of Iowa, a talented lot, as she described them, with much to say and divided, unequivocally, into two groups. One belonged to the "Bathtub School," which appropriated to itself the lower strata of behavior, the cult of vice. Mickey Spillane was their unnamed hero and Hemingway their god. To the alternate group belonged those who clung to emotions such as tenderness and devotion, who searched for philosophical attributes, and were

respectful of Freud and Jung. As teacher, Marguerite had encouraged the latter, gathering pleasure from their progress, and,
from both groups, she reported a high ratio of publication. Meanwhile she continued with her mammoth-sized novel, an important book, she assured us, to be published by Scribner's, and
running to more than a thousand pages. Miss Young was much
drawn to Van Wyck, whose own method of self-appraisal was the
inverse of hers and who sat, as she talked, silent in his garden
chair, courteous but somewhat remote, beneath the shade of a
hanging branch of magnolia. Within them both, nevertheless, was
a fecund perception of humanity in its bald state, of man as a
being looking toward hope.

The weeks went by, the months went by, confronting us with
one more Christmas, one more New Year, as Israel marched into the
territory of the Egyptians pulling England and France in her wake,
as Van Wyck worked on a book about American writers and
artists in Italy, and I corrected the proofs for a small book of mine
entitled *Gramercy Park*. To our Christmas party this year came a
young writer and his wife just then established in a house at
Bridgewater, the Norman Mailers. He had made a name for himself with his *The Naked and the Dead* and with *The Deer Park*.
We greeted him as a new member of the community; an intelligent,
quietly alert young man he seemed that evening, and we were
touched by his childlike pleasure in our candlelit tree. We were not
at that moment able to foresee the many unhappy circumstances
which were to engulf him and his wife later on. The Mailers were
the latest in a growing community of young writers arrived in our
village: Edwin Gilbert, William Styron, John Aldridge, and now
Mailer, a group of men who began as a harmonious unit but soon
traveled their separate ways. On the New Year's Eve of 1957, we
were bidden to a party given by the Styrons in their Roxbury house,
and it gratified me, as basically it pleased Van Wyck, to find that an
article of his, "Thoughts on the Avant-Garde," printed the previous
Sunday in the *New York Times Book Review,* had created a
favorable impression on the youthful writers present. They sur-

rounded him then, as he stood pressed against the wall, immensely embarrassed and at a loss for any words save "thank you, thank you," which he hurriedly repeated beneath his breath.

In February of 1957, Van Wyck's seventy-first birthday was marked in particular by the arrival of a letter from Lewis Mumford, a special delivery from Amenia and brought at 7:00 A.M. to the door of our small apartment at the Fifth Avenue Hotel in New York. It was a summary of sorts, relating to the friendship of the two men, and it summarized, as well, Van Wyck's influence upon his generation:

. . . the image of the true man of letters following his mission, is to stir up the creative forces in our life, in defiance of all that deadens the spirit. . . . If my own debt to you has been continuous . . . enlarging itself like a descending snowball over the years, what shall I say of our country's debt to you? Only that this land would be a drearier and emptier place, were it not for all the good things, the books, the places, the people, that your imagination and insight have brought to light. . . . You have enlarged both our past and our potentialities: and I anticipate the verdict of generations to come when I record my gratitude for all that your life and work has meant, and will continue to mean. . . .

The publication of Van Wyck's *Days of the Phoenix* in the early spring of 1957 gave the public the story of his life in the 1920's and ended with the chapter he had called "A Season in Hell." This opened the door on a period of protracted suffering which had lasted for four years when, in one sanitarium after another, my husband confronted and eventually vanquished the formidable thrusts of total darkness. It was a time, as he described it in his own words,

when the dome under which I had lived crumbled into ruin, when I was consumed with a sense of failure, a feeling that my work had all gone wrong and that I was mistaken in all I had said or thought. What had I been doing? I had only ploughed the sea. . . . I saw myself as a capsized ship at night with the passengers drowned underneath and the keel in the air. I could no longer sleep. I scarcely sat down for a year. When I napped for an hour or so I dreamed that I was about to be hanged. . . . The nadir of common depressions was a peak of mine. . . . One of the doctors whom I saw, and who had read *The Ordeal of Mark Twain,* asked me if I had considered that "reason or emotion" had been the determining element in my mind and work. . . . I replied, "Reason, I suppose," and the doctor smiled. He shook his head and walked away, and I saw at once that he was right. I had always worked by following my nose, I had never been able to think anything out but rather felt things out in a cumbersome fashion and, writing always intuitively, I was emotionally paralysed now. . . . The upshot was that, like Peer Gynt, I went back to the button-moulder. I was to spend four years in houses of the dead or, as one might say, the wounded . . . at Stockbridge, at Katonah, at White Plains and in England. . . . All I remember of Stockbridge now was a drive one day to Pittsfield and Herman Melville's farm on a lonely road . . . a house all in sagging disrepair. It was a dirtyish yellow, and some windows were broken. . . . Peeping through the boards that covered the windows, I saw some of his old folios within, together with a big ship's model on a bracket on the wall, which took me 70 years back to the day when this *exalté* had also undergone a season in hell.

Even after Van Wyck "came back to life and sailed out clear and free," he was conscious of standing on the brink of a "cold black draughty void." And over and above all the rest, there lodged in permanence, along with the feeling that his best years lay still before him, an awareness of those "dark caverns" which Hawthorne had known, "into which all men must descend if they are to know anything beneath the surface, or what he called the illusive pleasure of existence."

An evening spent with Jean Starr Untermeyer, the first of Louis Untermeyer's several wives, confronted us with the Colums, Lee Simonson, and the Geismars. Molly Colum was unusually quiet that night, in pain as she was from a wearing attack of arthritis. She remained in her corner, entering the talk now and then with the aloof pronouncements of a sage. Padraic, who now took the burden of conversation upon himself, emerged like a spring freshet from the mountainside, and Van Wyck, fit companion for his old friend

at moments such as these, retaliated in kind, the two playing together as ardently as two boys in a city back yard. "I think I enjoy
talking to Padraic Colum more than to anyone I know," said my
husband as, that night, we turned out the lights.

Before leaving town for Bridgewater, we went to Nyack, on the
Hudson, with Jack and Phyllis Wheelock and a young writer friend
of Jack's, by name Sonnenberg, to dine with Carson McCullers. We
were driven out by the young man on a wild evening of gusty
wind and rain which penetrated the doors and windows of his
ancient car, a car suitable to a poet. At Nyack we found our
hostess seated in a chimney corner of her house, a pale young
woman with smooth, short, black hair and a direct gaze. She
was ill from a disease which had partially paralyzed one arm, and
her eyes were marked beneath, as if by a heavy pencil, with the
dark lines of suffering. She was outgoing and affectionate and
confiding, telling us quite simply, over cocktails, of her solitude and
her longing to be married. She seemed to believe that Jack and Van
Wyck, to whom she turned, could without fail secure the missing
husband. I watched her, wondering how any husband could be of
use to her in the writing which was her life, in composing those
gaunt tales of poignance and sorrow such as the *Ballad of the Sad
Café* and *The Heart Is a Lonely Hunter*. At table she was aided in
the cutting of her food by a colored maid who later, at the hour
of nine, entered the living room, where we talked, to whisk her
mistress out and away, undressing her and bringing her back in
nightgown and wrapper that she might bid us good night. Through
the bedroom doorway, as we left, I had a glimpse of a large bed,
paper-strewn, locus of her working life, and I hoped that the play
she was in process of making might equal in success her recent
Member of the Wedding. It was being written for Julie Harris and
its title was to be "The Square Root of Wonderful."

The parkways of early spring were lovely in the lands about us
as we motored here and there on afternoon visits to our friends:
clumps of vernal benzoin, their flowers more delicate than those of
the forsythia, and maples that gradually opened their scarlet buds

to wash the tree in a mist of rose, while beside the curving borders
of streams the skunk cabbage unrolled their stubborn, purple heads.
On a day in early May at high noon we motored along the Saw
Mill River Parkway to cross the Tappan Zee Bridge and make our
way on the Hudson's west shore to the small and picturesque
house belonging to Elizabeth Shepley Sergeant at Piermont. Here
we found Robert Frost with Mr. and Mrs. Waller Barrett, he
a collector of writers' manuscripts, many of which he was in process
of giving to the University of Virginia. Frost and the Barretts
knew each other well, and Elizabeth Sergeant was at present adding
to her book of reminiscences of Frost, so the luncheon talk ran
freely, closely united as we were in the tiny house, with the Hudson
River as a binding background. Van Wyck, seated opposite Frost
and but ten or twelve years younger, looked a youth by comparison,
his quietly composed face almost unlined. At lunch I was beside
Frost. We spoke of the Bostonians among whom I had lived at the
time of my first marriage, and of Amy Lowell, an admired friend
of Frost in spite of her arbitrary ways. Of Robert Lowell, then a
young and rising poet, he spoke with possessive affection. "He's
one of my boys," he said. Later, reverting to the subject of
Barrett's collection of manuscripts, Frost said he had recently lost
a bet of one thousand dollars, a bet he had made in rather too haphazard a fashion. "But I had no trouble settling it," he said, "since
a man like my friend Barrett, here, will pay a thousand dollars for
a rough scribbled draft of one of my poems." Frost was soon to
leave for England to receive honorary degrees from both Cambridge and Oxford. He had managed well enough, it seemed to
me, to withstand the stresses of fame, to remain a human being
rather than become a personality.

A Sunday supper in the early summer of 1957 was a means of
persuading Katherine Anne Porter to our house. She had been
living near us for several months, shut away in a house on a hilltop
near Southbury, on the road to New Haven, without a car and
out of earshot of the telephone. "What courage!" I exclaimed. "No,"

she answered, "merely the means of getting my work done. I'd like to have someone share the house with me but only if that person would keep it in order and expect nothing of me as a social being." The book she labored on just then, labor of protracted extent, appeared difficult to bring to an end: *Ship of Fools,* to be published two years later with great acclaim and tremendous sales. We found her endearing and attractive to look upon, her hair gone entirely white and her very large dark eyes direct and appealing. Several of the younger writers were with us—the Edwin Gilberts, the William Styrons, and Norman Mailer—and it was an evening of general satisfaction, for we were bound by the camaraderie that exists between those of a similar and difficult trade.

An initial though unplanned summer holiday we were to spend at Boothbay, in Maine, a spot earlier known to Van Wyck when on another summer he and Eleanor had occupied a house there. We set out at the finish of an enduring wave of heat, when the sun's inescapable power seared the grassy stretches of our lawn and the windows of the house were day upon day closed against the torrid winds that blew as if they crossed a desert. The rear-guard engagement against forces from without had happened to coincide with an attack arisen from the buried places of Van Wyck's inner being. These occurrences, in the form of a clinging oppression based on the pattern of the long-endured, long-past "season in hell," came to thwart his spirit now and then, so that the daily order was diminished, its flowing function curtailed. At mealtimes, there was silence between us, or the few words which my husband spoke, his brow creased in trouble, were merely perfunctory. And entering his study at those moments, I found him seated in the visitor's chair that faced his own deep chair of industry, empty-handed, upright, his jacket and his hair in meticulous order, as though he awaited the coming of some important caller. Was it Mephistopheles whom he had summoned? On one of these afternoons, I went to him to ask if he would do me a favor. "Would you take me away to Maine?" I begged him. "Give me, give us both a change of scene?" He looked up and away from preoccupation as I moved to open the terrace door, thereby inviting the fresh breeze, and he fixed his eyes on me. For a moment they did not move.

"Maine?" he asked.

"Yes. I've not been there for a year and a day. I'd love to have you show me Boothbay. You like the place, don't you? You've spoken of it often."

"Yes, I like it. Not a bad idea, to get away for a short time."

"Oh, do let's go! All that delicious cool air. And you'll see fir and spruce trees in the distance instead of study walls."

"When shall we start? Tomorrow? I can be ready."

The plot was unrolling, and I was again able to breathe. Once the idea possessed my husband's mind, he was not willing to pause even for the purpose of securing a place to stay in a resort town during a summer month. "There'll always be something available," he said. "We won't have to sleep on pine needles."

We left in another deluge of heat, when the leaves of maples hung lifeless along the village green and the song of birds was stilled. Van Wyck in haste, his shirt wet with sweat, helped to pack the car, as though the escape into freedom might be denied us by delay, and he drove the first miles in much the same manner. At lunch in a Howard Johnson's, he faced me across a window table, and I saw that the insinuating spirit of fresh adventure had begun to bring him pleasure although the smile was still absent from his eyes. "I wonder what Howard Johnson's spaghetti might be like?" he murmured, menu in hand, and I welcomed the familiar joke engendered from our Roman past. We came in midafternoon into the town of Boothbay and stopped before the office of a real-estate agent, one familiar to Van Wyck, who entered while I waited outside. He soon reappeared walking beside the agent, who drove us to a cabin on a wide inlet of water rather removed from the main harbor. "Sorry I don't have the house you rented last time," the man said as we went, "but this is pretty close to it." Evidently, Van Wyck had made an impression. We stopped at a rustic bungalow, high-beamed, with a balcony that overlooked the water. Van

Wyck was delighted, almost exuberant, turning to me in eagerness for corroboration of his pleasure. Promptly, we signed a three-week lease. At the post office, when Van Wyck asked the postmistress if he could engage a box, she looked up at him, a broad-waisted woman of pleasant face, and said: "Oh, you're the writer. I remember you. You had box 129 last time. I'm sorry that's taken now, but you can have box 135."

We were soon established in the new quarters, the depression forgotten. The day began at 6:00 A.M. when Van Wyck, wrapped in the old bulky wrapper, went forth at sunrise, taking with him his book and the pot of early-morning coffee, which he set on the balcony rail at the side of the rustic chair lately become his own. Often, he called me from within to watch the glories of the sun's scarlet journey upward in the wide-flung sky. The air and the water were still, and we too were still while the pulse of our lives rose slowly along with the sun. Later, an itinerant lobster fisherman drove his boat over the water, and as the day went on, minor flotillas of little sailing skiffs appeared and an occasional aquaplanist, a young, slim figure standing astride his vehicle behind the swiftly moving launch, became the classic Roman Charioteer. An Indian trail curved among the spruces and oaks below the cabin, and we walked it on quiet afternoons, in single file, making our deliberate way while a confident kingfisher flew above our heads.

An excursion from Boothbay to Nobleboro we made in order to call on Henry Beston, he of *The Outermost House,* and his wife, who wrote under the name of Elizabeth Coatsworth. They lived just beyond a small village and up a long dirt road which, they later told us, was impossible to negotiate during the thaws of February and March. Also, in the dead of winter, they were frequently snowed in. This part of their existence, however, they loved, as who does not love to be confronted now and then with the rigors of frontier life? Their place was a dream spot, or so I felt it to be, not too far from a nearby scattering of farmhouses to be termed "lonesome," and yet possessing a cheerful kind of privacy, open to the wide sunshine, to gentle winds, to storms, as it stood on a low-swung hill overlooking the lake and beneath the spectacular clouds of the Maine skies. The house was painted red, and about the face of the front door there was carved ornamentation in high relief, painted white, the creation of one of Maine's craftsmen, a specialist in carving the figureheads for ships. It cast a beneficent spell over those who entered. Both Van Wyck and I felt this in no small way. The result of the visit to the Bestons and the return visit they paid us was the establishment of a new and pleasant friendship or, as Henry Beston termed it—he a great stickler for the proper use of words—"a close acquaintance."

The three weeks at an end, we returned to Bridgewater, our spirits edged with fresh green growth like that on plants which earlier had been pruned to the core. In September came the trip we had long planned, a stay at Wellfleet, on Cape Cod, in an unusual motel apartment designed and owned by Nathaniel Saltonstall, cousin of my children, who provided his guests with kitchen service as well as a central office where telephone messages were gathered so that we were spared a telephone of our own. Several old friends were nearby: the two brothers Biddle and their wives. Francis was then engaged in writing his memoirs, while George, active as always, was concerned with writing an essay on modern art. A friendship my husband renewed here, one dating back to the days of the *Freeman,* was that with Waldo Frank, the writer so much acclaimed in South America. In the past, the two had now and then done battle in the field of literature or had gone no more than partway to meet each other. Now, a new understanding appeared to fence them round, and on the afternoon that Waldo sat drinking tea with us, they eagerly talked for three hours.

On an evening before the Cape Cod stay ended, we dined with Edmund Wilson and his wife in their Wellfleet house. There was so much that Wilson knew, that his mind encompassed as poet, playwright, novelist, critic, it seemed hardly worth while to utter a word in his presence, and one searched dejectedly for a topic that might interest him, while a trivial utterance fell at his feet like a gust-blown willow leaf. Also, his unalterable countenance, oriented, often, in a direction other than one's own, did not invite confidence. One's ego suffered. But Wilson was attentive to Van Wyck's ideas, and the talk between these two flourished. After dinner, his charming wife, tall, graceful, and superior in all ways, of Russian-German origin and born in France, was briefly occupied with household affairs, and I was left to the two men, invited to sit with them in a back room giving off Wilson's study and holding books in Greek, Latin, German, French. There was also a section given over to Hebrew, his latest field of concentration, and he had been immersed here in Bible history through his study of the Dead Sea Scrolls. We were several times to return to Wilson's house before we left for home, and, presently, as he and Van Wyck established an understanding, I found my initial uncertainties giving way to a timid affection for him. And it amused me on our leave-taking at noon one day to find Wilson standing in his great bulk on the piazza clad in his pajamas. Seeing us, he came down the steps, one foot following another with graceful speed in a kind of meticulous gait of dancing-school tradition. Van Wyck got out of the car and stood, a little withdrawn, shy, yet with the manner of courtesy which was his: two dedicated men confronting each other. How difficult, how demanding, how desirable was the world of literature and how inexorable its effects on those who practiced it.

During our drive west toward home, we stopped at Brewster on a morning of windless sun to eat a supplementary breakfast at their charming Cape Cod house with Conrad and Mary Aiken. This meeting had been arranged at a party given by the Biddles, an instinctive attempt toward closer friendship between the poet and the critic, their relationship heretofore having been of the professional order, one in which the two men had not always felt a bond in common. The house drew us at once, a house with a clinging aura of the past. Its walls were hung with Mary Aiken's portraits, its furniture was of horsehair, and the best parlor held the bust of Conrad's grandfather on the top of an old-fashioned square piano with yellowed keys. Solemn and compelling, he maintained his dignity, as though still playing the role of Unitarian pastor to a New Bedford church. Our hospitable reception as the sun moved into the south, our talk over a breakfast of coffee, blueberry muffins, and jam, sent us happily on our way.

Awaiting us at the Bridgewater house at 5:00 P.M. at the end of our long day was Mahonri Young, elderly sculptor-etcher, born in Salt Lake City of the Mormons and grandson of Brigham Young. A humorous, caustic, but friendly old man, he was attired in wide, sagging pantaloons upheld by suspenders ill-concealed under his ancient jacket, and on his head he wore a wide-brimmed farmer's hat: Huckleberry Finn grown to an incredible age. With him was a young painter who had driven Mahonri from his house in Ridge-field to engage in a sketching trip. We greeted them, in spite of our fatigue, with simulated warmth, this a prerequisite of hospitality to the aging, an obligation practiced always by Van Wyck. Tragic, my husband felt, to toss away these last human years as of small account, to be intolerant of idiosyncracies, to overlook the plight, and oftentimes the charm, of a personality brushed with the lacquer deposited by time.

Padraic Colum telephoned us in late October to tell us that Molly had died, leaving him suddenly one morning as they sat engaged with a book they were doing together: *Our Friend James Joyce.* She had been wretched for some time from the pain of arthritis and she dreaded the prospect of invalidism and a future of possible poverty. Her death was a release to her but not to Padraic, who would long be desolate without her stormy yet familiar presence. The funeral Mass at St. Patrick's Cathedral was impressive for its solemn rites, and the attendance was noteworthy, many writers of the day going to pay their respects. Padraic himself, little more than five feet tall, looked a shrunken figure as he walked behind the great black coffin carried on the shoulders of stout men. I was able to feel the sorrow that emanated from Van Wyck, sorrow for the loss of an old friend, sorrow at the transience of life's unfolding, the certainty of its ceasing. "Sure and I saw the tears in Van Wyck's eyes when I passed him on my way to the altar," Padraic said to me later.

An event that overwhelmed us in that October of 1957 was the suffering of a cerebral hemorrhage by Polly Thomson, and her having to be shut away from the world, her active life curtailed. The stroke affected both eyesight and memory. She could not remember the names of her friends and was confused as to the passage of time, although her sense of values still held. Seated beside Helen as of old, she tapped out on her hand the answers Van Wyck made to her questions about the current state of the world, about the launching of the Russian satellite, the lag of scientific education in our schools, and so on. As Van Wyck said to me on the drive home, the minds of those two remarkable women, personal grief, illness or no, were always focused on the abstract, never on small or passing inconsequence. But there was something most touching in Polly's manner that day, in the wistful expression of her eyes, in the way she clung to us: a small girl seeking reassurance and direction as she groped for a path out of the woods and onto the main road. As for Helen, she was magnificent. She had entered the room with her customary dignity, gone to her sofa corner after embracing us, and sat, hands folded in her lap. But then I saw the change that Polly's illness had brought in her. Instead of the usual impulsive gestures, instead of a frequent and most charming search for Polly's hand, which for so long had transmitted conversation, keeping her in the center of events, she sat quietly apart, a figure of colossal resignation, an Atlas accepting the tragic weight of the world. It was only by the look of fatigue, in the way her lips were compressed, in the fleeting quality of her smile, the absence of glow—only by these means were we able to learn that Helen, even though so pre-eminently having "her soul to keep," was but mortal like the rest of us.

A happy note rang out at the end of the year in the marriage which united my young Jean with William Haussermann, Jr., Boston lawyer of equable, intelligent, and human qualities. It was a fine moment for me when my three New England children stood before the altar of the Unitarian church at Chestnut Hill, upright, serene, and handsome, all, as they took their respective parts in the ceremony. We bade them but a temporary farewell that afternoon, for we had made up our minds, Van Wyck and I, to move to Cambridge for the midwinter months in order to be near the Widener Library, where were the papers and books necessary to the biography of William Dean Howells now taking shape in my husband's mind.

XIX

Conversazioni

WE waited, during a January afternoon, for an hour or so in the lobby of the Hotel Continental at Cambridge, Massachusetts, like two immigrants, wrapped in our coats, packages in our laps, suitcases and cartons of books piled about our feet while guests from the floors above emerged from the elevators and others entered from the street to go upward. Presently, a familiar figure stepped through the revolving door and, in surprise, came over to greet us. He carried a florist's box in his hand.

"Why, here you are! How splendid!" he said. "I've come to welcome you to Cambridge, to bring you Josie's flowers. But is this as far as you've got?"

"Our rooms are not quite ready," I explained. "A woman with a sick baby whom they're moving to another apartment. It couldn't be done earlier, apparently. How are you and Josie? How lovely to have these flowers." All this in a rush of words as I smiled at the tall, handsome man standing above us, Dr. Henry Murray, professor of psychiatry at Harvard. Van Wyck, meanwhile, with a benign and slightly embarrassed smile sat immovable in hat and coat encircled by his burdens, but, as always, a figure to be noticed. It was to him that Harry spoke now, telling Van Wyck of his pleasure in a small book of his recently published: *From a Writer's Notebook,* a book of aphorisms, of precepts.

"It's stupendous! Prodigious!" Harry reiterated with the generous enthusiasm which was one of his marks. "How do you do it? How do you manage to go on as you do?"

Diverting the subject from himself, Van Wyck asked Harry a question:

"Are you able to get enough time from teaching in order to write?"

"Not enough, no," Harry answered briefly, looking troubled. It was he who changed the subject now, telling us that the Japanese scholar, Daisetz Suzuki, lived upstairs in the hotel; he led the Zen Buddhist cult, so much in evidence just then, among certain circles of the West. Harry said he was going now to call on Suzuki, and he handed Van Wyck a pamphlet issued by a member of the cult, a copy of which he had just then sent off to Dr. Carl Jung in Zurich, he informed us. He left us to go aloft, and not long after, we ourselves were carried upward with our possessions.

The small apartment was very pleasant, with its airy, fresh look, its broad windows giving out on a wide fence-enclosed spread of grass and a maple-protected house, foursquare, in the New England tradition, painted with the somber gray of Puritan dress yet vivid because of the continuing life within: a small oasis which would grow ever more compelling as spring came near. The pattern of our lives, established here to further Van Wyck's book in progress, differed from the one we had voluntarily set up during our eleven years together. It kept us apart at the hours of the working day, and this was not easy for me to accept, meaning, as it did, that I was much without the familiar presence, an enduring base from which to leap. Now, soon after breakfast, my husband left the hotel to walk across the Cambridge common as far as the Widener Library, where a study had been put aside for his use and where he remained writing and reading until late afternoon, except for the lunch which he ate, like any workman, before a counter. Meanwhile, my own daylight hours were spent either with my children or in renewing those friendships established during the Boston years of my first marriage.

A tea to greet our arrival took place at the Cambridge house of Mason and Florence Hammond, who had recently returned from their duties at the Academy in Rome. This party Van Wyck very much enjoyed because of the presence there of William James, son of the great philosopher, a delicate old gentleman of sensitive perception and acute mind. His wife had died a year previously, and he lived alone in the old James house. Of his uncle, Henry James, he said: "He wrote too many letters and many of them were not worth writing." "But his vitality was extraordinary," Van Wyck replied. "To have been able to write his books by day and attend to his correspondence by night." Another guest of the Hammonds was Professor William Alfred, who taught Anglo-Saxon at Harvard, a complex language more difficult to master, apparently, than Greek. Alfred, I decided, was a good name for one concerned with the Anglo-Saxon period. He later sent me a much-used copy of Richard Whately's *Elements of Rhetoric* published in 1866, this polite gesture following a conversation we had together on style in writing. A paragraph to which I opened drew my attention, a portion of a chapter entitled "Exhortation." It read: "There is an instance related . . . of a whole audience being moved to tears by a *minute detail* of the circumstances connected with the death of a youthful pair at the battle of Fontenoy; though they had previously listened without emotion to a *general* statement of the dreadful carnage in that engagement." Here was a challenge to any writer.

Before making his decision to spend the midwinter months in Cambridge, my husband had been aware of the hazards brought about by human kindness, of the possibly arduous hours awaiting him who did not go easily into company. Had he not somewhere written years before:

Why is "good society," or so much of it, insupportable, in spite of its charm of good manners, courage and grace? Because it consists so largely of people who . . . rationalize everything until it fits their pattern. . . . What did Ruskin mean when he said that "an artist should be fit for the best society and keep out of it"? In America, as Edith Wharton pointed out, writers and artists have usually fled from the world of fashion.

But the Bostonians, or many of them, had ever been assiduous in their attentions to Van Wyck. This, he realized, was in no small measure due to his books on New England. It had been difficult to persuade the New Englanders that he had not been born as one of them, although he doggedly clung to his identity with another portion of the East. "I come from Plainfield, New Jersey," he reiterated, "a suburb of Wall Street." His books continued to stand, however, as a means of identification, of association. "You have shown us our origins, our heritage," the Bostonians said. And so it happened that we were much with people, from the cocktail hour onward, swept along a most pleasant current, impossible to combat.

We went, on an afternoon early in the season, to drink cocktails with Charles and Patricia Warner, a bright young couple, he an instructor at Harvard. Here were Mr. and Mrs. W. H. Howells. We had been brought together because Mr. Howells, an anthropologist, was a grandson of William Dean Howells, whose life was at present so deeply engaging Van Wyck. Here, also, were the young Arthur Schlesingers, whom we had not met previously although he was already established as a best-selling biographer engaged at that moment on his life of Franklin Roosevelt. He was alert and slim and aware and he impressed me with the keenness of his perception. The shadow and the depths, however, seemed to be awaiting the future. I was glad to meet Schlesinger's wife, Marion, a talented painter of children's portraits and a daughter of Walter Cannon, author of *The Wisdom of the Body,* a book which possessed an enduring wisdom of its own. From the Warners' house, Van Wyck and I drove directly to the Arlington Street Church in Boston, where we parked our car under a still and icy night of full moon. In order to mitigate the impact of chill Puritanism sweeping us, we clung together as we walked to the entrance of what was once the old Federal Street Church, where William Ellery Channing used to preach. Channing's statue faced us across the street in the Public Garden, and now, in the shadow of the great man, my son, John Saltonstall, was to address a congregation gathered in the parish house. He spoke clearly and with a straightforward simplicity which seemed to please his audience, a speech which was a precursor to the many strewn along the path of the political career he prepared for.

On the next morning, a Sunday, Van Wyck decided to drop his work in favor of calling on his old friend Mark DeWolfe Howe, who lived in Boston's ancient Louisburg Square, where he gathered the fruits of his long literary life. He was at that moment ninety-two years old and confined to a wheel chair, but nothing had interfered with the perfect clarity of his mind, and he still delighted in good conversation.

"You look very well, Mr. Howe," I said from the sofa that faced his chair. "Even better than you did a year ago."

"That's what I'm told," he answered, "and it distresses me to hear it. The doctor gives me three more years but I don't want them. I'm ready to go at any moment."

"What a wonderful thing to be able to say!" I exclaimed. "I doubt if many people could."

Chiang Yee presently arrived in Cambridge for a few days, the same Yee, grown slimmer, his oriental composure even more pronounced. He took us out to dine with Dr. Suzuki, the Zen Buddhist established close to our rooms on the hotel's fourth floor. Yee had invited Dr. Suzuki's pretty young secretary and also a priest of the Zen order who derived from a monastery in Japan, a man with a beautifully chiseled countenance of calm. Dr. Suzuki was an elderly, shrunken, intensely earnest little person, able to speak, as well as to write, fluent English. His secretary, therefore, rather than being an interpreter, acted as worldly companion and nurse. She told me a little of her story as we sat facing each other at dinner. A girl in her early twenties, Miss Okamura had been interned with her family in California's Death Valley at the moment during the last World War when the Japanese of our land were, for security reasons, deprived of their possessions and held together in a vast encampment. "But I was happy there," she said. "I was six years old and I was able to make what seemed to me very beautiful gardens with the colored stones and plants of the desert." She possessed an engaging smile along with her composed oriental manner, and she attended with assiduous care to the needs of the important man who was her chief. The Buddhist priest, Hisamatzu, spoke no English, but his good will, combined with a gentle innocence, made him easily approachable. With him was an interpreter of rather limited linguistic powers who much resembled an American Indian in appearance. Our conversation had to do with their religion, with that particular form of Buddhism which was becoming a fast-growing enchantment to many in our land. None of it seemed easily grasped or easily adapted to our western mind, and we were told by Dr. Suzuki that only by means of prolonged study could the Zen philosophy be properly understood: a nirvana forever beckoning and always somewhat beyond grasp. At the end of the meal we all gathered in our sitting room at the hotel, and the talk, rather more relaxed now, flew about while the stolid interpreter took photographs of the company under the brilliant ceiling light. On leaving, Miss Okamura fetched from her kitchen an immense bag of oranges sent her that day from Florida, sharing them with us, and we exchanged our good nights with so much fervor that the entire floor rang.

Lovely for me it was to walk about the streets of Cambridge, as often I did, while Van Wyck worked at the library. I was reminded of Dublin, for in both cities there existed the aura of a university town, the potentials for mental excellence, the overflow of bareheaded boys and girls philandering in the streets between classes, the bicycles veering in complex and difficult traffic, the pleasant-faced shoppers, many of whom seemed to offer possibilities of new friendship. I enjoyed my strolls in the region of Radcliffe College and, walking south, I liked to linger before the fine, elderly houses of Brattle Street, those standing in the Bulfinch tradition of beauty and austerity which made one remember the lofty-minded, upright beings for whom they had been built. And I thought with pleasure of Van Wyck's description of life in Cambridge as it had been lived in the 1800's by Charles Eliot Norton at Shady Hill, "the gracious house with wide verandahs, surrounded by its rolling lawns, the beeches and the willows, filled with the clatter of crows, where the Cambridge circle met over a game of whist, for music or for conversazioni, suggesting the Dante evenings of the future." Now and then I went, by invitation, to meet my husband at the Widener Library in the study set aside that winter for his use, one named for Norton and holding his portrait. Here Van Wyck was lodged deep in the atmosphere of that enlightened time, while, day after day, he sat among the scholars in the row of studies, separated from the bookstacks by no more than an iron grille.

We dined one evening with the young Arthur Schlesingers in their Cambridge House and were happy to find the Edmund Wilsons there, briefly come to town from Cape Cod. Wilson we had seen the previous week when he dropped in at the Continental for a cup of tea with us, bringing his Harvard son, whose mother was Mary McCarthy, Wilson's second wife. He had talked to us then of the subject much on his mind, the plight of the Iroquois Indians who dwelt on a tract in the southwest corner of New York State and were about to be dislodged because of the advent of the St. Lawrence Seaway. Wilson had come into possession of ancestral lands in New York at no great distance from the renowned Oneida Community and he invited us to visit him there in July when he fled the Cape and the crowds of midsummer.

Toward the end of our stay in Cambridge, on a fair afternoon of late March, we drank our tea on the top floor of the Continental with Mr. and Mrs. Paul Sachs, he the great benefactor of the Fogg Museum at Harvard. It was a beautiful spot, an apartment composed of eight or ten rooms confronting the sweep of the compass, sunny, fresh, close to heaven, and holding a lovely choice of drawings from the Sachs collection at the Fogg, the finest single collection of drawing in our land. Then over eighty, Mr. Sachs had bequeathed it to the museum with the proviso that he might retain on his walls such pictures as he wished to enjoy. And so it was that we wandered from room to room in close proximity with Ingres, with Degas, with Tiepolo, Matisse, and Picasso, able to place a finger in quite offhand fashion on treasures of this magnitude. Perhaps, because "all beauty is akin," the drawings seemed to hold a tender camaraderie with the flowers placed about the rooms, the sprays of roses, sheaves of lilies, the daffodils of spring.

A final dinner took place in the heart of "the old Boston tradition," or old Cambridge, in this case, that region epitomized in many novels and tales, including Marquand's *The Late George Apley* and Santayana's *The Last Puritan.* Dinner was at the house of Edward Forbes, grandson of Emerson. He and his wife lived at "Gerry's Landing," in Cambridge, an expansive house forming a quadrangle with dwellings occupied by the younger family. There was also a greenhouse of unusual effect where plants grew on the second story above a darkened garage, so that driving up the winding hill, as we did after dark, we looked upon a blazing light suspended, apparently, in mid-space and falling on the flowers of amaryllis, clevia, and primrose. It was as though they were touched by a heavenly wand. The house proper, inside, held to an atmosphere of the country: floors laid with strips of India matting, furniture heterogeneous and unremarkable, bare floors unwaxed. We might have been beside the beach, sand brought in by untidy feet, faded parasols in a corner stand and all the rest. Indeed, the island of Naushon in Vineyard Sound, long a stronghold of the Forbes family, appeared to have set a permanent imprint on the manner of life here, the more so as, on that evening, we were fed venison killed at Naushon. Little by little, however, we became aware of treasure in place here and there along walls and on table tops: Chinese and Korean paintings of antiquity, ancestor portraits rich and deep in color, pottery from the beautiful early Tang period. There had ever been, I reflected, an intimate association between educated Boston and the orient, sprung, in the first instance, from the eighteenth-century days of the Salem-China trade. And now, Edward Forbes, long-time director of the Fogg Museum, carried on. Mrs. Forbes, also of the Boston tradition in the manner she had of speaking her mind, of going her way unperturbed, told us directly that she was not interested in the past, turning away from the talk of Emerson and family history. She was soon to set forth, she told us, on an expedition to Arizona, where she would confer with a specialist among the investigators of flying saucers, a man who counted these mysterious interstellar objects as emanations from a far planet. In the course of the evening Mr. William Jackson, of the Houghton Library, and Van Wyck were asked by Mr. Forbes to identify various faces in faded photographs and daguerreotypes among the Emerson family, these having been temporarily removed from a plush album on a nearby stand. Neither of the men was of much help, and my heart went out to our host, a gentle, ruminative man, who wore his hair brushed forward in a bang and who possessed the look of a questioning child. His playing at a game of nostalgia had not brought him the assurance he sought.

Our return home in early spring was enlivened by the presence of Frank Stimson. He had joined us in Cambridge when dismissed from the hospital, where he had gone for a check-up, and he was to remain with us until the day in early April when we bade him farewell in New York on the corner of Fifty-eighth Street and Madison Avenue as he boarded a bus which would drop him near the Yale Club. Soon after, he was to install himself on the slowly plodding ship bound for distant Tahiti. We had not been aware of finality at that parting on a day of sleet and rain, Van Wyck and I standing in the slush created by city traffic, as we waved to Frank, a massive figure on the bus step above. We could not know that we were not to see him again.

At home, a few days later, we drove to Westport to call on Helen and Polly, who, we hoped, might have somewhat recovered from the state which had so impaired her sight, her memory, her spirits. Sad to say, we did not find her improved. Arriving at the house, we came on the two, in the charge of a white-clad nurse, seated side by side in a sunny corner of an enclosed piazza. They were touchingly glad to see us, listening eagerly to our news, laughing at our small jokes. But in contrast to her former speed of light as she tap-tapped our phrases on Helen's pliant hand, Polly's present pace was halting, the slow letters formed with pauses between. It was Helen, now, who took the lead, became the teacher, the protector. With an expression of confidence and patience, she strove to help Polly in her fumbling attempts to communicate, murmuring aloud the words as one by one they reached her comprehension. And at the moments when Polly turned away, of necessity withdrew, Helen sat motionless, accepting life's inflictions, its wanton intrusions, with a dignity that could almost circumvent their power.

XX

Seven Maids with Seven Mops

$\mathcal{A}$S May of 1958 went rapidly toward June, our house in Bridgewater, inside a cordon of wood-and-rope barriers, was separated from village life, from its usual function during three days. This, for the making of a televised picture concerned with Van Wyck Brooks, with his books, his ideas, his philosophy. The film thus brought into being was one of several known officially as the "Wisdom Series," interviews with men and women whose names held an emanation of high accomplishment, of a "true and right knowledge and discernment": the dictionary definition of wisdom. Frost and Sandburg were among those already tabulated. Others were to follow.

On the morning of the opening scene, while Van Wyck and I were still at breakfast in the window of the dining room, an immense moving van drew up in the back driveway. This was followed by automobiles bringing technicians, property men, and, finally, two directors, a man and a woman, whom we were presently to know well. Under their orders the crew went to work with lively dexterity, removing furniture from the living room, stacking it in the hall and upstairs rooms, bringing in a massive camera on wheels, the sound units, and other equipment of motion-picture reliance. Our familiar room of everyday disappeared: tables, chairs, books, lamps gone; the well-polished hearth and-irons smeared with layers of grease to subdue their gleaming, while the view of trees and grass beyond the windows was obscured by lowered Venetian blinds. Nothing was to be included in the setting save our large sofa and accompanying coffee table, which were placed at the far end of the living room before a painted board depicting a rural landscape, one that mounted to the ceiling. Here, later, and for hours at a stretch, Hiram Haydn, Van Wyck's interlocutor, and he himself were pinioned side by side, in the interest of immobility, to the sofa legs. Hiram, publisher, editor of the *American Scholar,* a man of knowledge and tact, long associated with learning, with books, with the writer's craft, arrived each day from Westport in time to take his place: a happy arrangement but arduous. For, as the hours passed, it became evident that his role was the more difficult of the two, his the responsibility for keeping the talk alive, for discovering the questions best suited to the unlocking of Van Wyck's mind.

Twenty-odd men were assembled on the job of setting on tape the words spoken by these two, that they might be carried into the future, twenty men who worked there in our house for three long days. I thought of the Walrus and the Carpenter: "If seven maids with seven mops swept it for half a year/Do you suppose, the Walrus said, that they could get it clear?" The chief of the project, a man who arrived to stay only briefly, left the details, the routine, to a woman director, a most competent person. She stood without flinching, tall and thin as an asparagus spear, at work beside the camera on a taxing schedule that ran, usually, from nine to six, showing her exhaustion toward evening in small ways of acerbity while she released a little of the inner tension by unpinning a massive knot of dark hair, allowing it to fall about her shoulders. The crew, meanwhile, had a less restrictive time of it as the men took turns at the various jobs and, in free moments, sat out on the front lawn to play gin rummy, a most astonishing sight to the staid inhabitants of our countryside. My role consisted in keeping quiet and out of the way while the principal actors, Hiram and Van Wyck, faces smeared with pancake make-up, remained fixed slaves to the camera, a monster spewing venomous heat and light. Hiram was ever patient, malleable, and Van Wyck strove to do what was expected of him, becoming more and more engrossed as the discourse possessed him, as the goal to be reached came clearly into sight. I felt sure that his cheeks beneath the paste flamed high.

During the last morning, just before the cameras were shut off, I came in to say that lunch was ready. Haydn was questioning Van Wyck about his well-known aversion to Hemingway and Fitzgerald. "Can you explain this?" he asked.

"Well," Van Wyck said, "they were both boys. Hemingway was a boy and Fitzgerald was a boy. For that matter, we are a nation of boys. Our President is a boy."

At this point the cameras were abruptly stopped while a bland young man, one of the directors, went up to Van Wyck and dropped on a knee before him.

"Mr. Brooks," he said, "I wish awfully that you and Mr. Haydn would talk about the early influences on your work. That would be so interesting and we have so little time left. After the break, won't you begin there?"

It appeared that the young man had opened a pleasant path for my husband's further thought. It was obvious also that the reference to Eisenhower was to be eliminated. Van Wyck remained agreeable and apparently acquiescent. But after lunch, when the cameras were again wheeled into position, he opened the proceedings before Hiram had had a chance to question him.

"As I was saying, our President is a boy," he continued, as though he had not been interrupted. And the phrase remained in the final script.

The job came to an end, finally, the twenty-four hours of filming, with cuts, having been judged sufficient for a subsequent runoff of one half hour. The directors seemed satisfied, but they regretted, they told us, that the various components of the "Wisdom Series" had had to be made on a "shoestring." Only eighteen thousand dollars was allocated to each. We did not regret the removal of the street barriers from before our house, the reappearance of daylight in our living room, the loss of the painted trees, our own release from bondage. Some weeks later we followed the film on television at the house of a friend in New York, and it seemed to us, then, that the labor had been justified. I turned from the screen and glanced at Van Wyck, who watched himself with no more than mild distress as his voice rang out beyond us to reach any who would hear. "Pretty much of a waste of time," was his only comment.

A visit to Edmund Wilson at his family seat in Talcottville, New York, we undertook in August of that summer, driving along the newly completed Thruway, leaving it now and then when Van Wyck's interest in history and the human beings who had lived it impelled us toward some spot on a less-traveled road. There was, among others, a house near Amsterdam on the borders of the Erie Canal, one of several increasingly imposing residences built in the eighteenth century by the powerful ruler and trader with the Indians Sir William Johnson. Here on his vast New York acres he had lived a romantic life with his wife, the daughter of an Indian chief. I listened and looked attentively as Van Wyck led me into this man's existence, informed me of his unusual accomplishment. Also, en route, we stopped at Utica before the Episcopal Grace Church, imposingly designed in the Gothic manner by Richard Upjohn, who had been the creator of so many churches in our land and whose daughter Myra, a frail and appealing old lady possessing a beautiful use of the English language, lived as one of our neighbors in New Milford. There was, to my pleasure, our visit to the Utica State Hospital, "a grand building in the neo-classic style," the guidebook told us, built at the instance of the admirable Dorothea Lynde Dix, with whom I had become intimate in writing of her as one of the *Three Wise Virgins* whose achievements had been guided by the vision of William Ellery Channing.

At a late hour of the afternoon on a fine day, our sight-seeing at an end, we found ourselves on a plateau between far-reaching meadows of alfalfa that led us, finally, to Talcottville, where we drove through a street of ill-matched, inconspicuous dwellings to come to a stop at a corner bisected by a country road. Here rose a stone building of imposing form, Wilson's house. Of this we could be certain, for Wilson stood on the lawn waiting, with some impatience, for our arrival. It bore an authentic air of the 1800's and had been built to endure, built also with a fine fancy, the unyielding quality of the stone lightened by a delicate tracery of white-painted carved wood, while a graceful second-story verandah hung from the façade above the front portico. Wilson, meanwhile, immobile before it, appeared as one irrevocably attached to its present and guardian of its future. Elena Wilson came out to greet us as we left the car, and we were taken at once to our bedroom at the rear of the second story, square, high of stud, and equipped with the dark mahogany and walnut furniture associated with our grandfathers. This included an immensely tall dress cupboard, a wide bed, and a washhand stand with sprigged china bowl and slop basin. Our use of the washstand was intermittent owing to the recent installation of a bathroom off the hallway. This, and a few modern appliances in the rambling kitchen, were the only changes apparent in the house of Wilson's forebears, unless for fresh paint here and there. We found later that Elena had, herself, stripped the small dining room of its tattered paper and placed a coat of powder-blue paint along its walls in order, she said, to diminish the incipience of dampness clinging to a house of stone. The room possessed a little fireplace with coal grate, and into this she made a habit of throwing some of the debris of the day: paper, strips of cardboard, twigs, setting a match to it and thus inducing a brief, bright blaze when we ate about a circular table contentedly eying the fire and the pretty tufted sofa beside it upholstered in a frieze of vivid red.

This was the room, a small oasis, to which I became chiefly drawn, possibly because it pertained to Elena, to her hereditary European background, matching an air of elegance which, unconsciously, she wore. The rest of the house fitted her less well, its origins and hers remaining severely apart. Indeed, it was obvious that she was less happy here than in their home at Wellfleet, free of the ghosts adorning her husband's past. Wilson, however, had given himself entirely to the past. He led us about the grounds on that first afternoon to seat us beside him under a great dying elm, where we drank iced tea close to the flower bed in the back yard, a long untutored bed growing run-out phlox and one or two peony bushes and a few spears of hollyhock in a brave manner of continuity. The talk between Van Wyck and Wilson began as soon as they sat down and, no matter what the setting during our stay, did not readily cease: a persistent skirmish in which neither one managed to cripple the other.

For our entertainment, Wilson arranged that we lunch at the Oneida colony, the settlement initiated in 1850 by John Noyes, who, in the manner of other benign fanatics, envisaged heaven upon earth and hoped that this might be the more speedily brought about by a species of lofty selective human breeding, to be determined by a committee which would control physical relationships between the men and women members of the group. When this form of illicit love was interrupted by the arm of the law, Noyes fled to Canada, and the prospect of heaven was postponed. The colony was still much alive, however, its current charter in better keeping with our mores and its finances solidly backed by its connection with the well-established Oneida Silverware Company. At luncheon we were in the hands of Noyes's competent, handsome daughter and her husband. We were joined by one of the members who was a specialist on Indian life; this as a gesture toward Wilson and his study of the Iroquois.

That evening several of the neighbors came to dine. One of these, a professor of economics at Harvard, was well versed in the history of New York State, familiar with the events of its earlier

settlement and with the romantic and disastrous stories of those
refugees from political upheaval in Europe, many from the court
of France during the revolution, refugees whose names, for example that of Madame Scarron of Schroon Lake, had left an
enduring imprint on the names of towns and rivers of the district.
He suggested that on the way home we move through that upper
part of the state where man's losing battle with unrelenting nature
still haunted the deep gorges, the untamed, wooded slopes, and
he thought we might like to drive along a corner of the once
vast acreage presented to Baron Steuben by our young revolu-
tionary government in gratitude for his tenacious and generous
assistance.

When the guests bade us good night, Wilson took us across the
hall to the two rooms which he kept for his own use. The front
room was his study, holding a deep armchair, a card table strewn
with papers, and another piled with books. The back room was
furnished with a couch, where, in Elena's absence, he might sleep.
It was occupied now by a cluster of puppets representing Punch
and Judy and their retinue, and, mounting high, a classic-sized
theater awaited action, curtains drawn, a great gaudy shell cast
away at some earlier epoch in time. The puppets, limp and passive
in their familiar garb, lay abandoned and apparently forgotten.
This, plainly, was not their moment, and we did not press their
owner about past or future.

The drive away from Talcottville on a dark morning of intermittent squalls brought a brooding sense of the past, a sadness that
would not leave us. In vain I summoned the agreeable scenes of
the last few days: Elena's charming, firelit breakfast room; our
pleasant picnic at evening by the banks of the Independence River,
wading barefoot in the cool water, sniffing the odor of damp
fungus and pungent fir trees; the fair prospect of golden meadows
stretching away below us as we stood on the uplifted verandah.
Instead, come to haunt us as we went, was the memory of Wilson,
a solitary rain-wrapped figure on the lawn, half-awake in dressing
gown and morocco slippers while the continuum of the many other

days of rain, beating against the lonely valiant house, took their toll in our hearts.

So ended our midsummer saga except for a pause, on the way home, in Catskill at the house of Thomas Cole, one of the painters of the Hudson River School, who had lived and done his work there during the years 1830 to 1850. On what had become a torrid afternoon, we stopped here in order to please Van Wyck, who wished to pay a passing homage to the memory of a notable craftsman. We parked our car on the outskirts of a small summer-house wrapped in climbers and surrounded by trees and flower beds planted with coleus. At the large dwelling house a group of children and their mother sat on a piazza overlooking the river, and they invited us up. The mother made it known that the house was owned by her aunt, the granddaughter of Cole, who had lived here all her life. Presently, the old lady came out, small, white-haired, delicate, with bravely determined mien and an old-fashioned courtesy. She took us into the cool, dim, high-ceilinged interior and, by instinct deferring to Van Wyck and his instructed attention, she stood us before a quantity of shadowy landscapes hanging in semi-obscurity. It was apparent that her grandfather's best pictures had long ago been taken into the hands of collectors. But I was glad that this residue remained to her along with the family china, the Hepplewhite dining table, and her far-reaching memories. Outside, as we left, the younger generation, in rocking chairs on the piazza, sucked at popsicles and turned the pages of comic books, and, through a window opening on a small summer kitchen, the mother stood turning hamburgers over a kerosene flame.

At Sherman on an evening in late August, Van Wyck and I were among the fifty or so of his friends gathered to celebrate the sixtieth birthday of Malcolm Cowley. The weather was superb, with the wind out of the northwest, and a glowing light fell downward upon tree leaves and the intensity of green grass. It was a gay and loyal assembly gathered on the Cowley lawn:

writers, painters, journalists, publishers, librarians. A long white-clad serving table holding bottles of whiskey and gin had been placed against a background of shrubbery, and the pristine quality of the setting brought a kind of innocence to the carnival scene, as though shepherds had come into shelter above a stream to slake their thirst and exchange stories. Another celebration was a seventy-fifth birthday party given by James Laughlin of the New Directions Press as tribute to William Carlos Williams, the Rutherford, New Jersey, doctor who wrote poetry between attending his patients and who had been much celebrated by the avant-garde critics. He seemed touchingly pleased that Van Wyck should have come to the party. Many others were there to greet him, a quite splendid convocation gathered in two rooms before Laughlin's magnificent collection of modern French pictures. Before we left, a tall, bright young man, a frequent contributor to the *New Yorker,* attempted an interview with Van Wyck, who stood below him, cocktail glass in hand, cheeks a vivid red, eyes very much alive. In this encounter, I noticed that my husband had allowed impulse to dominate discretion, that perennial impulse inherent in his nature which, when he was a youth, John Butler Yeats had decried. He let himself go, on that afternoon, in his summary of a fellow writer while the interviewer took notes of each uttered word. On our way home, he was suddenly confounded, overwhelmed, disconsolate, and a letter was instantly dispatched to the young journalist begging for an erasure, for mercy.

The sad news reached us, on our return from an October trip to Canada, of Frank Stimson's death. Frank had written us from Tahiti of a threatened operation, of the possibility of cancer, but most of his information, hurriedly and scrappily conveyed, had seemed inauthentic, the more so as there had been several false alarms in previous years. So we had not taken it to heart. Now, he was dead. He had died on a Sunday at the hour when Van Wyck and I were on our knees in the chapel of the Ursuline Sisters at Quebec, listening to the lovely compline service. "Poor Frank," we kept on saying to one another. "So far away from his beginnings." We hoped he had been spared any great agony. We knew he had deeply loved his native wife, her long rose-decked hair falling about her shoulders, that she had been at his side. More than this we did not know except that much of his important work remained unfinished, that he had not lived to see it through, to acquire the fame due him. Years back, Van Wyck had written of Frank to Lewis Mumford: "Frank turns out to be the most exciting *scholar* I have ever met. He has a vitality and power like Agassiz's and he has put them both behind his Polynesian studies." These powers were no longer available. We were very sad. A month later came a letter mailed in Tahiti-Papeete from a friend of Frank's who wrote of the last days in the hospital. To the end Frank had buoyantly expected to live, and his wife, a confirmed Catholic, educated in the crude manner of her native island, where her father was king, and speaking neither French nor English, had been his continual support. Part of the letter brought us moving details:

. . . The funeral procession was so long that the casket was in the church and the service underway before the last of the cars arrived. Every pew was filled and the overflow crowd gathered in front of the church in Punaania. The Tahitian pall-bearers carried the casket from before the altar to the cemetery near the lagoon. The saddest part of it all was when Frank's beloved Tahitians sang their traditional farewell. His wife sat in a chair beside the grave, superb in her native dignity, and received the sympathy of those who tossed a blossom into the grave. I never realized before how majestic she was.

His wife disappeared not long after the funeral, gone, many believed, to hide herself away in the small island of her birth. In silence Van Wyck set the letter down, moving toward his study, taking refuge there in still more silence. I went to fetch my "Commonplace Book" to search for the insert placed in it eight months earlier by Frank:

Seven Maids with Seven Mops

Consciousness

With peril of loss
  not questioned, fully known.
Could we upgather, whole,
What we, perhaps alone
  in all the realms of Being unworthily possess,
  The essence, nothing less,
No dregs, no dross;
  The essence thrice-distilled of Consciousness.

If this were poured into a silver bowl
As beautiful as light
  (Call it our human Holy Grail)
Then held aloft against the threat of Night,
  would it avail?
Who knows? It might.
  If such a miracle could be
  Surely all men would see,
The very blind be struck with sight.

*(From James Norman Hall's personal
note-book-Papeete)*

Good Friday, 1958:
(typed by Frank Stimson for Gladys Brooks)

The Christmas of 1958 brought us the unexpected presence of Peter Brooks, who had shipped on a freighter in early autumn to seek his fortune in Italy, a precarious but ineradicable decision of his, bringing apprehension and sorrow to Van Wyck. The prospect of freedom and glorious new association in a foreign land had not materialized, as the boy wrote home of these things. There had been many shattered dreams, and he finally decided to return home, working his way on a freighter from Scandinavia to the port of New York. On Christmas Eve, without warning, he entered our front door to confront the tree standing lofty and magnificent in the bow window, embers still alive on the hearth, red curtains drawn. He set down his bag and paused at the broad entrance. "This is the most beautiful room in the world!" he said.

The intensities of winter, as "frosty winds made moan," drove us to New York, to the Hotel Grosvenor, at Fifth Avenue and Tenth Street. Our apartment was high above the avenue on a level with the belfry of the Church of the Ascension across the way, and its chimes each day brought a recurring pleasure to Van Wyck, who was ever captivated by the small adornments of traditional existence. We were often out of hearing of the Ascension bells, however, uptown in the houses of friends or attending plays, concerts, exhibitions of paintings. One of the excitements of that winter was the opening on Broadway of a play entitled *J. B.* by Archibald MacLeish. It was based on the book of Job, and its theme strove to establish in modern life a counterpart to the ancient Bible tragedy. The play was immensely popular and very moving to many people. Women wept as they followed the downfall of a prosperous family, as they watched J. B. reduced to his bed of ashes. A question put to Van Wyck by E. E. Cummings, who had not seen the play, seemed much to the point: "How could any sane man dare go into competition with this book of the Bible?" But the long run of *J. B.* spoke for MacLeish's success. We had been in conversation with the Cummingses on that particular day at their small ground-floor flat enclosed behind an iron grille in Patchen Place, where we drank tea and ate slices of bread and butter, English fashion, before a coal-burning grate. Cummings and Van Wyck had been acquaintances for some time, and I had known him since the days in Paris in 1922 when he came to lunch with a few French writers at my house in the Rue de l'Elysée. During these recent years Cummings had gradually changed his focus of interest from poetry to painting, discipline of another kind but equally relentless.

On February 16 of 1959, we celebrated Van Wyck's seventy-third birthday at a small dinner in Charles Brooks's great loft on West Broadway, a place resembling those primitive dwellings of northern Europe which, in early times, enclosed man and his livestock and his tools beneath the same roof. At the head of four flights of stairs, Charlie's shelter held a stone-walled room of wide dimension, to which had been appended a kitchen and bath. At the rear he stored the lumber and implements necessary for the chairs and tables and ornaments he was engaged in making for his clients. Since quitting California he had concentrated his superior talent on designing and constructing furniture. Seated with us before the fire were Julius Teller and Peter, as well as several of Peter's many friends, boys who flocked to the loft like humming bees. Indeed, in the dwelling at 506 West Broadway, near Washington Square, its master-owner in the course of his labors had so generously shared his prophetic wisdom with the young that they responded as though to the call for prayer. Pray they did not. Instead, they worshiped the muse, each his particular one: poetry, music, painting, sculpture, philosophy, or woman. They could worship as intensively as they chose, for here there were few rules or taboos unless against the commonplace or the unkind. Many of the fine precepts that drew them they learned by example.

We dined a few nights later with Isabel Bishop, the painter, and Harold Wolff, her neurologist husband. They sent a magnificent great hired limousine to convey us from lower Fifth Avenue to their ample house in Riverdale, and, on the way, at an apartment building opposite the Guggenheim Museum, the car also picked up Alan Dunn and his wife, Mary Petty, cartoonists for the *New Yorker,* agreeable and immensely talented, both. We had not known each other previously, but it was pleasant to exchange confidences with them, wafted as we were in the darkness for long minutes, beneath the night sky. At the Wolff house the dinner party flourished under the calm, detached manner of our doctor host aided by the charm of our hostess, her far-reaching and splendid collection of paintings surrounding us from the walls as we ate the very special food prepared and served by the Wolff's Chinese manservant.

In April, Van Wyck delivered a lecture before the members of the Corcoran Gallery in Washington. During the several previous months he had prepared for it, carrying the typed pages about, an unyielding and indigestible load lying athwart his heart. My own heart, when the occasion was upon us, underwent a turbulence difficult to tolerate. But this discomfort was succeeded, as always at these moments, by pleasure in my husband's simple and touching performance, one which seemed to draw the audience with something close to affection for his ingenuous manner. Being untutored in the art of the lecture platform, he lacked the veteran's approach: the polite introductory greeting, the opening joke, the crescendo and flourish embroidering the conclusion. All these were missing. Rather, he walked to the platform as though entering his study to go to work, placed his papers on the high desk, and began to read. When he had done he stopped, bowed slightly, poured himself a drink of water, drank it, and walked away, while, for the supplementary acknowledgment of applause, he was usually prodded by another for a return to the platform.

In Connecticut, a few weeks later, we had a two-day visit from Chiang Yee. He was the perfect guest, rising early to have a walk in the first morning, remaining in his room after a rather silent breakfast to work at his writing until, just before lunch, he and Van Wyck had a slow stroll which was more a mental and conversational than a physical exercise, one that entirely engaged my husband, whose mind was in easy, happy communication with that of Chiang Yee. At teatime we met, the three of us, and the talk around the small living-room table reached its daily height. Later, after dinner, in the quiet, as Van Wyck showed signs of becoming sleepy, Yee became politely sleepy also, and we ended the day by going early and unabashedly to bed. His visit coincided with the bloom in magnificence of our great magnolia trees, and he liked to tell us of the festivals customary to China during his youth, festivals in honor of the magnolia flowers which included walks beneath the moon when, with companions, he recited lines of verse composed for the occasion. Chiang Yee was nearing the end of his *Silent Traveller in Boston* and he hoped to have it done in time to go to England when summer came. We made plans to meet there, a repetition of our earlier meeting in 1951. In the garden one afternoon, the two men held a conversation which had a bearing on the future. Van Wyck had spoken of Ernest Fenollosa, the orientalist, of the sad lack of attention accorded a man so important in his field, the man who had first impressed on modern Japan the value of its mighty culture, its superb heritage.

"I'm tempted to write about him," said Van Wyck.

"You must certainly do so," Yee answered. "And in order to find your material you should make a visit to Japan, where Fenollosa is still a god in men's minds."

Here was an idea that thoroughly pleased us.

The spring meeting of the Academy was interesting to me chiefly for the presentation of the Gold Medal, "the Award of Merit for the Novel," to Aldous Huxley. In his acceptance, a graceful and amusing speech, Huxley compelled the attention of the audience, standing above us, tall, lanky, his almost blind eyes fixed on the inner man, his air of austerity setting him apart, while his unobtrusive English humor delighted us. He spoke of his life-long aspirations, deploring his lack of power to carry them out. He told us that Balzac, "who was a veritable monster of power, maintained that all men of genius had short necks. Genius, after all," Huxley continued, "is an alliance of head and heart, the shorter the neck, the closer the alliance." He regretted that, unlike Balzac, "who had one of the shortest necks on record," his own neck was "the wrong shape."

At the luncheon table my place was between John Cheever and Erskine Caldwell. Cheever possessed a mischievous kind of humor, readily available. My conversation with Caldwell went less fluently. He seemed averse to talk amid the din made by that assemblage. A silent man. On the other hand, I reflected, though inarticulate at this particular moment, he wrote a book a year. On the way home in late afternoon, driving Marian and Stuart Chase to their place in Connecticut, we talked of our coming trip to Holland, to England. A fine prospect, we all agreed. And as we arrived at our door, reaching the garden, lovely as a dream in the falling light, it seemed not to matter much whether we went or stayed so long as we were permitted to remain together.

A party of ours for several in the neighborhood, the Cowleys, the Blumes, among others, was enhanced one evening, unexpectedly, by the arrival of Van Wyck's son Charles, who drove out from New York bringing a recent friend, Charlotte Selver. Hers was a fine presence as she entered our room filled with strangers: poised, handsome and dignified, a professional of standing whose career was concerned with the growth of maximum health and vitality in her many eager students. Not long after, Charles and Charlotte were married, opening, thus, a fair prospect into the future for us as well as for them.

XXI

Storm Warnings

THIRD and last trip to Europe within the sixteen years of our marriage began with a visit to Holland. On board the *Nieuw Amsterdam,* a massive, comfortable vessel which sailed away on June 5, 1959, we were chiefly conscious of the quantity of ease afforded us, the padding of the human body, and, following as a matter of course, the difficulty of withstanding its insidious power to woo us. Was not sloth, I reminded myself, one of the seven deadly sins? Gluttony was, at any rate.

The undemanding days went by, free of that pursuing effort which attended our lives on land. Presently, however, interruptions sprang upon us as various among the passengers made themselves known, old friends and new, who brought the necessity of our application to their various personalities. One of the first to approach us was Russell Hitchcock, a remarkable man whom I had known in the days before my marriage to Van Wyck, professor of architectural history at Smith College and exceedingly knowledgeable. He was somewhat deaf and, because of this, had acquired

the habit of monologue, addressing us with a continuously in-
formative and compelling flow of facts, of imaginative ideas, as
though we had been among the more favored of his students. It
was very agreeable, and Van Wyck came to be much drawn to
Russell for the extent of his perceptions, to which he gave utterance
in the manner of a Buddha. Another passenger, an Englishwoman
married to a Russian and also of substantial presence, Cecilia Payne
Gaposchkin, was an important figure in the world of astronomy and
present head of this department at Harvard. Her husband was an
astronomer also. He had stayed behind to tend his garden while
she went to England to visit relatives. One could see that her
strength, tied as it was to persistence and enhanced by intellectual
vigor, had enabled her to go far. No dallying anywhere along the
road. I found myself full of envy for so much singleness of purpose.
It turned out that she and Van Wyck were often in conversation
at the long-drawn hour of tea in the large saloon, where music
was a background to their talk as they slumped in the deep
chairs.

Mrs. Gaposchkin happened to have a connection through her
English relatives with Fanny Wright, that remarkable young
woman who was born in Dundee soon after the fall of Waterloo
and was orphaned at the age of three. Miss Wright had early
picked up humanitarian ideas, falling under the influence of Byron,
and had later become a magnet and charming companion to several
conspicuous men, including Lafayette, whom she had been with
in America on his last trip there. But her life had ended in sad
obscurity and failure after years of labor for a high cause, that of
attempting to free and educate our Negro slaves. To this end she
had established a colony of colored and white, living side by side
in a mosquito-infested swamp in Tennessee, a project that ended
in disaster. Recently discovered, and now in the hands of Mrs.
Gaposchkin, was a trunkful of Fanny Wright's correspondence, including several letters from Mrs. Trollope, who had come out from
England briefly to join the Wright colony. All of this was of great
interest to Van Wyck, who had written of Fanny Wright in *The*

World of Washington Irving. Owing to the subsequent kindness of Mrs. Gaposchkin in making the letters available to him, he was soon to set down her story more fully in his book *Fenollosa and His Circle.*

The morning arrived when, glancing through the porthole of our cabin on the *Nieuw Amsterdam,* engines slowed, we saw a cow grazing in a meadow beneath a windmill and we knew that we had reached Holland. Our landing at Rotterdam, which followed a long interview of Van Wyck by a representative of the Holland Associated Press, moved smoothly in the hands of the quietly capable Dutch. We went at once by taxi to The Hague, where a room awaited us at the long-established and delightful Hotel des Indres. It proved to have an outlook over the square of fine houses and great trees, and frequently from our balcony we were to hear a hurdy-gurdy serenading us on mornings of sunshine. A great sheaf of peonies awaited us in our room, sent by the Baroness van Wassenaer, a sister of Eric van Lennep, the Dutch neighbor whose house stood across the street from ours in Bridgewater. She telephoned, presently, inviting us to make the circle of Holland with her in her car on the following day, a Sunday. We would leave at nine in the morning, she said, and be gone until evening. We accepted with alacrity.

On that first morning, Van Wyck and I set out before lunch to walk about the streets of the city, a proceeding which was important to him always because it brought the feel of a place. The Hague, as we had swiftly gathered it would, became a part of us in a short time. For one thing, Van Wyck resembled the Hollanders in appearance, with his high color and his dignified mien, and, instinctively, they made him one of them. During the course of our stroll, pausing in pleasure before the antique shops and the flower shops that were specialties of the city, we made our way to a tailor who had been recommended to Van Wyck. Here, while his measurements were being taken and samples for a suit shown him, I sat in the tailor's garden at the border of a narrow canal beneath rose-grown walls, and I sniffed the scent of stock and gillyflowers growing about me as I watched the occasional passer-by at the canal's edge, a boy or a girl on a bicycle, a sedate housewife on her way home from market. We were in Europe, in one of its beautiful cities, and we were together, Van Wyck and I.

The day of our touring Holland in Madam van Wassenaer's small Austin was sunny and wind-blown, crowded, exhausting, and memorable. It lasted for ten hours, and among our impressions were: cities marked by high-mounting cathedral spires; the isthmus town of Enkhuizen that projected far into the sea, where, beneath the wall built to restrain the impassioned waters from destroying their dwellings, inhabitants confidently took their quiet Sunday-morning stroll; the provincial museum of that northern district named Friesland, repository for the brightly colored crafts and the copper and brass utensils so much a part of early Dutch life; the Great Dyke standing against the furious wind athwart the ancient Zuider Zee. Our last stop was at Kampen on the Ijssel River, birthplace of Thomas a Kempis. By this time we were weary and hungry enough to find that the spirit of the Middle Ages was obliterated by the solid worth of the immense pancakes and several pots of tea set before us by a waiter of the local inn. Back at the Hotel des Indres that evening I had only to close my eyes in order to be overwhelmed by the masses of bicycles surrounding our passage all the way: bicycles pedaled by bright-cheeked youth, by young women whose babies were tucked in baskets fore and aft, bicycles equipped with small motors running smartly, whose various owners included a black-veiled nun, skirts decorously flying in the breeze; motorcycles with sidecars wherein were children and the elderly grandmother, while father and mother in leather jackets were astride the seat. A world of haphazard, friendly, yet tenacious motion.

Ten days of applied sight-seeing in the major southern cities brought our stay in Holland to an end. We made our journeys from The Hague by train, and I remember how greatly we enjoyed the aspect of a rebuilt Rotterdam following on the devastation wrought by war, the many glowing symbols of a new world placed in the form of modern sculpture within its central square. In Amsterdam there was our memorable visit to the studio of Rembrandt, who, during his later years, had gone to inhabit the quarter of the Jews. Nearby, was the graceful Portuguese-Jewish Synagogue, where the caretaker who took us through placed the traditional Jewish skullcap on Van Wyck's head, giving him a comically Aryan look. We were told, then, the story of Amsterdam's Jewish population at the hands of the Nazis, who put fathers, mothers, and their children to death either by exporting them to the furnaces of Germany or by the more direct method of lining them up at sunset against a wall to shoot them down. Haarlem we found to be a charming spot, with its crow-stepped, gabled houses—doorways and windows outlined in a fresh clean white—and its Frans Hals Museum, where, as we moved slowly through, we heard music arising from the garden, the recorded strains of a Mozart divertimento, played at the noon hour for those who came to rest here. And we long remembered the glorious sound of the world-renowned organ at St. Bavo Church as it was played by a famous organist on the afternoon of our visit, the high vaults echoing above our heads. Indeed, we were sorry to quit Holland and its lovely water-bound, circumscribed towns, its rows of bee-haunted lime trees, its gardens in miniature neatly set out like those to be had in the old-fashioned toy shops, the pleasant open faces of people about us showing contentment after protracted effort, children with hair as golden as that of angels in sixteenth-century painting.

We proceeded to Belgium, to Bruges and to Ghent, wishing to have a sight of these mediaeval cities and the work of their long-famed artists: Memling, Van Eyck, and the others. But we were caught in the complexities of travel, in unyielding, overrun spaces, continual noise, uncomfortable lodgings. The moment of summer vacation was upon us, and sight-seers from other lands, like ourselves, were everywhere. So, in spite of the splendor of Belgian monuments, we found that our vitality could not sustain the daily scene and we were not averse, a few days after quitting Holland, to board the Ostend ferry, which landed us on the shores of Dover among the cheerful, courteous souls who had been our forebears and who spoke our language.

Walking in the long English twilight on Dover Beach that evening, I thought of Matthew Arnold's "Ah, love, let us be true to one another. . . ." But the beach itself disappointed us, being composed of pebbles rather than sand, and broken in its expanse by jetties of unbeautiful concrete. In fact, Dover became for us little more than a point of embarkation for Canterbury, which was accessible by bus. During our first visit we walked about the town staring in wonder at the gate above the London road used by Chaucer's men and women, picturing their entrance on palfreys. Reaching the cathedral on foot, guided by its twin towers, we had its beauties much to ourselves at that early hour and we noticed that chairs were being set up in the choir. A verger who came our way informed us that there was to be a special service celebrated later for the annual reception of the lady Moral Welfare Workers. He said it would be a fine service, with the archbishop himself presiding. We resolved to be there also and went off to finish our sight-seeing. In a window of a restaurant we perceived a poster advertising two coming concerts that would take place under cathedral auspices during the weekend. "Oh, do let's move over from Dover so as to hear them," I said, and Van Wyck agreed. After lunch we followed the business through, purchasing our tickets from an affable young woman in the cathedral office who helped us secure lodgings for two nights at a private house where paying guests were accepted. We left Dover for good next morning and were presently installed in a splendid Georgian house surrounded by a spreading lawn and ample rose beds.

Meanwhile, we had become familiar with the cathedral during our afternoon with the Moral Welfare Workers. These ladies, a whole squadron of them, entered, as we stood near the cathedral door, on their way to the choir, or "quire," as it was there spelled. Rather timidly we followed behind, hovering near the entrance until we were found by our recent acquaintance, the verger, who beckoned us to seats just below the archbishop's throne. It seemed incredible and somewhat embarrassing that we should occupy so conspicuous a position. But my husband, whose shyness and civility restrained him always from seeking a vantage point within a crowd, was often singled out for attention by some discerning soul. At any rate, there we sat during an hour or so, minding our *p*'s and *q*'s beneath the eye of the ruler of England's church, while, one after another, the ladies approached him with their offering and their obeisance. We were rewarded by the music which embroidered the service, the lovely, clear singing of the choirboys, in their Elizabethan ruffs, their voices tumbling straight out of heaven. We were rewarded, further, by the entrance into the scene of Dean Hewlett Johnson, known, because of his outspoken admiration of Soviet Russia, as the "Red Dean" of Canterbury. He was a remarkable-looking gentleman of eighty-five, slim, upright, toweringly tall, walking with majesty in his clerical regalia. He possessed fine, sharply cut features and a fringe of white hair. He read the lesson in ringing tones, and it was difficult, in his presence, to be aware of anyone else.

Our weekend at Canterbury was pure pleasure for the amount of music and history pressed into and about it. The first concert took place in the cathedral on the Saturday evening, the second on Sunday in the Great Hall of King's School. Both were performed as a part of the festival commemorating the centenaries of Purcell (1659-1695) and of Handel (1685-1759), and on both occasions the program was largely given over to these two men—suites for strings, anthems of praise, a *concerto grosso*—beautiful music, beautifully performed before audiences of magnitude and of great enthusiasm. The evening at King's School—one of the oldest in England and the scene of David Copperfield's schooling—was the more delightful of the two because of its surroundings and the refreshing use of a students' orchestra as base. Among the pieces performed was a seldom played rhapsody of Brahms, a departure from the centennial music. It was composed shortly after he finished his great requiem and was written for contralto, small male chorus, and orchestra. Tender music, melancholy, moving as any could be. The touch of the amateur here, in the boys' orchestra and the chorus drawn from members of the school staff, as they supported the magical phrases of the soloist, enhanced the whole, bringing it a quality sprung from natural sources, a chorus of birds in a summer garden blending with the tones of a lady's soliloquy, a lover's sorrow. Adding to our pleasure was the presence once again of Dean Johnson, who sat in the front row, garbed in a flowing black cloak edged with scarlet; and his appreciation and applause exceeded that of the ordinary man. During the intermission, Van Wyck and I moved to the terrace beyond the Great Hall. Here, in the twilight, as the audience strolled about for half an hour, we noticed several of the schoolmasters, who drew us by their clever and agreeable aspect. One in particular, who was, Van Wyck decided, of Flemish origin, bore a resemblance, my husband found, both to Maeterlinck and to Verhaeren. Difficult to remain the strangers we were in such a gathering. I should have liked to open a conversation with one or the other, with Dean Johnson above all. I wanted to tell him of our admiration for his courage and vital presence, of our displeasure at his having been poorly treated by our State Department when it denied him a passport to our country. Van Wyck was firm in declaring I was not to do so, and I capitulated. But I should always, I reflected, regret it, remembering the advice given me by my teacher of English at the Brearley School when I was a girl. "If you feel an impulse of generosity you must act upon it," she said. "Otherwise it shrivels and dies a useless death within you." Offsetting this, as my husband knew, was the traditional English dislike of the barbaric Yankee who attempts to storm the citadel.

On a sad morning of hanging clouds, we packed our bags to board the first train for London, there to establish ourselves at a hotel in Chesham Place, making either this or the house in Cadogan Gardens of Van Wyck's stepsister, Dorothy Whyte, our headquarters until we sailed for home in the middle of August six weeks later. The London stay was frequently broken by trips afield.

One was to Buckinghamshire, where, with our friends the Nigel Laws, we briefly entered English history when, one afternoon, we drank tea at Windsor in the Tower of Henry III, climbing to the upper stories belonging to our host by means of the ancient circular stairway hewn out of the solid stone. Another visit, to a very old-style English hotel, resembling one in the epoch of Dickens, the Grosvenor at Shaftesbury, Dorset, we undertook in order to be near Tania and James Stern, who were living temporarily in a house nearby as they waited to become established in one of their own. The lobby of the Grosvenor, where on arrival we drank our evening cocktail, was a chill and drafty spot, and I awoke next morning with a cold and decided to spend the day in bed in a room overlooking a small, tree-edged cemetery. This room was locally celebrated for its large size and for the bath attached to it, the only such in the neighborhood, but on the basis of fair play it was allotted to guests for only one night each. The more reason for remaining where I was during that moment of good fortune. Van Wyck early went off with the Sterns to make a tour of the countryside, and I was left with an extended stillness broken occasionally by children who came to play an innocent game of bat-the-ball inside the cemetery walls, their upward-lilting English voices like those of some new species of bird singing above the gravestones. I went forth on the day following, but it was now Van Wyck who stayed behind to rest, while I was driven by Jimmy Stern through a romantic land of rich poetic association. We alighted for a moment to stand beneath a giant tree known as "Barnes's Oak." This was the tree celebrated in his verse by the rustic English poet, who was born not far from its protecting branches. And Jimmy slowed the car again to point out a nearby valley where stood the farmhouse said to be the birthplace of Hardy's Tess. Our third day in Dorset my husband and I spent together in the Sterns' small stone cottage, rose-grown and with floors of brick: "a poet's cottage," Van Wyck called it. Here, Jimmy's books, as always, wherever he might live, were a compelling lot, and when some subject under discussion required clarification he went off, to return with a volume and place it before Van Wyck, so that, after a time, my husband sat built about with volumes as a dwelling is with trees.

We drove southward out of Dorset in a hired, chauffeur-driven landaulet, waving good-bye to the Sterns on a day of vivid sun which was to embrace all that we saw: the magic of the countryside and the beauty of ancient cathedrals, Wells, Exeter, Glastonbury Abbey. At noon, we digressed somewhat from the straight line in order to make a call on Alyse Gregory Powys, who had had to abandon her far and lonely hillside after the death of a sister-in-law and had since settled in a small village of Devonshire, where her days were spent in a substantial house given her by a friend. We came on the house at noontime after a tortuous and lovely drive along narrow country roads. It stood in the hamlet of Morebath, a rustic spot dominated by its elderly church of lichen-covered stone placed on a knoll above. Alyse awaited us outside her door as, on that other, earlier day, and she moved quickly to greet us, the same small, gray-haired woman wearing the long skirt and the white-ruffed neckband of her custom. She gave us lunch in her kitchen, with its wide-open casement windows, and she told us of her present way of life, one of encompassing loneliness since the death of the friend who had brought her to this spot. Her nearest neighbors across a wide courtyard were the bailiff and his wife and their parrot. With these she had become intimate, and she took us to call on them. The bailiff's wife was a broad, shawl-wrapped woman who read the Scriptures every day, with moments off for the perusal of Rider Haggard, her favorite author. The parrot gave us small opportunity to converse, its own conversation being ceaseless. We drove on toward Exeter, later, waving our farewells to the gallant little figure in the dooryard. She and Van Wyck in their spoken exchange had somewhat made up for the years of separation, so much they had in common, not alone the long-past days of the *Freeman* and the *Dial,* but their love of books. Alyse's letters had always brought Van Wyck pleasure. "You have such a lovely way of capturing the impalpable things, recalling the blossom and the perfume," he had once written her. Two gentle and high-minded people. The day came to an end with the long drive back to Shaftesbury along beech and oak-laden hillsides where cattle "stood about the bars," where sheep were gathered in before the downward fall of night, and smoke from cottage chimneys pointed serenely to heaven.

Our stay was brief in London on the return. We remained at the house in Cadogan Gardens only long enough to pack a few fresh clothes and gather up our mail. The next objective was Cambridge, where we had been able to secure a hotel room for a stay of three days—a room, as it turned out, overlooking the Common, a wide expanse of green where much of the life of the community went on with conspicuous homogeneity and content. Van Wyck spent long moments out on our narrow balcony, looking down on the young at play, on the elderly with their dogs, on opposing teams of cricketers. He watched, unaware of the passing minutes, himself become a part of the scene. By contrast to this pastoral peace, the streets of Cambridge surrounding the colleges were crowded, noisy, and dusty under the summer's lack of rain, and it disappointed us to find that the punts on the River Cam followed close, one upon the next, while restless crowds sat watching the river traffic from the grassy slopes of the Backs. A few quiet spots were to be found: the solitary inner quadrangle at Corpus Christi College, where were carved the names of Marlowe and Fletcher and where, below rows of two-storied houses made of weathered stone, we trod upon cobbles that had been pressed by the feet of these Elizabethan poets. And there was the hanging silence about the library of Trinity College as we walked the lengths of aisles designed by Grinling Gibbon and paused, in the stillness, to hang over a first edition of Shakespeare's *Romeo and Juliet*. Again, at the Fitzwilliam Museum, the air of peace continued while we raised, one by one, baize covers which protected cases of manuscripts to find the revealing letters of many of the great writers and, a few aisles farther on, to come on the manuscripts of Haydn's Surprise Symphony, two pages from the rude and forceful hand of Beethoven, and the delicate, fragile script belonging to Mozart.

Sunday at Cambridge we spent with the daughter of Peyton Rous, Marion Hodgkin, married to a physiologist who taught at the university and who had a brilliant reputation. Him we did not see because of his absence in the Argentine, but a son of nine, who resembled the portrait of his paternal grandfather, appeared to have inherited the intensity, the tenacity verging upon genius. Young Marion, wise and kind and capable as she was, watched over us during our Cambridge stay, inviting us to several small parties of her friends. Among others we met Lord Rothschild, a zoologist and an interesting, outgoing man who had, we were later told, more or less adopted the small Hodgkin boy, intending to oversee his future career. He was, we discovered, a cousin of those Rothschilds whose great house, "Waddeston Manor," we had earlier visited under the aegis of the state's National Trust. Waddeston, a copy of the French châteaux Blois and Chambord, was filled with an incredible quantity of valuable objects of art, but it was cluttered, heavy, and dull in the German manner. There was nothing dull or heavy, however, about the Hodgkins' friend, a person who drew us to him with ease.

We left Cambridge on a hot morning of dry wind to go by train, in obedience to a complex schedule worked out by the station ticket seller, to Carlisle in Cumberland. As the journey turned out, we might as well have gone by eighteenth-century coach, so prolonged it was, so digressive. We were on our way to stay with the Lambs, nieces and a nephew by marriage of Dorothy Whyte. Christopher Lamb was a Catholic priest, a most companionable man whom we had known well during our winter in Rome. He had invited us to stay for a few days at Great Corby in the house inhabited the year round by his two maiden sisters. The fact of our ultimate arrival seemed a rather special dispensation. There being no direct line between Cambridge and Carlisle, we had three times changed trains and sat for four hours at a junction where the local porter, seeing Van Wyck, legs hanging from a platform baggage rack, had gone off, to reappear with a sugared bun, which he presented with his personal apologies for the delay. "These chaps don't have a proper sense of service," he said, presumably of the Cambridge ticket seller. Somewhere after seven in the evening we finally came into Carlisle station. But our spirits had risen on the last leg of the journey when, waking from a nap, we perceived that we had left drought and heat behind and run into a country of hills and valleys where the grass was of the darkest green and where sheep stood motionless beneath the new soft rain. It was a moment of rapture. This was followed, in the diner, by one of those tremendous teas for which the English are noted. It lasted well beyond an hour and was thoroughly restorative to body and mind.

Two impressions, gathered during our stay at Great Corby, remained agreeably with us. The first was a walk in the rain beside the Roman Wall, that great dividing line eighty miles long close below the border of Scotland, built by the Roman legions during the first century to keep the northern barbarians at bay. Here it was, now, for us to see, to sit upon, to walk along as we breathed the sweetest smells from moss and fern and quiet meadow grass. A second pleasure during our stay with the Lambs was an afternoon visit to Corby Castle, the great house of the neighborhood, wherein sections remained from the twelfth century, and the inhabited portions, in their magnitude and air of authority, were sufficient to impress two American pilgrims. A vast stretch of lawn before the house gave on ancient woods, and a path led sharply downward to the River Eden, a tumultuous stream divided here by a tree-grown island artificially constructed in the time of Edward I in order to effect what was called a "salmon coup," a sluggish strip of water inadvertently entered by the fish on their way upstream. There, more or less from inertia, the fish remained, rising easily to the fly, the scales tipped well against them, it seemed to me. At that moment in July, the household revolved about the salmon, and when, at teatime, the elderly lady of the manor was asked where her grandson had gone, she replied:

"I expect he's changing in the fish room." An unusual place in which to dress for the evening meal. But it was all romantic and persuadable, the life at Corby Castle, the more so as it had pursued its uninterrupted course for seven hundred years.

We crossed presently into Scotland and established a base in Edinburgh at a hotel in George Street, where rooms were so much in demand that we were made to change from one to another several times, these becoming progressively smaller, in order to accommodate people who had made "earlier bookings." This did not interfere with the enjoyment Van Wyck and I had in walking about the Edinburgh streets, in joining the bands of sight-seers that stormed through Edinburgh Castle, in having our tea and scones in company with the rest of the world. Several times, on days of morning rain that cleared miraculously in late afternoon to wrap us in brightness during the return through sheep-laden meadows, we boarded a bus at the city terminal to embark on a protracted trip. These trips were always a pleasure, freeing us, as they did, from the responsibility of driving ourselves, bringing us as well into the hands of expert guides to whom we listened as conscientiously or as casually as we chose. The stops for lunch and tea were in the nature of a surprise and almost always satisfying. We gave a day to the region where Walter Scott had lived, eventually reaching his house, "Abbottsford," which he built after attaining fame. The study here was a very small room encased in books and possessing an overhead balcony from where a secret entrance took Scott into his bedroom, passage to privacy. Van Wyck stood fascinated before the great two-storied desk, which held a set of indexed files gathered in boxes of fine inlaid wood. The room that moved my imagination was the dining room, with its broad bow window above the Tweed, where, during his final days, Scott had asked to be placed that he might look out, as he lay dying, upon his beloved river.

There came a Sunday when we rented a car, with chauffeur, to drive, in comparative magnificence, out into the neighboring country in order to lunch with an old friend, Ronald Campbell, an intimate of Nigel Law. His friendship and mine went back to Washington during the First World War, when he had been a youthful secretary attached to the British Embassy and my son was a baby in a carriage. We had neither one of us forgotten the high pleasure of many of the Washington encounters, and we were glad to be together again after the lapse of so many years. To meet us, Ronnie had asked the Marquis and Marchioness of Tweeddale and the Earl and Countess of Wemyss and March, names that resounded in splendid fashion as they were spoken to us. It turned out that Wemyss, a quiet, competent man, was a dignitary of the Scotch Presbyterian church, a position entailing each year a week's stay at Holyrood Castle, residence of Mary Queen of Scots. He was also head of the National Trust for Scotland, an institution belonging to the government, here as in England, which took over the management of ancient monuments, houses, gardens, and so on, when those to whom they belonged could no longer afford the responsibility of maintaining them, permitting entrance, also, to the paying public at certain hours of the day. The Tweeddales were especially approachable. He, an amusing man in his sixties, rejoiced, he said, in the present-day absence of servants, of cooks in particular. "We are no longer obliged to subsist on vegetables cooked in water," he told us. "My wife and daughters are freehanded in the use of butter. I myself am becoming proficient in turning out such things as braised lettuce and I hope soon to make a presentable soufflé." He went on to tell us that during the previous evening he had seen Shaw's *Doctor's Dilemma* in movie form and had delighted in its humor. When the play first appeared, years back, he said, there had been no difficulty in identifying the various Harley Street physicians, whom Shaw had spared not at all. Lady Tweeddale asked us to lunch with them on a day of that week, but we could not accept because of being on our way to London. A pity, it seemed to me, for their house, we were later told, was one of the great and beautiful ones of Scotland. Van Wyck, however, said he had had enough of adapting to British high life, the sample provided us having been pleasant, of course, but to him and to me unessential. Small opportunity here for the nurture of snobbery.

In London we once again sought refuge in the hospitable house of Dorothy Whyte and her daughter Ursula, a talented, handsome girl who was studying to become an opera singer. She was clever, as well, in making dresses for her friends, the basement of their house resembling a workshop in the manner of a French atelier. The voices of the young, inflections moving to the upper registers, English fashion, came to us from the open stairway as we sat with Dorothy in her living room. While staying in Cadogan Gardens, we were several times in the company of Chiang Yee, who came frequently to England. We went with him on various expeditions, accompanied by his son, whose blonde wife and small boy were attractive examples of an interracial alliance. On an afternoon of permeating sunshine—for the long drought of 1959 still held— we motored together into Kent to spend some hours at "Knole," the magnificent house of Elizabethan origin belonging to the family of Sackville-West. Unlike such gorgeous but forbidding residences —with their dark splendor—as Chatsworth and Blenheim, Knole drew us at once, a charming and captivating place. Here, as members of the public, we shared the wide, oak-grown park with small-sized deer of appealing aspect and, once beyond the high-walled, cobblestoned courtyard, we entered the house of civilized, home-loving people where in any corner, any room of our choice, we could have been happy. On our way through, following the guide, I thought of Virginia Woolf and her preoccupation with the passage of time, of her book *Orlando,* wherein during long years beneath this very roof at Knole the hero turned into the heroine, the man of action become a lady of reflection and repose. While the heroine was composing a poem to eternity here, in her sitting room, her verses were broken short one day, left unfinished when she dropped her pen to go to the window and, looking below, was "almost felled to the ground by the extraordinary sight which now met her eyes. There was the garden and some birds. The world was going on as usual. All the time she was writing the world had continued. 'And if I were dead, it would be just the same!' she exclaimed." The garden was there for us to see, as well. And the birds.

With Yee, on another day, after lunch in the Hong Kong Restaurant of Shaftesbury Avenue, we walked to Old Compton Street, that we might examine the façade of a house where Van Wyck had lived when first he came abroad on leaving Harvard in 1907. We were happy to find the building intact, with its small Italian restaurant at street level, and I thought of those early days when, on a very small allowance and holding a barely paid job with a literary agent, he had slept on the floor of a room in this house for want of a bed and had subsisted on a negligible amount of food in order to buy books and to write. He lived in a dream of literature and romantic poverty, sympathetic, as he told us he had been, to tales of "penniless assaults on literary fame, the story of Crabbe, who sold his clothes to pay for a last meal, and of Goldsmith, who was caught at home with his breeches at the pawnshop." During that time, Van Wyck had moved more than once to share rooms with various friends at several different addresses, but he managed in eighteen months to write his first book, *The Wine of the Puritans,* and to pay for its publication. One of his friends found him a room "with casement windows," in a farmhouse in Sussex, where he finished the book, living on "mutton hot or cold seven days in every week topped off with suet pudding." The farmhouse I did not see, but I stood as eagerly before the Compton Street house as Van Wyck, in that earlier time, had stood before the dwelling at 4 York Street where De Quincey had written *Confessions of an English Opium Eater.*

Now and then, before the sailing of the ship which was to carry us home at the middle of August, Van Wyck and I in continuing fair weather went off for the day, leaving London by train or bus, to visit some suburb of interest or a house listed under the National Trust. A day at Hampstead Heath brought us on foot to the house lived in by Keats not long before he went to Rome to die. At that moment it had been divided in two, one half occupied by the Brawne family, including the fair Fanny, the other by Keats and his friend Charles Armitage Brown. And it was here in a room giving on a small stretch of lawn that he had heard a nightingale singing in a garden tree and had sketched the lines that led, eventually, to the "Ode to a Nightingale." Very moving it was to sit on a bench in the garden with all this in mind. But no nightingale sang to us from any neighboring tree. We were to come on Keats's evanescent and poignant presence once more at an inn near Burford Bridge, in Surrey, where he had briefly stayed. We were there on a Sunday, and the inn was doing a thriving business, so that we were unable to have even a hasty glance at the room Keats had lived in: it was "occupied, Madam," as the clerk said when we enquired. Above Burford Bridge there stood "Box Hill," which had belonged to George Meredith. The box thus referred to was an abundant quantity of boxwood shrubbery, or trees they were there, growing along a hillside in the chalk of Surrey. Meredith's house just below this hill was almost hidden by the growth, and a succession of spiked posts bore chains leading to either side of a locked iron gate. The house, we were told, was inhabited by owners eager to keep literary pilgrims at a distance. I thought of that magical poem "Love in the Valley," and wondered where Meredith had found the setting for it. He had been happy, I hoped, when he wrote the lines "Could I find a place to be alone with Heaven."

August 14 of 1959 found us established at Chester, on the River Dee, near Liverpool, from where the *Media* was to sail two days later. Chester, a town of half-timber houses, held us with its beauty and its air of long tradition bound within ancient city walls. Our two days were spent chiefly in Wales, and my heart rose in an oblique sort of loyalty as we were flung into the Welsh panorama. Van Wyck laughed at me, his eyes alive with a teasing pleasure, when I spoke of myself as being Welsh, my name, Rice, or Rhys as it was spelled there, deriving from Wales. But a year or so before the trip he had presented me with a copy of George Borrow's *Wild Wales,* inscribing it to his "Wild Welsh Wife."

And now, he too enjoyed our drives through the Welsh country and he gave me excerpts from its history as we went, telling me of Llewelyn the Great and Owen Glendower, of Offa's Dyke and the fastnesses of Snowdon. He spoke of the minstrels of Conway Castle who beguiled the warrior resting from his labors in the great gaunt sea-bound hall. He told me the more recent story about the "Ladies of Llangollen" who had become a legend in their passionate loyalty each to each, living in a house on the River Dee. These romantic names blended with the loveliness of scenery: craggy hills pink with heather, gullies and streams and little pockets of grass folded away in privacy, the occasional farmhouse of stone and the long yards of stone wall, rigid and uncompromising, slim as a penciled line, drawing oblongs and squares about meadows of a green so intense as to need a name for a color as yet not designated by man.

On board the *Media* we found several friends, among them the Arthur Mizeners, he the biographer of Scott Fitzgerald, and a professor at Cornell. We shared a table with them in the dining saloon, and I was glad of their company, their help. For Van Wyck was not well on board. In fact, this was the first time since our marriage that anything on our journeys had gone amiss. The ship was not large, and our cabin was cramped, one bunk above another; the sea was choppy from the aftermath of a hurricane; the skies held rain and mists. Van Wyck seemed listless, and, two days before our landing in New York, he had an attack of vertigo and nausea which was apparently due to a disturbance of the inner ear. The ship's doctor gave him an injection "to quiet him," one so powerful that he slept for almost twenty-four hours. At first bewildered, then frightened, I sat at my husband's bedside wondering if he would ever wake again. He was obliged to leave the ship in a wheel chair, and we were not, as had been customary, helped by Charles Brooks, who in the past had gathered us and our rather large quota of luggage into the interior of his Volkswagon bus. He was vacationing in Mexico.

We reached Bridgewater in due time, our house the haven it

had ever been, and a few days later when Van Wyck had apparently returned to normal health, and certainly to normal routine, we were able to resummon the months past, to think back on the stable pleasures surrounding us in Holland, on the engaging qualities of the British, their manner of life so individual and not seldom eccentric. We laughed together over certain of the warning signs we had encountered on English highways: "Dead slow, Pray hoot," at one avenue entrance; "Bicycles forbidden because of possibly dangerous consequences," at another. On the lawn before Ely Cathedral rising in majesty, we found the sign: "Pray do not allow your dog to foul this green," and a notice at the heart of Edinburgh which read: "The amenity of our streets is recommended to your care." We spoke of places, of incidents come to lodge in our memory: the enduring masonry of the West Gate entrance to Canterbury used by Chaucer's pilgrims on the far road from London, and the spot within the cathedral where in the north transept occurred the martyrdom of Thomas à Becket. We spoke to each other of the flashing views from the windows of trains bearing us along English meadows embroidered with flocks of baby lambs beneath branches of young apple trees in fruit, and we remembered the spreading Saville Gardens at Windsor where flowers bore names that sang: campanula lactifolia, the blue cyanosis, the white mermaid rose. And there were the post cards we had purchased at the National Portrait Gallery in London, standing now in a pile at a corner of Van Wyck's desk, reproductions of the faces of famed English writers. My husband had taken me to this gallery when first we came to London, and we had lingered before the rows of portraits, those of the men who had bestowed fame upon England. We had lingered also at the revolving racks of post-card photographs on sale before the desk. Indeed, we bought so many between us that the attendant, a benign, elderly man, thought we had miscounted. "You have two cards of Swinburne, sir," he said to Van Wyck. "And I have two of Laurence Sterne and three of Keats," I answered, and smiled at him. "It's on purpose." And now, here they were safely in our possession: Ruskin in youth, Ruskin in age; William Cowper in his nightcap; Scott before the fire, his collie at his feet; Jane Austen from a drawing by her sister, large black eyes intently fixed, mouth small and tight; Charles and Mary Lamb in touching proximity; Emily Brontë, painted by Branwell Brontë, vehement, beautiful, tragic; Keats, as Severn had sketched him on his deathbed; Sterne with his lanky body and his humorous mouth; De Quincey, gentle, delicate, his eyes fixed on far visions; Carlyle, shaggy, intent on posterity, uncompromising.

All this and more we had between us, seated of an afternoon on the terrace where, below us, the center pool became a focus for thirsty birds while for Van Wyck and me at sunset it was a wishing well that functioned to keep us close in an eternity shared.

XXII

Desolation and Diversion

*I*N a room at the back of our house, over the kitchen—a
servant's room when the house was built—I placed a pair of small,
gilded metal eagles given me by my husband on a soft October
day. They brought a gay sort of challenge to inertia, a bright
sense of purpose to future occupancy, to the work which I hoped
might emanate from this room, recently become my writing room.
Though not large, it was as charming as any in the house. It had
been the bedroom of young Peter before he went off to school,
and he had turned it over to me on his recent departure. It
faced east, thereby collecting the rays of early sun, and it faced
south through a window overlooking the garden. A haven this
spot had become, its chief component being a writing table of
walnut made for my use by Charles Brooks, graceful as a young
sapling can be graceful or a lithe maiden, its curving stretchers
a feat of carved beauty.

An evening in New York not long after Thanksgiving was the
occasion of fresh honors for Van Wyck, and he returned home on

the following day bearing an engraved bronze plaque mounted on wood. The caption read:

Casa Italiana of
Columbia University
Merit Award
Presented to
Van Wyck Brooks
for Outstanding Service in
Promoting Cultural Relations
Between Italy and America
1959

The book thus selected for merit was *The Dream of Arcadia,* the story of those Americans who from the early moments of our developing nation had looked toward Italy and Italian culture to assist them in their growth. Such disparate names as Longfellow and Edith Wharton, Bryant and Henry James, Washington Irving and Hawthorne, Fenimore Cooper and Emerson and Henry Adams had received sustenance from their various visits to Rome, visits oftentimes of several years' duration. Van Wyck had enjoyed the Casa Italiana party. He returned from Columbia on that evening to the Wheelocks', where I waited for him, to tell us about it as we toasted him in Spanish sherry. He seemed quietly pleased, in a reflective mood, his boiled shirt somewhat creased, his hair rumpled. It had been an exciting moment for him, I could see, but, characteristically, he did not give us any details. The Italians, he said, were full of a charming gusto. "What gratifying natures they have," he exclaimed, referring to the nation as a whole and thus diverting from himself the enthusiasm bestowed upon him, the hero of the evening. The Italian ambassador had been present, he said, the cultural attaché, the president of Columbia, and several of the professors. "But isn't it getting rather late?" he asked, bringing the account to an end. "Shouldn't we all be in bed?"

In the country again, we drove the ten miles between us to dine with the Cowleys, and the talk was much about the novel and of the writers who made novels. In rereading *Anna Karenina,* Malcolm remarked that the young novelists of our day failed to come within seven leagues of the Tolstoy standard. "Is this not due to a lack of stature allied to paucity of experience?" he asked. Tolstoy possessed a lofty and compassionate soul, and his experience of the world, compared with the one of the average American writer, was that of master to apprentice. Shortly after this evening Malcolm and Glenway Wescott were appointed a two-man committee by the Academy to choose a candidate for the Gold Medal given the writer who, during the last five years, had written the best novel. The choice lay among John Hersey, John Cheever, Robert Penn Warren, Vladimir Nabokov, for *Lolita,* and James Gould Cozzens. The last was decided upon for *By Love Possessed.* In the course of their ruminations, Malcolm wrote a précis of Cozzens's work. It was a delight to read. He acknowledged that several deterrents stood in the way of the judges' choice: Cozzens's politics were conservative, his religion was institutional rather than personal, his background was inescapably conventional. However, he knew his trade from the bottom to the top, he was a master of form and a prodigious craftsman, and for these attributes alone he deserved recognition.

During the holiday season Polly Thomson fell and broke her hip. She had been placed in the Bridgeport hospital, where her mental state was rapidly deteriorating. Helen was continually in our minds. How to reach her? How to help her? Through her nurse, we invited her to come to us on Christmas, but she preferred to spend the day beside Polly's hospital bed, holding her hand. On an afternoon somewhat later, when we drove to Westport to call at the house, the attendant on duty went off to ask whether Helen would like to see us. After a long wait word came that "Miss Helen says she will be glad to see Mr. and Mrs. Brooks." She entered the room with confidence, instinctively finding her sofa corner, and we sat beside her, one on either side. She placed her fingers on Van Wyck's mouth and waited for what he would say. When he spoke she smiled, then dropped her hand. I gave her a small bunch of sweet-smelling flowers, and slowly she pronounced the word "free-si-a." We were unable properly to talk to her, but we contrived to communicate our love and our sorrow. She spoke to us once again, and we managed to understand. "Poor Polly is not well," she said, carefully uttering each word like a lesson learned, shaking her head as a child does who tells a sad story. "Polly cannot spell." This meant that Polly could not be aware of Helen's need, that her once busy fingers, for so long Helen's gateway to life, lay now useless upon the bed sheet. We rose, finally, embracing Helen in farewell, leaving her alone in her world of darkness. Turning at the door, I saw that she sat motionless, the flowers held upright in her two hands.

At the end of January we drove away from Connecticut en route to Savannah, where we planned to spend the winter months. I was somehow sad in quitting the house, where my newly restored study, dominated by the shining golden eagles, spelled a happy continuity. We had three days of driving, much of it along Route 301, where motels and gas stations lined one's path, in the way the primrose and hawthorn line the roadsides of the English countryside, and the monotony of signboards dulled our sensibilities and our communication with each other. We managed an occasional joke, and I laughed aloud when Van Wyck, apparently dozing, awoke to utter the words "Come just as you are," reading them from a recurrently prominent advertisement. "A rather unpleasant idea, don't you agree?" he asked. At Savannah we entered an apartment made of two immensely high-ceilinged, old-fashioned rooms in the De Soto Hotel. They looked out over cherry trees and magnolias and camellia bushes soon to be in flower. It was very pleasant. Once settled, and our relations with the friendly colored people who looked after us well established, we promised ourselves many weeks of uninterrupted work.

The work began well enough. Van Wyck was in process of writing *Fenollosa and His Circle,* while I had become engrossed in a book of my reminiscences which followed naturally on those described in *Gramercy Park.* Several pleasant people looked us up, and we spent a long afternoon with the mistress of a plantation beyond Savannah, a widow who took us through her park of some eight hundred acres, now gradually reverting to the wild for want of the labor that once had kept them spruce and alive. The frame house, painted white, was growing dim, and the Spanish moss hanging from the live oaks surrounding it made it into a place of sorrow, or so I felt, as on another day I felt the melancholy of the beautiful Bonaventure cemetery, a spot which seemed to please my husband as he led me here and there, pointing out the graves of especial beauty or interest. We left the plantation in the late afternoon, our hands filled with camellias, as the dusk began to gather. Our hostess stood alone on the gallery of her large, empty house, and I thanked the benign spirit protecting me for the near presence of my husband, whose hand held mine.

Van Wyck's birthday came and went in quiet recognition of these happy occurrences. Ten days later he was stricken with an ailment which at first we thought to be a winter virus but, which, continuing as it did, was pronounced by a doctor to be something more grave. An examination revealed that a lump existed in his lower left colon, and it seemed best that he go immediately to the hospital for a more thorough investigation. A room was promptly obtained for him at the Memorial Hospital, a fine modern building eight or ten miles from town, and we moved him out. A series of tests followed, so familiar to many and as yet unfamiliar to us, tests that lasted for two days, that were not only disagreeable but often painful. My heart bled for my husband, who was, however, equable and patient throughout. Two episodes remain forever fixed in my memory of those hospital days. One was the quantity of iced water brought, in the Southern tradition, by a succession of small, curly-headed colored girls. The other was a conversation I had with the doctor in charge of Van Wyck. Seated on a window seat at the far end of the corridor beyond Van Wyck's room, he said: "You know, Mrs. Brooks, I believe the growth in your husband's colon may be cancer."

"Oh, no!" I spoke to myself, pushing the doctor's words away, forbidding them entrance to my inner being. "Why do you think so?" I asked aloud, quietly enough, I believe.

"Because we've pretty well eliminated any other cause. I advise an exploratory operation at once. The sooner the better."

It was now necessary to break the news to Van Wyck. I managed it somehow and without his being drastically shaken, I hope, although I never could be certain, so great was his control. His confronting the inevitable, his courage, as the next few years showed me over and over again, coincided with that of the mediaeval knight who, besieged and surrounded, gallantly countered the attack of far outnumbering forces.

"Merely an exploratory operation," I said once again.

"I understand," Van Wyck answered. "When will it be performed?"

"The day after tomorrow, probably. You'd rather they did it here than at home?"

"The results of all the tests are here. Why begin again?"

My heart sank. We seemed very far from family, friends, all the familiar things. "Yes, of course," I heard myself answer. "And this is a splendid hospital."

With characteristic Southern generosity, a recently made friend, owner of a local bookshop, had invited me to stay with her during the ordeal, to quit my room, temporarily, at the De Soto. The surgeon was introduced to us, and the matter seemed closed. But on the morning following, the telephone rang in our hotel sitting room, and Van Wyck's voice came through.

"How would you like to make plans for our going home?" he asked in a small questioning tone. My heart rose to meet his.

"Oh, I'd love to," I answered in a rush of words. "I'll be at the hospital in less than an hour."

Together, we arranged for our departure that same evening, and we journeyed northward overnight. In Savannah, it was explained to the kind and understanding doctors that we thought it best to have the operation performed nearer home. By telephone, we alerted our children, and a surgeon, attached to the Grace New

Haven Hospital. Van Wyck and I smiled at each other when all this was accomplished. We had a fine sense of reprieve and, undressing that night in a stateroom of the Atlantic Coast Line Railroad, we both felt we were escaping calamity, our lives intact. We were met by Charlie Brooks and driven to Bridgewater, reaching our flower-filled house at lunchtime. Kenyon took over from here, and on the next afternoon Van Wyck was established in an agreeable room in the New Haven hospital, which held a comfortable sofa for me to sleep on in case of emergencies.

The operation took place on a morning in early March. The tumor was removed, and most successfully, the surgeon assured us. Several of my children had arrived from Boston to sit with me during the ordeal, waiting with me in a small corridor room where the television unfolded its charms without pause for the benefit of ambulatory patients. In the next three weeks, doctors, nurses, interns, friends were continually attentive, and Kenyon Brooks, during the black days of uncertainty, acted as my stand-by. He flew to Savannah and drove our Peugeot station wagon home, and he remained on call when any fresh necessity arose. Meanwhile, Van Wyck became the perfect patient. He accepted pain, dragging discomfort, small oversights in treatment, with the uncomplaining equanimity which had first been evident in Savannah. "You are at the mercy of these people," he said to me one day. "Why not let them be?" Happy moments there were when his progress, and what appeared to be an assured future, became visible facts. The small daily pleasures increased as we set up our routine together. There were the hours when I read aloud: *Tom Jones,* Sherlock Holmes, the travel books of Somerset Maugham, Henry James, and Freya Stark. There were our games of Chinese checkers at the moments when my husband sat in a comfortable corner of the sofa, there were my trips on his behalf to the Yale Library, and, on my return, there was the spilling out of books from his red baize bag over the bed.

We returned to Bridgewater on a fair day at the end of March, the first day of spring, and we took up our residence on the first floor of our house, the stairs being forbidden Van Wyck. The dining room became our bedroom, and we awoke each day to see the sunrise through the wide easterly window and seemingly for our benefit alone. Van Wyck went happily to bed on the first night of being home, sleeping without a break for eight quiet hours. He knew that the study was but a few paces down the hall and that soon he could take his seat before the writing table. Indeed, his first act on arriving home, following the long fatiguing drive from New Haven, had been to go and sit for a moment in the deep reading chair, empty during so many weeks, to place on the bench beside it the two published volumes of his autobiography: *Scenes and Portraits* and *Days of the Phoenix.*

His strength, his vigor, returned in remarkable fashion, and although perforce he kept his pace somewhat below the former one, he felt entirely himself and looked better than he had of old. Our first undertaking beyond the limits of Bridgewater was a night spent in Morristown that Van Wyck might receive an honorary degree from Fairleigh Dickinson University at Rutherford, New Jersey. This ceremony was performed in the grand manner. In robe and mortar, Van Wyck marched to the platform with other dignitaries, preceded by Scottish pipers in full array. The citation read was also magnificent, stating as it did that Van Wyck was "one of the world's great literary critics of all time." I sat a little to the left, facing the platform, which had been placed on a grassy plateau out of doors, and I looked with pleasure on a group of splendid trees: mulberries, beeches, cut-leafed oaks, retinisporas, Sargent hemlocks. These superb plants had been set out years back, when the place belonged to a granddaughter of Commodore Vanderbilt, and their selection had, I could guess, been influenced by my old friend and tutor, Charles Sprague Sargent, of Boston's Arnold Arboretum.

A day came presently when we drove to Westport to lunch with Helen Keller. Polly Thomson had died at the moment of Van Wyck's return from the hospital, and this was our first meeting with Helen since she had been bereft. We found her far from crushed. She appeared to have added another dimension to her already heroic stature; her early Swedenborgian training, at the hands of a young assistant of Alexander Graham Bell, now stood her in good stead. Did she not believe that Polly awaited her at the gate to heaven? How be deterred from happiness when this prospect shone bright? Helen's younger sister, Mrs. Tyson, had arrived from Montgomery, Alabama, their childhood home, and the two talked together as they had when they were small, the deaf-and-dumb manual having been instilled into the sister's awareness at that moment. Her fingers, as we watched, carried on what seemed to us a gay, almost irresponsible dance, while Helen's face, as the process continued, lighted with swift pleasure or darkened in despair, according to what they told her.

Several weeks of the summer we spent on Martha's Vineyard in my son's house at West Tisbury, for which he had exchanged the Silo, my gift to him and to his family a few years before. Van Wyck went each day to swim and to lie in the sand, his strength growing more and more certain, so that we came almost to forget those days of shadow at Savannah and New Haven.

The Christmas of 1961 was embroidered round about with grace and with humor, and held at its heart that lovely aura of permanence, that sense of rightful continuity which the presence of family can bring. We celebrated it in Bridgewater with two of my daughters and their husbands, the Catlins and the Haussermanns, as well as with young Ephron Catlin and Peter Brooks. They all arrived in time for the lighting of our nine-foot spruce and they became an instant part of the glow of candles, in company with those friends who had gathered to drink mulled wine over the fire. On the day of Christmas, Kenyon joined us for present-giving, for dinner, and for laughter which became a corollary to the swiftly unfolding hours of their stay. Then, on Twelfth Night we dismantled the tree and took our leap into the New Year, which was to bring completed books for Van Wyck and me. In fact, we went on January 10 to New York, each of us bearing a manuscript for our publishers. Van Wyck's was the third installment of his autobiography, *From the Shadow of the Mountain,* and mine was a second book of reminiscence, which Atheneum was to publish under the title *Boston and Return.* On January 18 we had expected to go to Washington to attend the ceremonies surrounding the inauguration of John Kennedy. Our trip had been arranged in pleasant detail, the more so as the invitation had made it clear that our President-to-be was to bring into new prominence the long-neglected world of the arts. The telegram sent Van Wyck read in part:

During our forthcoming administration we hope to seek a productive relationship with our writers, artists, composers, philosophers, scientists and heads of cultural institutions. As a beginning, in recognition of their importance, may we extend to you our most cordial invitation to attend the Inaugural ceremonies. . . .

As things turned out, we stayed at home. On the day before we were to leave, as I was taking a walk with Van Wyck in the snow, my foot slipped and I twisted my knee, incurring acute pain from what proved to be a torn cartilage. So, the phrases accompanying the inauguration proper we heard at home, spoken on radio, obliged as I was to stay in the house and, at that moment, possessing no television. Van Wyck was chiefly interested in Robert Frost's informal entrance on the scene, his appearance on the Presidential rostrum, his wind-tossed utterances of concern for the future, and his disregard for the amenities of the moment. "Always a good showman," my husband said.

An entry in my journal under the date of February 22, 1961, reads: "Several people told me I looked very happy. Indeed the evening was one of the high spots of my life. . . ." These words referred to a party given Van Wyck by the Academy of Arts and Letters on his seventy-fifth birthday, a gathering of some sixty writers, artists, and musicians, which, in spite of its size, held the effect of spontaneity, of affection and love. The party was the focal point of what turned out to be three days of celebration. It began for us at lunch after our arrival in New York when, seated beside Van Wyck on a restaurant bench, I read aloud a long article by Malcolm Cowley from the current issue of the *Saturday Review*. It was a summary of Van Wyck's lifework and was most moving for its grasp of his intention, for making the intention clear.

. . . Set down that he was a pioneer in the study of American literature. . . . Set down that his judgments have been reached independently, oftentimes in defiance of fashion. Set down that his aim has always been to lend courage to American writers with the aim of producing great leaders among them . . . but chiefly set down what he has done and continues to do by example rather than precept. The example is that of an author who has followed a single line of development with complete integrity. . . .

The dinner was held in the Academy library, where circular tables had been set against the mounting rows of books which served as background to the spoken words. Glenway Wescott was the general manager of proceedings, and Mark Van Doren was toastmaster. In his introduction, Mark said of Van Wyck:

Although he is utterly accessible and utterly affectionate he also has unspeakable dignity. . . . What he has said in book after book, no matter what the subject . . . has been something about truth, the truth concerning man which doesn't seem to be available to us often enough. It is Van Wyck's interest in the truth and search for it and serious regard for it—with wit, to be sure, and sanity—it is this that I admire him for above all. . . . I have seen him here at the Academy and Institute, where he has been so useful, helpful and necessary for many years. I've seen him at meetings . . . saying almost nothing while everyone else talked. And once in a while I would look at him and ask myself what Van Wyck was thinking. . . . I suspect that he was thinking about what we were saying and finding it not quite adequate. He was relating our talk to larger things and placing it in a pattern which was so wide indeed that the name for the whole of it might be truth itself.

Jack Wheelock made the opening address. He went to stand behind Van Wyck's chair, placing a hand on his shoulder, speaking without show of oratory, as if telling a story to the uninitiated. His reminiscences of the days shared with his friend at college were touching and amusing, and his summary of Van Wyck's work, it was generally agreed, was memorable for its penetration.

In a period of defeatism, of clever cynicism, Van Wyck Brooks has kept the banner of faith and hope and courage flying for many more of us than he will ever know. . . . I was mailing a package to Van Wyck Brooks from the little village post office at East Hampton last summer and took it to the young clerk at the postage stamp window to be weighed. He glanced at the address and murmured "Ah! *Flowering of New England!*" I smiled and said, "You've read his books?" "Many of them," he replied. And then he added, "He's a good writer."

Lewis Mumford followed, opening his speech with the words:

Van Wyck, if I don't manage to say anything else tonight . . . let me say what's in our hearts, what fills us this moment with delight. We love you and we're grateful for the fact that you have lived!

There were others who spoke, among them Chiang Yee, who looked impressive in his oriental garb when he rose from his place beside Pearl Buck to quote Confucius on the blessings of growing old. Finally, wearing a white carnation in his buttonhole, Van Wyck stood to make his speech of thanks, an unprepared speech spoken with the humor that appeared so continually in the glint of his eyes but was not often uttered. He charmed us with his obvious happiness, his simplicity, and his fresh, youthful appearance. George Biddle later said that Van Wyck reminded him of a kitten confronting a saucer of cream. When the speeches were over, Glenway Wescott read many of the letters and telegrams from those who had not been able to come, reading from a large black folio stamped with Van Wyck's name and later placed in our hands. One message which particularly pleased Van Wyck was from Will Durant, in Los Angeles; others came from James Farrell, from Allan Nevins, then at the Huntington Library in California, and from Allen Tate, at the University of Minnesota. On the day following the party a letter arrived from John Hersey, who was currently living in a house built by Van Wyck twenty years back in Weston, Connecticut. "I feel above all," he said, "in the atmosphere of this place, your gift of serenity in work—and I thank you for having left a touch of that here. It helps me. . . ."

In May of 1961, we had a second bout of hospitalization when, at the advice of the local doctors, Van Wyck went to Roosevelt Hospital in New York for the elimination of a small benign tumor in position near the earlier one, which, it was decided, should for safety's sake, be removed. "It's the right moment to get rid of it," they said, "now that you're in such good shape." There was the same early-morning trip for my husband on a stretcher to the operating room, the same wait for me in the corridor. But the outcome was entirely reassuring. "Mr. Brooks's condition is splendid in every way," the surgeon said. And, by June 1, we were back in Bridgewater, where not alone the doctors, but everyone, handed plaudits to my husband for the pluck and the stamina which had done so much to pull him through the two assaults made on him.

XXIII

A Kiss for Caroline

*V*AN WYCK and I sat on the terrace under a wide umbrella above the garden, where iris and vivid double poppies and the gentle bleeding heart fought for supremacy, their roots carpeted with the star-flowered woodruff, whose leaves brought a pungency to the brew of May Wine. It was the second day of June, and we had been married fourteen years. There was, that evening, to be a party at the Herseys' house, the house built by Van Wyck, a party for several, beside ourselves, who had been married on that day. But it seemed wiser for Van Wyck to remain at home, free of added effort. In late afternoon, Peter and Ebie Blume came by, their hands filled with presents. Wrapped in silver foil and bound with a sprig of Cotoneaster was a pair of minor-sized champagne bottles, and the bouquet set down beside them, gathered by Ebie from her garden, was a collection of sweet odors emanating from a jug of gray pottery. Later, Kenyon appeared, bringing a splendid shad, fresh caught, with its roe, from the Connecticut River. After dinner, with Kenyon, we sat talking of Asa Gray, the botanist who once had swung his knowledge of plant life toward Darwin and his theory of evolution, thus bringing assistance to the Englishman in the famous controversy with Louis Agassiz. We spoke also of the intricately made glass flowers in the Peabody Museum at Cambridge and of Ibsen's play *Hedda Gabler,* recently put on to perfection in New York. Gradually our talk diminished, our gestures slowing like those of mechanical toys unwound. Kenyon arose for the final effort of home-going, and we went to bed, our gratitude for manifold favors come, seemingly, into full flower.

One more flowering, *The Flowering of New England,* composed by my husband in the days before we met, established a frame of reference for an episode that took place in our summer garden. This had been visited by a woodchuck, who, each morning while we slept, left his burrow beneath the piazza floor to seek nourishment among the flowers in our borders. Devastation everywhere as, from an erect position on his hind legs, he nibbled and destroyed our carefully tended blooms. Finally, after a trap baited with lettuce had failed in its intention, the woodchuck was brought to his end by the rifle of Dan Hammond, husband of our Agnes. A single shot at evening accomplished the deed, and he lay on his back, paws in the air, plump and dead and full of my flowers, most particularly lupine blossoms not yet uncurled. And then we could not but feel sad for the creature's fate. Van Wyck murmured the words of Emerson, who had told his friend Thoreau "that it was not for him, a follower of the Brahmins, to effect the transmigration of a woodchuck." Thoreau himself had once made friends with a woodchuck, to whom he had spoken in "a sort of sylvan baby-talk." Thoreau offered him checkerberry leaves. He was "one of the natives. His family had certainly lived in Concord longer than the Emersons or even the Hoars. . . ." But we had saved some of the flowers of our summer garden.

Padraic Colum came to stay for a few days. He was in his eightieth year, still vital and strong, traveling the earth as though in his teens, living cheerfully enough the life of loneliness forced on him by the death of his wife, aware of all history through his exceptionally knowledgeable mind, while his vast store of poetry flowed through him like a continuing spring freshet. Together, the three of us attended a party given William McFee on his eightieth birthday. Mac looked grandly imposing, seated motionless and unhearing in his chair, erect, ruddy, a sea god brought to earth or a captain mariner for whose commands there was no longer a crew. His books, sadly, with the sea for their hero, were no longer being kept in print, although many others had followed the early and famous *Casuals of the Sea*. A day or so after the celebration Van Wyck received a letter from McFee: "I think the party was one of the happiest I have ever known, Republicans and Democrats, Catholics and Jews, all got on together. I can now slide into octogenarianism with a clear conscience. . . . I was delighted to see Padraic Colum again after all these years and to see Van Wyck so completely recovered from his operation. The gifts were superb. I am spoiled with the generosity of my friends. I shall never forget this party."

A midsummer holiday of a month at Stonington, Maine, in a house at the edge of the bay, was a great boon to Van Wyck, for whom Maine was his compensation for all things difficult or unpleasant. We had driven eastward without plan, in the pattern of his choice, and we moved imperceptibly into a land of conifers and salt water and white-painted farm buildings wherein the well-stacked woodshed was a component part. At Stonington, situated on the tip of our map, we could go no farther without driving into the sea, and here we remained, gathered into a bungalow house as though by predestination. With giant rocks and open meadows about us and only a causeway to the larger world, we were safe from intrusion. Van Wyck sat at a card table in an easterly living-room window, working on the Fenollosa book, while in the bedroom, I made the revisions suggested by Hiram Haydn, the editor of my book *Boston and Return*. For days no one came to interrupt our exile save two friends with whom we collided at the post office. These, however, lived in even greater seclusion than we, as we found when we visited them on adjacent Bare Island, where, in the rafters of their cabin, they sheltered a newborn baby bat as yet unable to fly and a family of minks that moved unconcernedly past their door. Our holiday lasted for three weeks. Van Wyck was blissfully happy. So was I. He said he was "living outside of time."

Returned to the everyday world once more, in November we attended a meeting of the American Philosophical Society, at which Van Wyck read a paper, a condensed version of his essay on Fenollosa. It went very well, because things Japanese and the Zen philosophy were much in men's minds, and the fact that Ernest Fenollosa had been an outstanding agent in helping to preserve the art of Japan served now to bring him into focus.

In January of the ensuing year, we set out to spend the cold months in Tucson. This entailed a protracted drive in Van Wyck's newly purchased Corvair, through Virginia, North and South Carolina, Alabama, Mississippi, and the ubiquitous Texas. Here, on the outskirts of Fort Worth, we were held up, because of icy roads, for three days and nights in one of the lesser motels. The hours passed well enough, however, as Van Wyck, in the easy chair, applied himself to Volume IV of Gibbon's *Decline and Fall of the Roman Empire* and, propped with pillows on the mammoth bed, I got on with my "work in progress." At last we reached the Arizona desert, where its hills and hollows of far-flung sand, the manifold thorns of the far-spread cholla plant, the immense, intense sky, the leaves of the inevitably assured century plant were all as compelling as tradition had described it.

In Tucson proper we settled into an apartment giving on a patch of green lawn and garden beds watered each day by a meticulous gardener. This we enjoyed, for neither Van Wyck nor I was thoroughly won over to the insinuations of the desert in spite of Joseph Wood Krutch, whose two books *The Desert Year* and *The Voice of the Desert* were provocative and moving. Krutch had more or less left behind his concern with the New York stage, and, with his generous French wife, lived in a hospitable house outside the heart of Tucson. It stood beneath a mountain which cast a benign sort of guardianship over their daily existence, while the desert grass surrounding them was the abode of birds and lizards and the occasional wild flower, all of which Krutch examined and protected. We presently met at their house the director of the Desert Museum, a remarkable place which was a repository for the animal, bird, reptile, and plant life of the region. We met also the director of the great and famed zoo at San Diego. This was at an afternoon tea party, when he arrived bringing guests from Ireland: Mr. and Mrs. Alec Reed. Reed, a drama critic in Dublin who held a chair at Trinity College, was interested in desert plant life as well as the stage, so Krutch's house was a magnet. He was a curious-appearing man with huge vitality, white-haired but with a complexion like a flaming sunset, and the possessor of a brogue which delightfully infiltrated the conversation. Reed and Van Wyck had much to say to one another, the more so when the Irishman discovered that in 1951 we'd spent a month in Dublin among the writers and playwrights there. He told us that our friend Ria Mooney, for so long directress of the Abbey Theatre, had herself given a magnificent performance of the wife in O'Neill's *Long Day's Journey into Night*. One of us innocently asked the Reeds what their objective was in the United States, and Mrs. Reed, with enviable simplicity and composure answered: "We brought our boy over to the Mayo Clinic to see could something be done for his heart. But he died there."

On our walks about Tucson at the spectacular hour of sunset we sometimes attended vespers at the Convent of the Benedictines, listening to the service sung by a priest attired in gold and the responses intoned in the high, lucid sound of the nuns' voices. At other hours we liked to stop in, sharing the silence with the sister on her knees, motionless before the altar in "perpetual adoration" of the Virgin above her. Never was the Virgin left untended; each half-hour of the day and night, one of the nuns came there to kneel, taking the place of her who had gone before, a rite performed with silent and respectful regularity while the minute hand of the wall clock went on its quiet round. Another religious service, less formal, less practiced, with a cruder, more impassioned mode of performance, we witnessed at the end of Lent in the territory of the Yaqui Indians. The Yaquis had been among the last of the tribes to arrive from Mexico, and it was rumored that they had been expelled for their rites of cannibalism. At any rate, they lived on the outskirts of Tucson, independent of others of their kind, belonged to no reservation, and were pitifully poor. The Lenten and Easter celebrations, an annual enacting of the crucifixion, burial, and the rising from the dead, were of the most primitive kind but deeply felt. Van Wyck and I had been taken in charge by a patron of the Yaquis, Mrs. Painter, a writer and a resident of Tucson who had secured the confidence of these proud people and had made attempts to increase their well-being. On the evening when we took part in their rites a cold rain fell, and we sat wrapped in blankets inside a small building shaped like a barn, widely open at one end, while a procession of men and boys entered carrying a roughly fashioned platform of whitewashed wood as base for the Virgin, a doll clad in tinsel-trimmed white. This they set down before an altar, and during the next several hours they took turns kneeling, genuflecting, chanting, drawing their wooden swords in an attitude of protection for their Lady. The onlookers about us watched each move with the intensity of people whose lives depended, quite literally, on the action. Even the children were borne upward with the rest, standing or sitting motionless until, at the moment of summons, they too joined the pageant.

At the end of March we bade farewell to the several friends, including the Krutches, who had taken us in during the winter; we paid a last respectful visit to the grove of great saguaro trees in the reservation outside Tucson; we had a final meal in the Mexican quarter of the town; and early on a fine morning, we drove out of Tucson. Our road to the East led us along the Gulf of Mexico, and several of the Texan settlements that overlooked the water, the meadows about them vivid with flowers, invited us to visit them again. A sandwich lunch in San Antonio, at the edge of the river that coursed through the city, made us think we were once more in Amsterdam or Venice, so much did the scene, with its curving footbridges and its leisurely pedestrians, resemble scenes in Europe. A stop of two days in New Orleans at the Pontchartrain Hotel, a minor Ritz with an added touch given it by the easy ways of the South, allowed us a rest which Van Wyck seemed very much to need. He had been lacking, recently, in his characteristic intensity; often tired, he did not wish to take the wheel of the car when it fell to his turn. But we had our little jokes, as usual on these journeys, and I submitted with all enthusiasm to being instructed in the events of history as they arose to confront us. In New Orleans, as we passed the Cotton Exchange, Van Wyck had informed me that the brother of Degas, the French painter, had been a member there, and beneath an advertisement for Lord Calvert Whiskey he murmured that this gentleman was descended from Rubens.

In the mound of mail awaiting us at home, there was an invitation to dine at the White House on Sunday, April 29, to meet the Nobel Prize winners. Van Wyck, in his customary way of being unimpressed by grandeur and wishing to get on with his work, at first wanted to refuse. I, on the contrary, was eager to accept. Furthermore, as I asked my husband, was not an invitation to the White House in the nature of a command? He relented, and our acceptance went forth. We were both glad, later, that things happened this way, for we had a lovely time in Washington from beginning to end. We went down by Pullman from New York a day ahead of the party. Already there was an air of festivity in our car, filled as it was with Nobel Prize scientists and their wives.

In Washington we stayed at the Mayflower and we lunched on Sunday with Francis and Katherine Biddle. Their house and garden in Georgetown had an authentic flavor of the elegant past. Alexis Léger, whose pen name was St.-John Perse, and his wife lunched there also. It turned out that Léger and Pearl Buck were the only writers who had received the Nobel Prize to be present at the White House that evening. Science far outweighed literature in being thus recognized. The Louis Untermeyers were at lunch, and Louis, then Consultant in Poetry at the Library of Congress, was effervescent and amusing as always.

When evening came and we were dressed for the party, we met our Connecticut neighbors Rose and William Styron in the lobby of the Mayflower. This we had arranged earlier, and the Styrons had brought James Baldwin with them. We all went briefly to the bar for a drink before going on to our further entertainment. Across the table, Van Wyck looked handsome and distinguished in his well-cut dinner coat, his hair *en brosse,* as the barber termed it, his special air of intensity and preoccupation and latent humor somehow accentuated. Entering the grounds of the White House in our taxi, circling the illuminated fountains, we might have been approaching the Place de la Concorde in Paris. It was all massive and splendid as we moved through the grounds toward the elegant circumspect white building surrounded by stillness.

We were among the first to arrive, and after leaving our wraps, Rose and I were each taken in charge by a correct marine who escorted us in heel-clicking style up the grand staircase. I felt I was Eliza Doolittle in *Pygmalion,* my whole future depending on gracefully reaching the head of the stairs and, once arrived, averting any lapse into Cockney. We were received by a lady who was tall, stylishly clad, and full of dignity, a social secretary of very special talents. She wafted us toward the famed East Room, where the party collected as we awaited the President and Mrs. Kennedy. The first person to see us was Fredric March, who, later in the evening, we found, was to entertain the company by reading aloud excerpts from the writing of several literary Nobel Prize recipients. Gradually the room filled with many friends, and we wandered about sipping our cocktails, greeting the Samuel Morisons and James Farrell and Pearl Buck, John Dos Passos, the Gerard Piels, of the *Scientific American,* and Katherine Anne Porter, who was at that moment having a huge success with her long-awaited novel, *Ship of Fools.* The Alexis Légers arrived presently, and Robert Frost, his white hair tousled, wandered in last of all. Finally a band struck up "Hail to the Chief," and the President and Mrs. Kennedy stood at the entrance. Under the guidance of the marines the company was formed into a long queue and instructed to move forward, the husbands preceding their wives. During the initial moments of the slow forward march, I noticed a large alabaster urn suspended above me from a wall bracket and filled with flowers: iris, narcissi, tulips, red and purple anemones, branches of cherry and yellow mimosa, a fair and fragrant gathering arranged as though a group of children had brought the flowers from the fields and thrust them in. It made me happy.

Our turn to be introduced to the Kennedys came in due course, and I heard Van Wyck's name being announced and saw him shake hands with the President and his wife, the polite, abrupt handshake of the shy person who wants to get it over. Rapidly he moved on, and I followed rather more slowly. For I had a message to deliver from Helen Keller, who, a few days earlier, when told we were to meet the President, had said: "Give him my love and a kiss for Caroline." The Kennedys smiled, and the President, holding onto my hand for a moment, called out to the receding Van Wyck: "I read *New England: Indian Summer* when I was in the hospital." He had read it during his recovery from the serious injuries he had received in the near-tragic PT-boat accident. Turning back to me, President Kennedy said: "We'll be seeing you later." I did not know what this meant but I had been charmed, in our brief encounter, with Kennedy's good looks, his spirit, his awareness. Mrs. Kennedy had had a smaller part to play in our meeting, and the impression of her on that evening was less pronounced.

Moving next through the Red Room, I saw with pleasure several small round tables with their white cloths set up near the fire beneath the portraits of our past Presidents. Van Wyck and I were not to remain here, however, as our cards summoned us to the large dining room. At one of the tables for eight, I sat beside Arthur Schlesinger, who had become a stand-by to Kennedy, temporarily dropping his career of professor-writer. On my other side was Dr. Detlev Bronk, director of the Rockefeller Institute. Mrs. Linus Pauling, on Schlesinger's left, was a small, frail woman whose eyes were rather sad. This seemed to me natural enough, because her husband, the recalcitrant Nobel scientist, had been all day picketing the White House and carrying a placard which read: "Ban the Bomb." He had ceased this occupation only in time to change for dinner, arriving with his wife to join the line that led him to the President. Here, he had apparently made some perfunctory apology for the day's role, to which the President is said to have replied: "We're glad to have your views." I turned presently to Mrs. Pauling, a very appealing person to whom I was much drawn, and I asked her a most personal question. "Are you happy?" I said impulsively, thinking of her husband's role. "*So* happy," she answered. "I should like to have life go on just as it is, forever." At the large center table, Kennedy sat with Mrs. George Marshall, widow of the general, on his right and Mrs. Ernest Hemingway on his left. Just before dessert was brought in, the President rose to make a speech, and the company fell into silence. "This," he said, "is the most extraordinary collection of talent . . . that has ever been gathered together at the White House—with the possible exception of when Thomas Jefferson dined alone." When the meal ended we were asked to make our way back to the East Room. We moved to the sound of violins, and presently, in a rotunda off the hallway, we came on a bevy of violinists, who stood about eight feet apart, lining the wall the whole way round. They were young, slim, elegantly dressed in dinner coats, and, an anomaly, they played as fiddlers play at country fairs, unaccompanied, with the harsh, rasping sound of hair scraping gut. They might have been the male counterparts of Ziegfeld Folly girls, so carefully matched were their figures and uniform accomplishment.

In the East Room again, the President and his wife had taken chairs in the front row of the group arranged for the company, and soon after, when we were in our places, Fredric March came to stand before us. During a half hour he read portions of the works of two of the Nobel Prize winners, beginning with an address made at Harvard by General Marshall in 1947. This had to do with the forming of the Marshall Plan. It was followed by excerpts from an unpublished manuscript of Hemingway, which was much in the vein of the writing we had associated with him in recent years. I was sorry that none of the illuminating poetry of St.-John Perse was given us. The language barrier doubtless had something to do with this. At the end of the reading, the Kennedys rose and moved toward the door, where certain among the guests gathered about the President, asking for autographs, while the young violinists struck up a brightly swinging tune and a few people went off to the floor of the rotunda to dance. Glancing back over my shoulder, I saw that in an attempt to elude the autograph hunters, the President had more or less forced a passage out and away. The party seemed to be over for us, at any rate, whose hour of rising next morning would necessarily be early. And we had had so much real pleasure that to stay longer might well be an anticlimax. Going to pick up our wraps we encountered Dos Passos and his wife on their way home, and we bade each other good night outdoors under the fountains' flowing light.

At the hotel, as we undressed, we kept on repeating: "What a lovely evening! What a perfect party!" We did not at the time know that we had missed an hour with Kennedy, who had invited the various writers present, and their wives, to his private rooms for conversation, a quite wonderful occasion, we were later told.

"The President said, 'I'll be seeing you later,' when we were shaking hands in the queue line, Van Wyck," I told my husband. "But I didn't know what he meant."

My husband's answer was not very clear, for his mind was on the book he held in his hand.

XXIV

The Meaning of God

*T*HE summer of 1962 took its course, outwardly, within the
pattern we had come to depend on, our fifteenth summer together,
made of work, usually serene, now and then harassed, of leisurely
walks, of tea drinking with companions in the garden, or of
evening meals at the house of a friend. One of these evenings was
given over to William Shirer and his wife. Van Wyck admired
Shirer's penetrating work and he liked the man. So he was not
averse to driving the thirty miles or more to his place, on the
last day of June, the latter part through authentic farming country
where, at dusk, the women and young boys helped stow bales of
hay. For long minutes we sat on Shirer's lawn beneath ancient
maples, looking off into a far valley of tranquillity and we
watched white masses of early garden phlox become wraithlike
under the falling sun. We were in the company of friends, Mark
and Dorothy Van Doren, Marian and Stuart Chase, and the charms
of our hostess enlivened the talk and deepened our content. She
was a native of France and a great linguist, able to read the

Odyssey in Greek. She possessed, as well, a soothsaying gift which gave her a subtle sort of agreeable power.

Our midsummer holiday we spent at Little Compton, Rhode Island, in a cottage belonging to the Carl Bingers, those friends whose garden in New York had been the setting for our wedding breakfast. It was in Rhode Island at the end of August that I noticed my husband's lack of staying power, that the pain over his heart became more frequent, more prolonged. He seemed unequal to much effort, preferring to sit reading in a wind-sheltered spot from where he could follow the daily performance of a flock of wild white swans, descendants of a pair brought years ago from England, stately, wise, and confident. All day they flew in to ruminate on the fresh waters of the cove below, rising again with a ferocious sound of vibrating wings, and it amused Van Wyck, slumped in his chair, high-crowned Panama shielding his eyes, to observe the dividing line, set up by their mores, whereby in enviable tranquillity the elder swan occupied one shore of the inlet, adolescents the other.

We cut the holiday short when it became clear that Van Wyck should be nearer to his doctor, who at once, on our return, ordered a week's rest for him in the bedroom of our house. The week did not drag for Van Wyck as, at a card table in a window over the garden, he worked on an introduction to a group of essays from the *Paris Review* soon to be published in book form by the Viking Press. Released from confinement, he returned to his study, but on a morning not long after, he was set back still further by a slight stroke, which for the moment paralyzed a leg and an arm. He soon recovered in his inimitable way, one that was deceptive not only to me but to his doctors. None of us realized the extent of the ills which assailed him. It was as though he had been granted a leave for good conduct from the prison of declining health, as though courage and fortitude and a mind wound by thoughts of a non-personal and absorbing kind allowed his turning back from disaster, granted him the reward of his own choosing—namely, continued hours of labor and life.

At Grace New Haven Hospital, where he was then given a brief examination, he was told he might have two weeks in which to finish a piece of work before he returned for more prolonged tests. Thus dismissed and for the moment free, we walked down the hospital steps in a most hopeful mood and took our way home. We stopped off at a stationer's to buy a new copybook for me, one intended to serve as journal, and Van Wyck, as always, inscribed the title page, handing it back to me with a smile:

For Gladys
on a happy day.
Sept. 25th, 1962

Presently, the *Paris Review* piece completed and the hospital tests still a week away, we set off in the Corvair for our customary autumn tour of New England. Our focal point was an inn in northern New Hampshire, but there was nothing to deter us from leaving the highway for smaller roads when they seemed agreeable, from getting lost now and then, from pausing in order to pay a visit to some friend. In Hanover, New Hampshire, we stopped at a house near the grounds of Dartmouth College where Rudolph Ruzicka had gone recently to live—the elderly Bohemian craftsman-designer of magical powers who had been responsible for the type occurring in several of my husband's books. The two men talked of the past and they were quietly glad to be together. Driving eastward that afternoon, along the Vermont shore of the Connecticut River, we told each other that the meadows of alfalfa and well-tended grass, with the Green Mountains beyond, were lovely as any landscape could be. The sight brought us a renewed feeling for the earth and all its bounties. The air was still, holding the scarlet and gold of leaves in a tension of glory, and I knew, with a curious sense of undemanding yet irrevocable finality, that nothing could ever have been intended to bring a greater happiness to Van Wyck and to me than the pleasure of our being together beneath so much beauty.

On the way home, after two restful nights at our inn, we

guided the car at noon up a sharp mountain road in Madison,
New Hampshire, the setting for a house belonging to Professor
Ernest Hocking, the philosopher. We found it eventually, a place
where the great man had lived winter and summer since the
death of his wife some years earlier, an old-fashioned frame house
of simple design and upkeep, of the kind men built in the
nineties for their families to occupy in the mountains or by the
sea during the summer months. Professor Hocking awaited us at
the summit of nowhere, as it concerned the active world, but this
position, we later discovered, was entirely suited to his cast of
mind. An outgoing man in spirit and bearing, tweed-clad, he had
a magnificent physique for one entering the ninth decade, walking
each day along the steep mountain roads, rowing on the lake
below. We had arrived, by invitation, at the lunch hour, and we
entered the verandah dining room to be joined by Hocking's
daughter and granddaughter. We stood, then, behind our chairs,
and at a signal from our host, wide enough to include the universe,
we held hands, the five of us, during his blessing, which seemed
to induce the flow of a benign current between us. I had not known
that Hocking's philosophy involved so strong a link with religion,
but Van Wyck later told me that the title of his first book was
The Meaning of God in Human Experience. The talk at lunch
was of William James, Van Wyck's great admiration. "It was
James," Hocking said, "who helped transplant me from the Midwest and brought me into contact with the superior minds in
Cambridge such as those of Royce and Palmer, as well as making
of me an ardent disciple." Whether James or another was responsible, this man's nature was as lofty as the high hilltop on
which he dwelt. Following lunch the two men went to the study
to discuss the dilemma of a writer friend whose output had fallen
off, his work hanging in the balance. I had a glimpse of the two
at the hour of our leaving: Hocking broad-shouldered, assured,
an equable Father Time; Van Wyck a smaller figure and more
youthful, eager yet troubled by the problem confronting them,
intent on replacing a thing lost. We drove off, waving our farewell

as the car rounded a large maple in the center of the driveway, to the ladies on the piazza and to Ernest Hocking, who stood alone at the edge of a small copse, upright, steadfast, his roots deep in the soil, a leader pushing upward toward the light.

There was an amusing experience that afternoon when we stopped at a motel to ask for accommodations, and met a well-meaning man who came over to our car to speak to me while Van Wyck was in the office.

"Pardon me, ma'am," he asked, "but was that gentleman Van Wyck Brooks?"

"Yes, he is," I answered.

"Van Wyck Brooks in the flesh?"

"Yes," I smiled.

"To think of that!" he said. "Why, I read his books." He stared toward the motel. His expression was rapt. Quickly, I roused him.

"I'm hoping we can get a room here. We've come a long way today, and my husband is rather tired."

"You won't be able to get in here, ma'am. There's a plumbers' convention on. Everything's taken. But maybe I could help you get in somewhere else."

"Oh, could you? We do need help." I had begun to worry about Van Wyck once again.

The man left me to go in search of my husband, and ten minutes afterward they came out together. Van Wyck looked bewildered and not altogether pleased, being wary, always, of obtrusive strangers.

"This gentleman has kindly engaged a room for us at a Howard Johnson motel down the road," he said to me. "We can't get in here." His manner was blunt as he opened the car door. I smiled my thanks, hoping to propitiate.

"How do we find the Howard Johnson?" I asked. "Which of all these motor lanes should we take?"

"Ma'am, you just follow me. It's kinder complicated."

We set off, the stranger in the lead, and later, while Van Wyck was again negotiating for a room, he came over, handing me his card. "It's been a pleasure to meet you," he said politely. "Here's my card. I'm sure glad to have shaken hands with Van Wyck Brooks." He went off, and I read the name of our benefactor, followed by the words "Fleet Manager of the Chevrolet Motor Division."

The trip homeward on the two days following went easily enough, but the bright pleasure of our flight away was not open to us now. Ahead, lay the new hospital encounter, the tests, the possibility of misfortune, even catastrophe. Of these dark things we did not speak, but they lay about our gestures and permeated our hearts. I drove on while Van Wyck, silent and undemanding, seemed to be confronting places far beyond our vision. Deliberately, we accomplished our tasks at Bridgewater; soberly, we set about our packing for the coming brief journey; and on the appointed day we drove to New Haven almost as though becalmed, aiming for that skyscraper building which was the Grace Hospital. The room given Van Wyck now, because of crowded space, was small and airless, facing a noisy pantry. Here he remained for two long weeks, patient in every sense, even docile, but failing a little more in stamina each day. He was in process of recovery from an operation on the carotid artery performed soon after our arrival, which had been decided upon by a group of doctors, in order, they said, to circumvent a second stroke. This had been labeled a "minor" operation and was carried out under a local anaesthetic, but it took its toll, nonetheless, of his person. I like to remember the words spoken by my husband from the recovery room soon after the ordeal, words repeated to me in amusement by the surgeon. "Will you be good enough to have me wheeled back to my room so that my wife can read to me?" he politely requested.

Van Wyck returned by ambulance to Bridgewater, and, weak though he was on arrival, he moved slowly about, examining familiar places: the living room filled with branches of crimson oak leaves; the dining room, its geraniums and begonias flowering on sun-bound shelves; the study where the large window chair and his writing table awaited him. Lying on the center blotter were ten or twelve pages of manuscript in his narrow, nervous, distinguished hand, the start of a book on Lewis Mumford. The book was not to progress much farther. Only a few more lines had been written before there was a renewed call to the hospital. This time it was the small hospital at New Milford, near home. It seemed, in contrast to our recent experience at New Haven, where all was huge and hurried, to be a gracious English country house, and we felt like guests invited for a pleasant stay. Our spirits rose. Our luck would turn, we believed. Or so it seemed, though I could never be certain what in his deepest being my husband believed. He continued to spare me. He knew that I loved him.

The tests began again, the trips to the X-ray room, the taking of blood samples, all the familiar procedures. It had now become almost impossible for Van Wyck to eat, to digest what he was able to swallow. The growth in the colon had returned, it was found. The one chance of survival was a further operation. And so, at Thanksgiving, I gave him my kiss, my blessing, as he was again wheeled on a stretcher to an operating room. He survived, a fresh miracle. At the end of a seven-hour wait, walking the cold lanes of Bridgewater under the sparkling stars, I was finally able to take his hand in mine, to kneel at his bedside, to tell him he would live. "You will get well, darling," I said.

On New Year's Day we went back to Bridgewater. "Let's go home," Van Wyck had kept on saying. We went home to the transformed dining room, that spot of sun and hope where Van Wyck's hospital bed stood beneath the portrait of his grandfather and faced those of his great- and his great-great-grandfathers—and where his grandson Peter came presently to be near him. Here was security, the base for a gradually diminishing existence which lasted four months. Each day he walked, and later was wheeled, to the study to sit in his chair, and when the book in his hand became too heavy to hold he listened as I read to him. "Read to me," he would say from his bed, flat on his back, in a voice I could barely hear, and the trip to the study followed. This had always been the spot dedicated to reading, to writing. None other was to his liking. And so, slowly, laboriously, we moved down the hall to stay for an hour, a half hour, sometimes only for ten minutes, and I read on. A sad, subdued, and yet intensive life based on depths, preparation for departure, preparation for grief.

The long winter was upon us and then came spring. Our magnolias opened their flowers and they dropped one by one. The grass turned green. A robin built its nest in the Virginia creeper climbing our verandah, a baby rabbit nibbled at the new shoots of our garden. Van Wyck was little aware of these things but he did not suffer. He gave himself over to the final act required of him, to the weakness that wound itself gently, at first, then irrepressibly about him. We were together by day and by night, united as before, as in the buoyant times. At Easter, and thereafter, until a day before the end, I read to him from his *Scenes and Portraits: Memories of Childhood and Youth*. It seemed the moment for him to live again in that far past, so close to the present. He listened, speaking one word now and then, the word "pause."

On the early afternoon of May 2, 1963, I was obliged to pause for always. Van Wyck had died. Quietly, he went, after whispering, as I leaned over him: "You must have rest." And then grief began.

Index

Adams, Henry, 66
Adams, John, 12, 13
Adams, Léonie, 53
Adenauer, Konrad, 209
Age of Reason, The (Paine), 12
Aiken, Conrad and Mary, 249
Aldridge, John, 217, 240
Alfred, William, 255
American Academy in Rome, The, 215, 217, 218, 219, 231
American Academy of Arts and Letters, The, 78, 121, 191, 223, 277, 302, 309
American Civil Liberties Union, 48, 176
American Language, The (Mencken), 63
American Philosophical Society, 76, 316
American Scholar, 264, 265

Ames, Elizabeth, 186, 189
Anderson, Judith, 79
Anderson, Karl, 38
Arvin, Newton, 54
Auden, W. H., 191
Audubon, John James, 11
Aurep, Baroness Alda, 229
Ayer, Harriet Hubbard, 182, 191
Aylmer, Rose, 65, 66

Baedeker, 125
Baldwin, Evelyn, 27, 47, 92
Baldwin, James, 320
Baldwin, Roger, 27, 47–48, 92, 175–76
Ballad of the Sad Café (McCullers), 243
Balzac, Honoré de, 50, 153–54, 277
Barnes, Djuna, 49
Barrett, Mr. and Mrs. Walter, 244

Basso, Hamilton, 38, 39, 53–54, 120, 211
Basso, Toto, 38
Beard, Charles, 78
Beebe, William, 176
Bell, Alexander Graham, 183
Benét, William Rose, 48
Benton, Rita, 27, 91
Benton, Thomas, 27, 91, 92
Berenson, Bernard, 225, 228–31
Beston, Henry, 175, 247, 248
Biddle, Francis, 248, 319
Biddle, George, 165, 174, 193, 194, 248, 311
Biddle, Hélène, 165, 174, 193, 194
Biddle, Katherine, 232, 319
Biddle, Michael, 174
Binger, Carl, 15, 325
Binger, Clarinda, 15
Bishop, Isabel (Mrs. Harold Wolff), 275
Bishop, John Peale, 53
Bloch, Ernest, 70
Blume, Ebie, 313
Blume, Peter, 84, 109, 120, 278, 313
Blumenthal, Joseph, 184
Bogan, Louise, 53
Boston and Return (Gladys Brooks), 309, 315
Botteghe Oscure, 233
Bradlee, Benjamin, 152, 238
Bradlee, Benny, 152, 238
Bradlee, Jean (*see* Haussermann, Jean)
Braille, Louis, 183
Bread and Wine (Silone), 233
Brecht, Bertolt, 49
Bronk, Detlev, 322
Brooks, Ames, 97, 98, 217

Brooks, Charles, 29, 89, 159, 274–75, 278, 297, 300, 306
Brooks, Edith, 215
Brooks, Eleanor, 4, 6, 16, 38, 206, 245
Brooks, Inez, 89, 159
Brooks, Kenyon, 29, 50, 90, 91, 120, 159, 169, 238, 306, 313–14
Brooks, Oliver, 215
Brooks, Peter, 23, 30, 89, 90, 159, 160, 161, 162, 177, 238, 273, 275, 300, 308, 330
Brown, Monsignor, 140–41
Buck, Pearl, 319, 320
By Love Possessed (Cozzens), 302
Bynner, Witter, 212, 213

Caetani, Princess Marguerite, 232–33
Calder, Alexander, 84, 109, 110, 223–24
Calder, Louisa, 224
Caldwell, Erskine, 277
Campbell, Ronald, 292–93
Cannon, Walter, 256
Capote, Truman, 53
Carey, Mathew, 10
Carrel, Alexis, 98
Carroll, Georgia, 60, 61, 62, 113
Carroll, John, 60, 61, 62, 113
Casa Italiana, Columbia University, 301
Cass Timberlane (Lewis), 121
Casuals of the Sea (McFee), 315
Cather, Willa, 78, 209, 211, 212
Catlin, Ephron, 308
Catlin, Priscilla, 28, 308
Channing, William Ellery, 257, 267
Chapman, John Jay, 46

Charles Scribner's Sons, 98, 185, 240

Chase, Marian and Stuart, 277, 324

Cheever, John, 277, 302

Chilmark Miscellany, A (V. W. Brooks), 23, 42, 73, 104, 149

Clark, Eleanor, 218

Clark, Walter, 177

Coatsworth, Elizabeth (Mrs. Henry Beston), 247

Cobb, Frank I., 19

Cobb, Margaret, 18, 54, 117, 182

Cole, Thomas, 270

Colum, Mary (Molly), 46, 47, 117, 171, 198, 242, 250

Colum, Padraic, 44, 46, 47, 79, 117, 129, 171, 198, 242–43, 250, 314–15

Committee on Un-American Activities, 73

Commonweal, 90

Conant, James B., 209

Confessions of an English Opium Eater (De Quincey), 295

Confident Years, The (V. W. Brooks), 84, 92, 120, 121, 157, 170

Cornell, Katharine, 28, 183

Cowley, Malcolm, 84, 109, 121, 157–58, 168, 270, 278, 301–02, 310

Cowley, Muriel, 84

Cozzens, James Gould, 302

Croce, Benedetto, 235–36

Cry, the Beloved Country (Paton), 185

Cummings, E. E., 40–41, 52, 274

Cummings, Marion Moorehouse, 53

Curran, C. P., 133, 134

Damrosch, Walter, 78

Davidson, Florence, 152, 154, 165

Davidson, Jean, 224

Davidson, Jo, 8, 37, 72, 74, 105, 152, 153, 154, 155, 159, 165

Day, Father, 109

Days of the Phoenix (V. W. Brooks), 159, 214, 241–42, 307

"Dead, The" (Joyce), 129

Death Comes for the Archbishop (Cather), 209

Dehumanization of Art (Ortega y Gasset), 77

Desperate Hours, The (film), 196

De Vries, Peter, 53

Dial, The, 288

Dickens, Charles, 171

Dickinson, Emily, 171, 188

Dilk, Dora, 10, 21, 22, 30, 84, 87

Dinsmore, Leslie and William, 27

Dinsmore, Professor William, 219, 235

Dix, Dorothea Lynde, 194, 266

Doctor's Dilemma, The (Shaw), 293

Doll's House, A (Ibsen), 217

Dos Passos, John, 52, 320, 323

Draper, Ruth, 155

Dream of Arcadia, The (V. W. Brooks), 301

Dunn, Alan, 275

Dunsany, Lord Edward, 133

Durant, Ariel, 199

Durant, Will, 199–200, 311

Eastman, Eliena, 52, 92, 93

Eastman, Max, 52, 92, 93

Edgeworth, Maria, 142

Edison, Thomas, 183

Eisenhower, Milton, 172

Eldridge, Florence (Mrs. Fredric March), 119
Elements of Rhetoric (Whately), 255
Eliot, T. S., 52, 75–76
Ellison, Ralph, 219
Emerson, Ralph Waldo, 191, 314
E. P. Dutton and Company, 45, 90, 121, 158

Fairleigh Dickinson University, 307
Farrell, James, 51–52, 311, 320
Farren, Robert, 129
Fenollosa and His Circle (V. W. Brooks), 281, 303
Fenollosa, Ernest, 277, 315, 316
Fiedler, Leslie, 161
Fineman, Irving, 202
Fitzgerald, F. Scott, 265, 297
Fitzgerald, Robert, 53
Flexner, Simon, 98
Flowering of New England, The (V. W. Brooks), 102, 157, 198, 314
Flynt, Josiah, 170
Foote, George, 15
Forbes, Mr. and Mrs. Edward, 260–61
Force, Juliana, 36
Fosdick, Raymond, 52
"Fragment of a Meditation" (Tate), 50
Frank, Waldo, 248
Freeman, The, 47, 248, 288
From a Writer's Notebook (V. W. Brooks), 254
From the Shadow of the Mountain (V. W. Brooks), 309
Frost, Robert, 184, 244, 263, 321
Fuller, Buckminster, 70

Gaposchkin, Cecilia Payne, 280, 281
"Gardener, The" (Wheelock), 164
Gardner, Mrs. Jack, 225
Gauss, Christian, 77
Geismar, Anne and Maxwell, 191–92, 242
Gibbon, Monk, 133, 137, 138
Gilbert, Edwin, 240, 245
Gonne, Maud, 138–40
Grace New Haven Hospital, 306, 326, 329
Gramercy Park (Gladys Brooks), 240, 303
Gray, Asa, 313
Greek Commonwealth, The (Zimmern), 102
Gregory, Alyse (Mrs. Llewelyn Powys), 149, 150, 288
Gregory, Lady, 141
Grolier Club, 73

Hackett, Francis, 85
Hall, James Norman, 273
Hamilton, Edith, 172–73
Hamilton, Nancy, 183
Hammond, Agnes and Dan, 180, 314
Hammond, Florence, 223, 255
Hammond, Mason, 218, 219, 235, 255
Hanson, Polly, 186, 189
Hardy, Thomas, 148–49, 287
Harvard *Advocate,* 177
Harvard Monthly, 96
Harvard University, 39, 231
Haussermann, Jean, 28, 152, 182, 238, 251, 308
Haussermann, William, Jr., 251, 308
Hawthorne, Nathaniel, 191, 242

Haydn, Hiram, 264, 265, 315
Heart Is a Lonely Hunter, The
(McCullers), 243
Hellman, Lillian, 48
Hemingway, Ernest, 265, 323
Hemingway, Mrs. Ernest, 322
Herbert (aide to Helen Keller), 60
Herrick, Robert, 116–17
Hersey, John, 191, 302, 311–12, 313
Hibbard, Henry, 97
Hisamatzu, 258
Hitchcock, Russell, 279–80
Hocking, Ernest, 327–28
Hodgkin, Marion, 290
Hotel Earle, 170
Hotel Hay-Adams, 66
"House in Bonac" (Wheelock), 164
Howe, Mark DeWolfe, 257
Howells, William Dean, 252
Howells, Mr. and Mrs. W. H., 256
Huntington Hartford Foundation, 193, 196, 202
Huxley, Aldous, 167, 277
Huxley, Maria, 167
Huxley, Matthew, 167

Ibsen, Henrik, 217
Institute of Historical Studies, Rome, 235
Invisible Man (Ellison), 219
Iroquois Indians, 259, 268
"I Tatti," 225, 228–31
Ivins, William, 115–16

Jackson, William, 261
J. B. (MacLeish), 274
James, Henry, 53, 255
James, William, 34, 205, 327
James, William (grandson), 255

Jeffers, Robinson, 203, 204, 205
Jeffers, Una, 204
Johnson, Eastman, 185
Johnson, Dean Hewlett, 285, 286
Johnson, Sir William, 266
Josephson, Eric, 83
Josephson, Hannah, 191
Josephson, Matthew, 82, 87, 109
Jung, Carl, 254

Kaye, Danny, 197
Keats, John, 188, 295, 296
Keller, Helen, 28, 58, 59, 60, 79–80, 154–55, 183–84, 202, 209, 251, 262, 302–03, 307–08, 321
Kennedy, Caroline, 321
Kennedy, Jacqueline, 321
Kennedy, John F., 309, 321, 322, 323
Kenyon, Eliza, 125, 165–66
Kinsey report, 52
"Knole," 294
Koestler, Arthur, 75
Krutch, Joseph Wood, 191, 316–17, 318

La Farge, Oliver, 211
Lamb, Christopher, 290
Landor, Walter Savage, 65–66
Larson, Karl, 211
Last Puritan, The (Santayana), 260
Late George Apley, The (Marquand), 260
Latour, Father, 211–12
Laughlin, James, 271
Lavin, Mary (Mrs. William Walsh), 131, 132
Law, Nastia, 145–46
Law, Nigel, 144, 145–46, 287, 293
Lennep, Eric van, 281

Levy, Julien, 109
Lewis, Sinclair, 121
Leyda, Jay, 187, 188
Life, 90
Life of John Sloan (V. W. Brooks), 211
Limited Editions Club, 184
Lindbergh, Anne Morrow, 98, 99
Lindbergh, Charles, 98, 99
Literary History of the United States (ed. Spiller *et al.*), 157
Lives of the Painters (Jamieson), 71
Longford, Lord, 128
Longworth, Nicholas, 61
"Love in the Valley" (Meredith), 296
Lowell, Amy, 244
Lowell, Robert, 244
Lys dans la Vallée, Le (Balzac), 154

MacBride, Sean, 138
MacDowell Colony, 197
MacDowell, Mrs. Edward, 197-98
MacLeish, Archibald, 191, 208, 274
MacManus, Francis, 129, 131
Macrae, Elliott, 45, 158
Macrae, Marjorie, 158
Madame Sans Gêne (film), 196
Mailer, Norman, 240, 245
Makers and Finders (V. W. Brooks), 120, 157, 158
Malady of the Ideal, The (V. W. Brooks), 49
Mann, Thomas, 122, 222
Mannes, David, 91
Mannes, Leopold, 91, 92
Manship, Paul, 113
March, Fredric, 118, 184, 196, 197, 320, 323

Marcus Aurelius (Sedgwick), 225
Mariano, Nicky, 228, 229, 230, 231
"Marius Amid the Ruins of Carthage" (Vanderlyn), 58
Marshall, General George, 323
Marshall, Mrs. George, 322
Marti, Miss, 219
"Mass at Acoma, The" (Cather), 209
Massingham, H. J., 104
Mather, Frank Jewett, 191
Maynard, Theodore, 49
McCarthy, Senator Joseph, 179-80
McCarthy, Mary, 259
McClintic, Guthrie, 28
McCracken, Robert, 172
McCullers, Carson, 243
McGreevy, Thomas, 129
McFee, William, 109, 112, 166, 315
Meaning of God in Human Experience, The (Hocking), 327, 328
Means, Marjory, 119
Meiklejohn, Alexander, 47, 48, 206
Melville, Herman, 187, 191
Melville Log, The (Leyda), 187
Member of the Wedding (McCullers), 243
Mencken, H. L., 63
Meredith, George, 296
Miller, Henry, 205-06
Mills Hotel, 168-69
Miss MacIntosh, My Darling (Young), 53, 240
Mizener, Arthur, 234, 297
Montagu, Ashley, 173
Mooney, Ria, 128, 317
Moore, Marianne, 48
Moral Welfare Workers, 284
Moravia, Alberto, 234
Morison, Samuel, 320

Moyne, Lady, 136
Moyne, Lord, 133, 134, 135, 136
Mumford, Lewis, 42–43, 78, 112, 114, 241, 272 311, 330
Mumford, Sophia, 112, 113
Murray, Henry, 106, 107, 253–54
"Muse of Cortona, The," 227

Nabokov, Vladimir, 302
National Institute of Arts and Letters, 48, 78
Natural Superiority of Women, The (Montagu), 173
Nevins, Allan, 311
New Directions Press, 271
New England: Indian Summer (V. W. Brooks), 66, 111, 321
New Republic, The, 85, 157
New York *Herald Tribune,* 41, 157
New York *Times Book Review,* 240
New Yorker, 271
Niebuhr, Reinhold, 191
Nine Chains to the Moon (Fuller), 70
North Country School, 177, 178
Northeastern University, 160
Norton, Charles Eliot, 259
Noyes, John, 268

"Ode to a Nightingale" (Keats), 296
Okamura, Miss, 258
Oneida Colony, 268
O'Neill, Eugene, 191
Opinions of Oliver Allston, The (V. W. Brooks), 5, 12, 36, 41, 76
Orlando (Woolf), 294
Ormsbee, Richard, 161

Ortega y Gasset, 77
Ostroff, Anthony and Miriam, 206
Our Friend James Joyce (Colum), 250
Outermost House, The (Beston), 175, 247

Pach, Walter, 19
Paine, Thomas, 11
Paris Review, 325, 326
Pascal, Blaise, 92
Paton, Alan, 184–85, 189
Pauling, Linus, 322
Pauling, Mrs. Linus, 322
Peabody Museum, Salem, 189, 239
Pearson, Dr. Mabel, 117
P.E.N. Club, 168
"Penrose Memorial Lecture," 76
Père Goriot, Le (Balzac), 154
Perkins, Maxwell, 15, 16
Perse, St.-John (Alexis Léger), 319, 320, 323
Petitpas restaurant, 35, 102, 137
Petty, Mary (Mrs. Alan Dunn), 275
Phelan, Kappo (Mrs. Kenyon Brooks), 90, 159, 169
Phelan, Senator James, 204
Phi Beta Kappa Society, 208
Piel, Gerard, 320
Pierre (Melville), 187
Plainfield, New Jersey, 67, 97
Poe, Edgar Allan, 11, 37
Pope, Alexander, 12
Pope Pius XII, 224
Porter, Katherine Anne, 244–45, 320
Powys, Llewelyn, 149
Powys, Mrs. Llewelyn (*see* Gregory Alyse)
Praz, Mario, 233–34, 235

Prendergast, Charles, 37, 38
Prendergast, Eugénie, 37, 94
Prendergast, Maurice, 37, 38
Princeton University Press, 77
Pusey, Nathan M., 208

Reed, Mr. and Mrs. Alec, 317
Rice, Durant, 118
Richardson, H. H., 66
Richter, Gisella, 219
Rights of Man, The (Paine), 12
Roberts, Laurance, 218, 235
Roberts, Justice Owen J., 172
Robinson, Edward G., 194–95
Robinson, Edwin Arlington, 36, 49
Robinson, Lennox, 128, 134
Rockefeller Foundation, 52
Rockefeller Institute, 98, 322
"Rocky Mountain Roundup of the Arts," 161
Roethke, Theodore, 233, 234
Rogers, Bruce, 78, 85, 86
Rome and a Villa (Clark), 218
Roosevelt, Archibald, 176
Roosevelt, Eleanor, 184
Roosevelt Hospital, 312
Rospigliosi, Princess Marguerite, 218, 235
Rothschild, Lord, 290
Rous, Marion, 101
Rous, Peyton, 101, 290
Rucellai, Countess, 46
Ruzicka, Rudolph, 73, 326
Ryder, Albert, 37

Sachs, Mr. and Mrs. Paul, 259
Saint Bernard's School for Boys, 9, 39, 62
Saint-Gaudens, Augustus, 80
Sainte-Beuve, 31
Saltonstall, John, 144

Saltonstall, John, Jr., 28, 108, 160, 257
Saltonstall, Nathaniel, 248
Saltonstall, Stephen, 23, 24
Salvemini, Gaetano, 154, 155
Sandburg, Carl, 106, 107, 119–20, 160, 184, 263
Santayana, George, 155, 260
Sargent, Charles Sprague, 307
Saturday Review of Literature, 42, 158, 310
Scenes and Portraits (V. W. Brooks), 102, 181, 223, 307, 331
Schlesinger, Arthur, Jr., 256, 259, 322
Schlesinger, Marion Cannon, 256
Schnackenberg, Henry, 109, 232
School for Scandal (Sheridan), 128
Scientific American, 320
Scott, Sir Walter, 292
Selver, Charlotte, 278
Sergeant, Elizabeth Shepley, 244
Sherwood, Robert, 191
Ship of Fools (Porter), 245, 321
Shirer, William, 41, 324
Shock of Recognition, The (Wilson), 5
Short, Marie, 203, 204, 205
Silent Traveller in Boston, The (Yee), 276
Silent Traveller in New York, The (Yee), 146
Silone, Ignazio, 233
Simonson, Lee, 70, 71, 242
Sinclair, Upton, 200–02
Sloan, Helen, 117
Sloan, John, 19, 72–73, 80, 117, 137, 197

Soul, The (V. W. Brooks), 206, 207–08

Spanish Loyalists, 74

Spiller, Robert, 39, 49, 173

Spirit of St. Louis (Lindbergh), 98

Spring-Rice, Tom, 144

"Square Root of Wonderful, The" (McCullers), 243

Stanford University, 102

Stephan, Ruth, 40, 54, 239

Stern, James, 47, 131, 148, 149, 287

Stern, Tania, 47, 148, 287

Stimson, Frank, 189–90, 238–39, 261, 271–73

Stockton, Frank R., 53

Studs Lonigan (Farrell), 51

Styron, Rose, 320

Styron, William, 240, 245, 320

Sullivan, Anne, 183

Sullivan, Louis, 80

Sullivan, Noel, 204

Suzuki, Daisetz, 254, 257

Swanson, Gloria, 196

Swift, Jonathan, 129–30

Taggard, Genevieve, 49

Talma, Louise, 219, 222, 231

Tate, Allen, 7, 8, 9, 50, 53, 75, 76, 311

Teller, Julius, 108, 159, 173, 275

Theodore Roosevelt Association, 176

This Singing World (Untermeyer), 115

Thompson, Dorothy, 169

Thomson, Polly, 28, 58, 59, 60, 79–80, 154, 183, 184, 209, 251, 262, 302, 303, 307

Thomson, Virgil, 79

Thoreau, Henry David, 191, 314

"Thoughts on the Avant-Garde" (V. W. Brooks), 240

Three Essays on America (V. W. Brooks), 55

Three Wise Virgins (Gladys Brooks), 202, 266

Thurber, James, 106

Tiger's Eye, The, 54

Times of Melville and Whitman, The (V. W. Brooks), 19, 23, 41

Toksvig, Signe (Mrs. Francis Hackett), 85

Tolstoy, Leo, 302

Too Late the Phalarope (Paton), 185

Tone, Aileen, 66

Torrence, Ridgely, 49

Tower, Elizabeth (Betsy), 28, 203, 238

Trask, Katrina, 185

Trask, Spencer, 185

Tweeddale, Marquis and Marchioness, 293

Tyson, Mrs., 308

Uccello, Paolo, 46

Undset, Sigrid, 39

Union College, 170

University of Montana, 159, 161

University of Pennsylvania, 39, 49, 172

Untermeyer, Jean Starr, 242

Untermeyer, Louis, 48, 109, 115, 242, 320

Upjohn, Myra and Richard, 266

Vanderlyn, John, 58

Van Doren, Mark, 48, 106, 107, 310, 324

Verses by Two Undergraduates (V. W. Brooks and J. H. Wheelock), 96
View from Pompey's Head (Basso), 211
Vincent, Mr. and Mrs. John, 196
Voice of the Desert, The (Krutch), 316
Vray Mistère de la Passion, Le, 151

Wallace, Henry, 74
Walsh, William, 131, 132
Wampanoag Indians, 93
Ward, Aileen, 188
Warner, Charles and Patricia, 256
Warren, Robert Penn, 302
Wassenaer, Baroness van, 281, 282
Weems, Parson Mason L., 10
Wemyss, Earl and Countess, 293
Wescott, Glenway, 48, 302, 310, 311
Wheelock, John Hall, 4, 6, 50, 53, 79, 96, 97, 98, 163, 164, 184, 185, 223, 237, 243, 301, 310–11
Wheelock, Phyllis, 4, 6, 50, 101, 163, 184, 223, 237, 243
Whitman, Walt, 81, 190
Whyte, Dorothy, 126, 127, 128, 224, 286, 294
Whyte, John, 127, 128
Wild Wales (Borrows), 296
Wilder, Thornton, 78, 110, 219, 222–23
Willard, Frances, 170
Williams, William Carlos, 49, 271

Wilson, Edmund, 5, 31, 157, 248–49, 259, 266, 267–70
Wilson, Elena, 267, 268, 269
Wine of the Puritans, The (V. W. Brooks), 295
Winternitz, Felix, 6, 7–8
Wisdom of the Body (Cannon), 256
"Wisdom Series," 263–66
Wolff, Harold, 275
World of Washington Irving, The (V. W. Brooks), 10, 12, 280–81
Writer in America, The (V. W. Brooks), 43, 156, 171
Wyeth, Andrew, 208
Wyman, Florence (Mrs. William Ivins), 115–16

Yaddo, 72, 185–89, 206
Yeats, George (Mrs. W. B. Yeats), 137, 139, 141
Yeats, John, 130
Yeats, John Butler, 35, 36, 102, 113, 129, 137, 271
Yeats, William Butler, 137, 139–40, 141
Yee, Chiang, 146–47, 165, 189, 190, 223, 257, 276–77, 294, 295, 311
Young, Mahonri, 250
Young, Marguerite, 53, 239–40

Zimmern, Sir Alfred and Lady, 102, 103